Librarian Putnam inaugurates an interlibrary loan service and the sale of the Library's printed catalog cards.

The Library of Congress becomes the first American library to contain over one million volumes.

1914 A special Legislative Reference Service is established.

1925 The creation of the Library of Congress Trust Fund Board enables the Library to accept gifts and bequests for the benefit of the institution.

1930 Congress authorizes construction of the Annex Building.

1939 Archibald MacLeish becomes Librarian of Congress.

1940 Librarian MacLeish appoints a special Librarian's Committee to analyze the institution's operations and organization. The Committee's recommendations lead to a major reorganization.

1945 Luther H. Evans becomes Librarian of Congress.

1946 A Legislative Reorganization Act expands the Library's Legislative Reference Service and makes it a separate department.

1947 The recommendations of the Library of Congress Planning Committee, appointed by Librarian Evans to examine the Library's national role, are submitted to Congress.

1954 L. Quincy Mumford becomes Librarian of Congress.

1962 At the request of Senator Claiborne Pell, Harvard librarian Douglas W. Bryant prepares a statement about the national functions of the Library of Congress. The Bryant memorandum and Librarian Mumford's lengthy reply are published in the Library's 1962 annual report.

1965 Congress authorizes construction of the James Madison Memorial Building.

1966 Librarian Mumford inaugurates the MARC (MAchine-Readable Cataloging) program and the National Program for Acquisitions and Cataloging.

1970 A Legislative Reorganization Act expands the Legislative Reference Service, renames it the Congressional Research Service, and gives it increased autonomy within the Library.

1975 Daniel J. Boorstin becomes Librarian of Congress.

1976 Librarian Boorstin appoints a staff Task Force on Goals, Organization, and Planning and eight outside advisory groups to review the Library and its activities and make recommendations for improvement.

The Library of Congress
in Perspective

By the mid-1890s, when this photograph was taken, the Library's principal room in the west front of the U.S. Capitol was overflowing. Photograph courtesy the Library of Congress.

The Library of Congress in Perspective

A Volume Based on the Reports of the 1976 Librarian's Task Force and Advisory Groups

Edited by John Y. Cole

R. R. Bowker Company
New York & London, 1978

Published by R. R. Bowker Company
1180 Avenue of the Americas, New York, N.Y. 10036
Printed and bound in the United States of America

Library of Congress Cataloging in Publication Data

The Library of Congress in perspective.

    Includes index.
    1. United States. Library of Congress.
I. Cole, John Young, 1940–   II. United
States. Library of Congress. Librarian's Task
Force on Goals, Organization, and Planning.
Z733.U6L494   027.5753   78-5000
ISBN 0-8352-1055-3

Contents

Preface

In 1976 a new Librarian of Congress, Daniel J. Boorstin, initiated a self-study of the Library of Congress. The twelve-month review, which soon became the most comprehensive in the institution's history, was carried out simultaneously by a staff Task Force on Goals, Organization, and Planning, of which I was Chairman, and by eight outside advisory groups.

The 1976 review is related to four earlier Library-wide assessments. The reviews carried out by the Librarian's Committee of Librarian of Congress Archibald MacLeish (1940) and the Planning Committee of Librarian of Congress Luther H. Evans (1947) were, like the Task Force effort, formal in nature. They also relied heavily on outside advice. Two informal reviews carried out by the Library itself have received less attention. The first is Librarian of Congress L. Quincy Mumford's report on a memorandum written by Harvard librarian Douglas W. Bryant (1962); the second, a paper written by the staff of the Library for the National Advisory Commission on Libraries (1967).

Despite their differences in scale and emphases, the five reviews share a common concern with the legislative and national roles of the Library of Congress. The reason is clear. The gradual growth of the Library of Congress, part of the legislative branch of the American government, into the de facto American national library has created special problems—as well as opportunities. Each of the five reviews thus addresses, in varying fashion, certain basic questions, including the Library's leadership role, its governmental and organizational structure, its relationships to its various constituencies, and the nature of its services to its users.

This volume approaches these questions historically, for, more than is the case with most institutions, the basic direction of the Library of Congress has been shaped by its historical development. An outline of the Library's history (Chapter 1) presents at least a partial explanation of how and why the Library acquired the many functions it now performs. The 1940, 1947, 1962, and 1967 assessments are part of that story. The emphasis in the volume, however, is on the 1976 review. The report of the 1976 Librarian's Task Force on Goals, Organization, and Planning is published in full (Chapter 2). Appendix B includes the final reports of two of the Task Force's fourteen subcommittees (Services to Congress and Services to Libraries). The reports of all eight outside advisory groups (Arts, Humanities, Law, Libraries, Media, Publishers, Science and Technology, and Social Sciences) are in Appendix C.

Debates about the Library of Congress, its roles, and its services, will continue. It is my hope that this volume will make a positive contribution to those discussions, both now and in the years ahead.

The Task Force review could not have taken place without the whole-hearted support of Daniel J. Boorstin, the Librarian of Congress. Special thanks go not only to the ten Task Force members but also to the hardworking chairpersons of the subcommittees and advisory groups. The names of Task Force, subcommittee, and advisory group members are listed in Appendix D. Finally, I am especially grateful to the staff of the Library of Congress, which contributed to the Task Force endeavor with enthusiasm and faith.

January 1978   John Y. Cole

The Library of Congress
in Perspective

Introduction

The Library of Congress is probably the largest library in the world. Its collections contain over 72 million pieces of research material including at least 18 million books, its staff numbers over 5,000, and its annual appropriation for FY 1978 exceeded $150 million.[1] It is the most diverse library in the world, serving six principal constituencies: the Congress, the federal government, the general public, authors and publishers, scholars and researchers, and the professional library community. Thus the Library brings together the common concerns of government, scholarship, and librarianship. This is a unique and beneficial combination, but one that also provokes unique expectations—and problems—relating to the institution's legislative and national roles.

Since its creation in 1800, the Library of Congress has been part of the legislative branch of the American government. Even though it is recognized as the de facto national library of the United States, its primary purpose is and always has been reference and research service for the Congress. Nonetheless, as a review of the Library's history makes clear, both the legislative and the national functions are inherent parts of the institution's basic fabric. The Library of Congress, primarily because of the unique circumstances of its origin and early development, is a product of American nationalism. That nationalism is the unifying force between the Congress, the Library, and the nation and is the reason why the Library and its services never have been the exclusive property of the legislative branch of the American government.[2]

In his remarks at the 1950 banquet honoring the Library's sesquicentennial, Librarian of Congress Emeritus Herbert Putnam pointed out that the unique governmental position of the Library of Congress had precluded the necessity for a constitution or written charter—a condition Putnam viewed as a great advantage for it gave the Library a flexibility it might not otherwise enjoy:

> [The Library's] enabling authority depends on the appropriation bills, that is to say, on grants from Congress in aid of what it proposes to do. But it's always a proposal to do something. The grant isn't a definition of

1

function, nor any evidence that Congress meant to define the function of the Library, or put a limit such as would be in the case of a Constitution.[3]

In 1962 Librarian of Congress L. Quincy Mumford asserted that Congress "has recognized the national responsibilities of the Library in a way that matters most—with understanding and consistent support."[4] By and large, Mumford's claim was accurate. The normal pattern has been for the Library to grow in stages, usually with alternating emphases between legislative and national functions. Naturally there have been periods of retrenchment, but on the whole the growth of the institution has been remarkably steady. Congressional committees occasionally have expressed unhappiness with the Library, but such instances usually have been followed with a reemphasis on the institution's legislative role that eased the situation. Concurrently, Congress frequently has taken a direct interest in national services performed by the Library for the constituencies served by both institutions—the general public, the library community, scholars, and federal agencies. In fact, many of the Library's new programs in recent years have originated not with the Library but with requests to Congress from groups such as the Association of Research Libraries (ARL) and the American Library Association (ALA).

The conservative approach of the Library, particularly its reluctance to initiate new programs without specific authorization from Congress, naturally draws criticism from "national library" advocates. It should be pointed out, however, that since there is no single, precise definition of a national library, the Library of Congress finds itself in the difficult position of performing national services for a variety of clientele, each with its own idea of what the Library should be doing.

Generally speaking, the major barrier to the expansion and improvement of the Library's collections and services has been lack of space, not lack of congressional support. The major periods of the Library's growth have occurred during the administrations of three Librarians of Congress: Ainsworth Rand Spofford (1865–1897), Herbert Putnam (1899–1939), and L. Quincy Mumford (1954–1974). Each eventually succeeded in obtaining approval for a major Library building. The Main Building was authorized in 1886, the Annex or Thomas Jefferson Building in 1930, and the James Madison Memorial Building in 1965. While waiting for construction to be completed, these three "expansionist" librarians endured badly crowded conditions that curtailed services and brought criticism from users. It is also worth noting that all three of these men enjoyed excellent relations with Congress.

Since 1865, when the "modern" history of the Library began, there has been a period of consolidation and reorganization after each major period of growth. In this sense, the immediate successors of Spofford and Putnam, Librarians John Russell Young (1897–1899), Archibald MacLeish (1939–1944), and Luther Evans (1945–1953), can be considered the consolidators, for the Library's two principal periods of administrative reorganization were 1897–1899 and 1940–1947. A further contribution of Evans, who tried to be an expansionist librarian, was his budget justification document for FY 1947, a blueprint for the Library's future that was offered too soon.

An understanding of the historical evolution of the Library, and the ambiguities, compromises, and personalities that have shaped it, is a prerequisite to understanding what the Library of Congress may or may not be able to do in the future. This volume emphasizes the development, inter-relationship, and perceived conflicts of the Library's legislative and national services.[5]

Notes and References

1. U.S., Library of Congress, *Annual Report of The Librarian of Congress for 1976* (Washington, D.C.: Library of Congress, 1977), p. A-58 (Hereafter referred to as *LC Annual Report*). "President Signs Legislative Appropriations Act," U.S., Library of Congress, *Library of Congress Information Bulletin* 36: 561 (August 19, 1977). Hereafter referred to as *LC Information Bulletin.*
2. For a more extensive discussion, see John Y. Cole, "For Congress and the Nation: The Dual Nature of the Library of Congress," *Quarterly Journal of the Library of Congress* 32: 118–138 (April 1975). Hereafter referred to as *LC Quarterly Journal.* Also see Charles A. Goodrum, *The Library of Congress*, Praeger Library of U.S. Government Departments and Agencies, no. 38 (New York: Praeger Publishers, 1974).
3. Putnam, "Remarks at the Conclusion of the Banquet Rendered in Behalf of the American Library Association and Associates to the Library of Congress, Mayflower Hotel, Washington, D.C., December 12, 1950," Putnam Papers, Library of Congress.
4. "Report of the Librarian of Congress on the Bryant Memorandum," *LC Annual Report for 1962* (Washington, D.C.: Library of Congress, 1963), p. 96.
5. The principal source for dates and other factual information is John Y. Cole, *For Congress and the Nation: A Chronological History of the Library of Congress* (Washington, D.C.: Library of Congress, 1978).

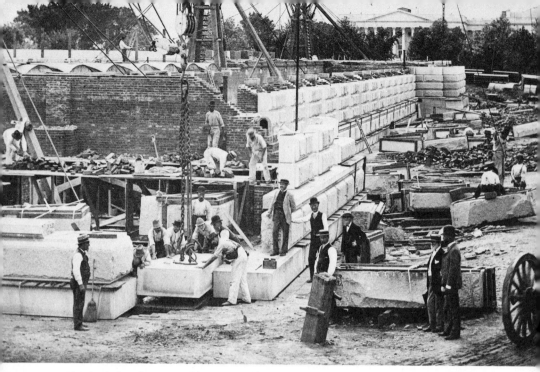

The cornerstone for a new Library building was laid in 1890. The monumental structure, located across the east plaza from the Capitol, was opened in 1897. Photograph courtesy the Library of Congress.

A view of the James Madison Memorial Building, under construction, as seen from the roof of the Thomas Jefferson Building (formerly called the Annex Building). The Madison Building is scheduled to open in 1979. Photograph courtesy the Office of the Architect of the Capitol.

1

The Library of Congress, 1800–1975

The Origins and Early Years

The Library of Congress was created by the national legislature as the first library of the American government. The Library was established at the same time that the American legislature prepared to move from Philadelphia to the new capital city of Washington, D.C. In section five of "An Act Making Further Provision for the Removal and Accommodation of the Government of the United States," signed by President John Adams on April 24, 1800, a sum of $5,000 was appropriated "for the purchase of such books as may be necessary for the use of Congress at the said city of Washington, and for fitting up a suitable apartment for containing them." From the beginning, however, the Library assumed more than a legislative role. On January 26, 1802, President Thomas Jefferson approved the first law defining the role and functions of the new institution. This measure created the post of Librarian of Congress and made it a presidential appointment. It set up a joint congressional committee to establish appropriate rules and regulations and supervise the Library's operation, but it also granted access to the Library to the president and vice-president, as well as to members of Congress.

On January 29, 1802, Jefferson appointed his friend and former campaign manager John Beckley as the first Librarian of Congress, in addition to his post as clerk of the House of Representatives. In April, Beckley published the Library's first catalog. It described a collection of 964 volumes and nine maps and charts.

From its first years the Library has been shaped both by the president and the Congress. President Jefferson kept in close touch with Library business, even preparing a desiderata list that served as the basis for its early acquisitions. In 1806 Library Committee Chairman Samuel Latham Mitchell urged the expansion of the Library: "Every week of the session causes additional regret that the volume of literature and science within the reach of the national legislature are not more rich and ample." The New York senator argued that "steps should be taken to furnish the Library with such materials as will enable statesmen to be correct in their investigations and, by a becoming display of erudition and research, give a high dignity and a brighter luster to truth."[1]

An important step was taken shortly after Mitchell's speech when, on February 21, 1806, President Jefferson approved an act of Congress that "continued" the earlier appropriation "made to purchase books for the use of Congress." Moreover, an additional $1,000 a year for a period of five years was authorized, the expenditure to be supervised by the Joint Committee on the Library. However, the use of the books was still a controversial issue, for on March 14 the Senate rejected a House of Representatives proposal that the privilege of taking books out of the Library be extended to include the secretaries of state, treasury, war, navy, and the attorney general.

John Beckley died in office on April 8, 1807, and on November 7 Jefferson appointed the new clerk of the House of Representatives, Patrick Magruder, as Librarian.[2] For the next seven years the Library grew at a modest pace. It did, however, with the approval of Congress, slowly become accessible to a wider range of users. In 1812, for example, a joint resolution authorized the justices of the Supreme Court to use the Library in accordance with the "same terms, conditions, and restrictions as members of Congress." In the same year members of the general public were permitted, for the first time, to borrow books—subject to the discretion of the Librarian and provided that a security deposit was left.

The Purchase of Jefferson's Library

In August 1814 a catastrophic event occurred, one that would have a far-reaching influence on the Library. The British army captured Washington and burned the Capitol, including the 3,000-volume Library of Congress. That event led ex-President Jefferson, then in retirement at Monticello, to offer to sell his personal library to the Joint Committee on the Library in order to "recommence" the congressional Library. The first Library of Congress collection consisted chiefly of historical and legal works. Jefferson's library contained books that reflected his own comprehensive interests in philosophy, history, geography, science, and literature, as well as political and legal treatises. Anticipating the argument that his library might be too comprehensive in scope to be truly useful to a legislative body, Jefferson used a phrase that, to this day, justifies the comprehensive collecting policy of the Library of Congress: "I do not know that [my library] contains any branch of science which Congress would wish to exclude from their collection; there is, in fact, no subject to which a member of Congress may not have occasion to refer."[3] There was opposition in the House of Representatives to the Jefferson purchase, both for political reasons and because individual congressmen objected to specific works in the library, including the books by Voltaire, Rousseau, and John Locke. But the vote in the House was 71–61 in favor, and President Madison signed the act authorizing the expenditure of $23,950 for the library on January 30, 1815.[4]

Proponents of the Jefferson purchase had argued that his library would make "a most admirable substratum for a National Library," expressing a new cultural nationalism being felt in the United States. Many Americans, aware of the cultural dependence of the United States on Europe, were anxious that their country establish its own traditions and institutions. A pronational library article in the Petersburg *Courier*, reprinted in the Washington *National Intelligencer*, stated one aspect of this national pride: "The objections made by the Federal members of Congress to the purchase of Mr. Jefferson's library are certainly not only extraordinary and illiberal, but reflect the greatest discredit upon the national character of this country. What can be a greater stigma upon the members of our National Legislature than to assert that books of a philosophical description are improper for their perusal?"[5]

The purchase of Jefferson's 6,487-volume library not only doubled the size of the Library of Congress, it also changed the nature of the collection and the institution. The broadening of the scope of the Library's collections has been the cornerstone for the extension of the Library's services to both the Congress and the rest of the nation. The purchase of Thomas Jefferson's library was the most important expansion of the collections in the institution's history.

National Aspirations

Patrick Magruder resigned his position of clerk of the House of Representatives and, by inference, the office of Librarian of Congress, on January 28, 1815, two days before President Madison approved the Jefferson purchase. The resignation came after an investigation relating to the loss of the Library in the 1814 invasion and the use of the funds under Magruder's control. On March 21 President Madison named a new Librarian. He was George Watterston, a local novelist and journalist and the first Librarian who did not also serve as clerk of the House of Representatives.[6]

The new Librarian did all he could to promote the idea of the Library of Congress as a national library, taking advantage of the arrival of Jefferson's library and his own connections in the newspaper business. During Watterston's 14 years as Librarian, the Washington press gave great support to the idea—sometimes in articles penned by the Librarian himself. The rhetoric in the July 31, 1815 (Washington, D.C.) daily *National Intelligencer* is a fair example:

> In all civilized nations of Europe there are national libraries, the selection and increase of which occupy much governmental attention. In a country of such general intelligence as this, so laudable an example should by all means be instituted, and the Congressional or National Library of the United States become the great repository of the literature of the world.

In November 1815 the Library published a new catalog, which, of course, was essentially a catalog of Jefferson's library. While prepared by Watterston, the catalog was arranged according to a classification scheme devised by Jefferson that, in turn, followed Sir Francis Bacon's classification of knowledge. The new classification scheme, as modified by each Librarian, would be used by the Library of Congress until the end of the century.

The title of the volume reflected Watterston's view: *Catalogue of the Library of the United States*. The Joint Committee on the Library was critical of the expenditure—600 copies were printed at a cost of $2.25 each—but had nothing to say about its title. However, in the same report, dated January 26, 1816, the committee was critical of the presidential role in Library affairs, observing "not without astonishment, that by an act passed the 26th of

January 1802, the Librarian of Congress was to be appointed by the President of the United States solely. It is difficult to conceive why an officer of both Houses of Congress . . . should not be appointed by the authority to which he ought to be amenable." The committee therefore recommended that, in the future, it make the appointment.[7]

In early 1817, in an attempt to permanently remove the Library from the Capitol, the Joint Library Committee sponsored a resolution calling for a separate Library of Congress building. The measure was defeated by the House Committee of the Whole. Watterston naturally was disappointed, taking the occasion to remind the readers of the *National Intelligencer* that in other countries similar institutions were objects of national pride and that "edifices are erected for the accommodation of national libraries." There was no doubt in his mind that the United States should have a library building "equal in grandeur to the wealth, the taste, and the science of the nation."[8]

Librarian Watterston's plea for a separate building went unheeded, but for the next decade and a half the Library continued to expand its collections and its clientele. A separate annual appropriation for the purchase of books was initiated in 1820. In 1824 the amount of the appropriation was increased from $2,000 to $4,000. On January 13, 1830, a joint resolution granted use of the books in the Library to "the Secretary of State, the Secretary of the Navy, the Postmaster General, the Secretary of the Senate, the Clerk of the House of Representatives, the chaplins of Congress, and ex-Presidents (when in the District of Columbia)." The extension of the Library's collection beyond that needed by a legislative library was tacitly acknowledged by an act of Congress in 1832 that established a separate "apartment" for the law books within the Library of Congress.

The Conservative Antebellum Years

In politics Watterston was a Whig, and an outspoken one. His librarianship came to an abrupt end on May 28, 1829, when newly elected President Andrew Jackson, a Democrat, replaced him with another Democrat: John Silva Meehan, a local printer and publisher. Meehan was an efficient and passive Librarian of Congress who demonstrated none of Watterston's ambition for the institution. Under Meehan, who served as Librarian until 1861, the legislative function of the Library of Congress dominated. This was particularly true after 1845, when a conservative and strong-willed Democrat, Senator James A. Pearce of Maryland, became chairman of the Joint Committee on the Library.[9]

Pearce, however, was not the only committee member who took a passive view of the Library. The bookmen and intellectuals who served on the committee in the middle years of the nineteenth century, men such as Benjamin Tappan, George Perkins Marsh, and Rufus Choate, were nationalists who favored the creation of an American national library; interestingly enough, they never viewed the Library of Congress as that library or even as its nucleus. For example, on June 7, 1844, the committee rejected the proposed purchase, for an advantagous price, of one of the choicest private libraries of Europe because the acquisition was not "suited to the purposes of Congress." In 1845 Senator Choate, then Library Committee chairman, presented the case in Congress for establishing the projected Smithsonian Institution as the national library, since the annual appropriation granted the Library of

Congress could never enable it "to fulfill the functions of a truly great and general public library of science, literature, and art."[10]

The Smithsonian Institution was established in 1846 "for the increase and diffusion of knowledge among men." The new Board of Regents was to make, from the interest on the bequest of James Smithson, "an appropriation not exceeding an average of twenty-five thousand dollars annually for the gradual formation of a library composed of valuable works pertaining to all departments of human knowledge." The new law also authorized the Library of Congress, along with the Smithsonian, to receive as a deposit one copy of each copyrighted "book, map, chart, musical composition, print, cut, or engraving."[11]

Indeed, in the early 1850s it appeared that the Smithsonian Institution might well become the American national library. Its talented and aggressive librarian, Charles Coffin Jewett, tried to move the institution in that direction, building on the materials brought in by the copyright law and urging an increased allocation of Smithsonian funds for book purchases. He also advocated (1) a system of centralized cataloging using stereotyped plates prepared by the Smithsonian; (2) uniform cataloging rules; and (3) the creation of a national bibliographical center. Jewett's efforts were opposed, however, by Smithsonian Secretary Joseph Henry, who insisted that the Smithsonian focus its activities on scientific research and publication. In fact the secretary, unlike members of the Library Committee, favored the eventual development of a national library at the Library of Congress, which he viewed as the most appropriate foundation for "a collection of books worthy of a Government whose perpetuity principally depends on the intelligence of the people." On July 10, 1854, Henry dismissed Jewett, effectively ending any possibility that the Smithsonian might become the national library.[12]

In all, the Library of Congress suffered difficult times during the 1850s. In the first place, the growing intersectional rivalry between the North and the South was not conducive to the strengthening or enlarging of any government institution, especially in a "national" direction. Furthermore, on December 24, 1851, the most serious fire in the Library's history destroyed about two-thirds of its 55,000 volumes, including two-thirds of Jefferson's library. Congress responded quickly and generously, appropriating a total of $168,700 to restore the Library's rooms in the Capitol and replace the lost books. Its attitude toward the Library remained ambiguous, however. Two days after the fire, the House of Representatives approved an investigation into its origin only after changing the wording in its resolution from "the National Library" to "the Library of Congress." Moreover, the lost books were to be "replaced" only, with no particular intention of supplementing or expanding the collection.[13] This policy reflected Library Committee Chairman Pearce's conservative philosophy.

Senator Pearce believed in keeping strict limits on the Library's activities. He was proud of the institution and did his best to protect it. As chairman he exercised his privilege to control the Library's acquisitions and its rules. According to one chronicler, in 1857 Pearce rejected the proposal that the Library subscribe to the new journal *Atlantic Monthly* because to do so might "inflame sectional feelings" between the North and the South.[14] In the same year, Pearce rejected a resolution that would extend borrowing privileges to the judges and solicitor of the Court of Claims, noting: "The list of those who are entitled to take books from the Library of Congress is very large; and the privilege is often abused by those who are entitled to it, using it for the supply of others than themselves and their own families." Apparently the public no longer was allowed to borrow books, for Pearce continued his report by pointing out that visitors were allowed "the use of books by reading them while they are there, and the means of making notes of what they read are readily furnished. They also are cheerfully aided by the Librarian and assistants in making researches."[15]

In the late 1850s, with the consent of Senator Pearce and Librarian Meehan, the Library of Congress gave up several governmental functions acquired in earlier years. On January 28, 1857, a joint resolution of Congress transferred responsibility for the distribution of public documents to the Bureau of the Interior, and responsibility for the international exchange of books and documents to the Department of State. On February 5, 1859, the 1846 law designating the Smithsonian Institution and the Library of Congress as repositories for U.S. copyright deposits was repealed.[16]

Senator Pearce also felt protective about the Librarian of Congress and his staff. On March 8, 1861, he informed newly elected President Abraham Lincoln that for the past 15 years the president "has always deferred to the wishes of Congress" regarding the appointment of the Librarian of Congress, and that the wish of the Library Committee was to retain Librarian Meehan and his entire staff.[17] Pearce's plea, however, was ignored and on May 24 President Lincoln appointed John G. Stephenson, a physician from Terre Haute, Indiana, and a political supporter, to be Librarian of Congress. The new Librarian soon hired a new Assistant Librarian, Ainsworth Rand Spofford from Cincinnati, and left the operation of the Library to Spofford while he served for extended periods of time as a volunteer aide-de-camp at, for example, the battles of Chancellorsville and Gettysburg. Stephenson had little impact on the Library during his three and a half years in office, but Assistant Librarian Spofford pushed forward several improvements that prepared the way for future accomplishments.[18]

Stephenson submitted his resignation on December 22, 1864, and on December 31 President Lincoln appointed Spofford as the sixth Librarian of Congress. At the time the Library had a staff of seven, a collection of approximately 82,000 volumes, and an annual appropriation of about $20,000.

Spofford and a New National Role

The modern history of the Library of Congress began when Spofford became Librarian, for during his 32-year administration (1865–1897) he transformed the Library of Congress into an institution of national significance. Spofford permanently linked the legislative and national functions of the Library, first in practice and then, through the 1897 reorganization of the Library, in law. He provided his successors as Librarian with four essential prerequisites for the development of an American national library: (1) firm congressional support for the notion of the Library of Congress as both a legislative and a national library; (2) the beginning of a comprehensive collection of Americana; (3) a magnificent new building, itself a national monument; and (4) a strong and independent office of Librarian of Congress. It was Spofford who had the interest, skill, and perseverance to capitalize on the Library of Congress' claim to a national role. Each Librarian of Congress since Spofford has shaped the institution in a different manner, but none has wavered from Spofford's assertion that the Library was both a legislative and a national library.[19]

Spofford revived the idea of an American national library, which had been languishing since Jewett's departure from the Smithsonian in 1854, and convinced first the Joint Committee on the Library and then the Congress itself that the Library of Congress was also a national institution. Spofford and Jewett shared several ideas relating to a national library; in particular, both recognized the importance of copyright deposit in developing a comprehensive collection of a nation's literature.[20] Yet there was a major difference in their views. Spofford never envisioned the Library of Congress as the center of a network of American libraries, a focal point for providing other libraries with cataloging and bibliographic services. Instead, he viewed it, in the European model, as a unique, independent institution—a single, comprehensive collection of national literature to be used both by congressmen and by the American people. Congress needed such a collection because, as Spofford paraphrased Jefferson, "there is almost no work, within the vast range of literature and science, which may not at some time prove useful to the legislature of a great nation." It was imperative, he felt, that such a great national collection be shared with all citizens, for the United States was "a Republic which rests upon the popular intelligence."[21]

Immediately after the Civil War, American society began a rapid transformation; one of the major changes was the expansion of the federal government. Spofford took full advantage of the favorable political and cultural climate, and the increasing national confidence, to promote the Library's expansion. He always believed that the Library of Congress *was* the national library and he used every conceivable argument in convincing others. One favorite, reminiscent of Watterston, was repeated often in the Librarian's annual reports: "In every country where civilization has attained a high rank there should be at least one great library."

In the first years of his administration Spofford obtained congressional approval of six laws or resolutions that ensured a national role for the Library of Congress. The legislative acts were:

1. an appropriation providing for the expansion of the Library in the Capitol building, approved in early 1865;
2. the copyright amendment of 1865, which once again brought copyright deposits into the Library's collections;
3. the Smithsonian deposit of 1866, whereby the entire library of the Smithsonian Institution, a collection especially strong in scientific materials, was transferred to the Library;
4. the 1867 purchase, for $100,000, of the private library of historian and archivist Peter Force, establishing the foundation of the Library's Americana and incunabula collections;
5. the international exchange resolution of 1867, providing for the development of the Library's collection of foreign public documents; and
6. the copyright act of 1870, which centralized all copyright registration and deposit activities at the Library.

Finally, in his 1872 annual report, Spofford presented a plan for a separate Library of Congress building, initiating an endeavor that soon dominated his librarianship.[22]

Spofford's most impressive collection-building feat, and certainly the one that had the most far-reaching significance for the Library, was the centralization of all U.S. copyright deposit and registration activities at the Library in 1870. The copyright law ensured the continuing development of the Americana collections, for it stipulated that two copies of every book, pamphlet, map, print, and piece of music registered for copyright in the United States be deposited in the Library. This act also eventually forced the construction of the separate Library building for by 1875, as described in the Librarian's annual report of that year, all shelf space was exhausted and the books, "from sheer force of necessity," were being "piled on the floor in all directions."

In the long struggle for a separate Library building, Spofford enlisted the support of many powerful public figures: congressmen, cultural leaders, journalists, and even presidents. The speeches and statements of these gentlemen usually endorsed not only a separate building but also the concept of the Library of Congress as a national library. For example, in his annual message to Congress on December 3, 1879, President Rutherford B. Hayes observed: "As this library is national in character and must from the nature of the case increase even more rapidly in the future, than in the past, it cannot be doubted that the people will sanction any wise expenditure to preserve it and to enlarge its usefulness." In a similar manner, on December 12, 1882, Speaker of the House of Representatives Thomas B. Reed informed Congress: "This nation has become great enough to meet the expectations of this people. Among these expectations is the establishment of a library large enough for the needs of the whole of this great nation."[23]

To Spofford must also go primary credit for establishing the Library's tradition of broad public service. In 1865 he extended the hours of service, so that the Library was open every weekday all year. In 1869 he began advocating evening hours of opening, but this innovation was not approved by Congress until 1898. Finally, in 1870 Spofford reinstated the earlier policy of lending books directly to the public if an appropriate sum was left on deposit, a procedure that remained in effect until about 1894, when preparations were started for the move into the new Library building.

Because Spofford's administration was dominated by the unceasing flow of materials into cramped quarters, other Library activities suffered. To the dismay of many, Spofford's carefully conceived scheme for a complete index to the documents and debates of Congress was abandoned about 1877, after several years of work. In 1880 he stopped publication of the Library's alphabetical catalog after only two volumes had been published. During the same period the Librarian also neglected the Library's recordkeeping, including that of the copyright department. This situation led, in 1895, to a U.S. Treasury Department investigation of the copyright accounts; Spofford was exonerated of any intentional wrongdoing, but was deeply embarrassed.

As the new Library building neared completion, Congress asked Spofford for "a full report touching on a complete reorganization of the Library of Congress." Spofford's lengthy report, dated December 3, 1895, concluded with a summary of his reorganization proposals and an interesting comparison between the Library of Congress and other institutions:

Respecting the general question of the reorganization of the entire Library service, it may be gathered from what has been laid before Con-

gress that the following departments or divisions are deemed important:
(1) printed books; (2) periodicals; (3) manuscripts; (4) maps and charts;
(5) works of art; (6) catalogue department; (7) binding department; (8)
copyright office and records; (9) superintendence.

[I desire] to place before Congress some view of the relative expenditure in other libraries and departments, that it may be seen how extremely small has been the working force allowed in the Library of
Congress. The Boston Public Library, with two-thirds as many volumes
and no copyright business, has 140 employees. The Congressional
Library had in 1885, 25; in 1890, 26; and in 1895 it has 38, of whom 5,
however, are employed in detached service in the law library and the
Smithsonian exchanges. . . . The British Museum, with no copyright
business and no circulation, but with 1,600,000 volumes, and with large
exhibits of antiquities, etc. employs 220 attendants in its eight departments, besides 160 engineers, electricians, laborers, window cleaners,
police, etc.[24]

In his next budget request, submitted on February 7, 1896, Spofford asked for
97 positions, "58 for the general Library administration and the remainder for
the proposed copyright department, to be headed by a register of copyrights."[25]

By this time, Spofford also was able to use his own accomplishments as a
justification for the Library's national role:

Gathered as it has been by appropriations of public money, supplemented for more than a quarter of a century by the steady acquisitions
coming in under copyright law, [the Library] has become to a degree the
representative of the Nation's literature. As the only Government library of comprehensive range, every year of its existence should be
marked by incessant progress toward completeness in every department. In the new and splendid home for the Nation's books provided by
the far-sighted liberality of Congress, readers whose pursuits are end-
lessly varied should be assured of finding the best possible literature
of all lands.[26]

For the most part, Spofford operated quite independently from the
American library movement and the American Library Association (ALA).
The primary reason was, quite simply, that he did not have the time to participate. By 1876, when ALA was founded, Spofford's Library of Congress
already was the leading library in the United States and he was completely
absorbed in the struggle for a new building. Spofford was a charter member
of ALA but could not get away from Washington to attend many of the annual
meetings. His independence from other libraries and librarians was accen-
tuated by his idea of a national library as well as by his personal tempera-
ment. He believed the Library should be, essentially, a comprehensive
accumulation of the nation's literature. He did not view it as a focal point
for cooperative library activities and was not inclined to exert leadership
in that direction. Furthermore, his personal enthusiasms were acquisitions
and bibliography, while many younger librarians were more interested in
problems of library organization.

These facts, along with Spofford's advancing age, created restlessness
and unhappiness among the leaders of the profession. They looked to the

Library of Congress for a new type of leadership. While cognizant of Spofford's problems and appreciative of his accomplishments, ALA was anxious to move the Library of Congress in new directions. As the new Library building neared completion, the organization, led by Melvil Dewey and Richard R. Bowker, decided to try to influence the reorganization that obviously would take place once the new structure was occupied. In late 1896 the Joint Committee on the Library provided the association with the perfect opportunity.

The Reorganization of 1896–1897

From November 16 to December 7, 1896, the Joint Committee on the Library held hearings about the Library of Congress, its "condition," and its organization. Although Spofford was the principal witness, ALA sent six librarians to testify, including its president, William H. Brett, librarian of the Cleveland Public Library; Melvil Dewey, director of the New York State Library; and Herbert Putnam, librarian of the Boston Public Library. The testimony of Dewey and Putnam on the desirable features of the Library of Congress was of special interest. Both men avoided direct criticism of Spofford, but it was obvious that their view of the proper functions of the Library differed from that of the aging Librarian of Congress. Putnam wholeheartedly endorsed Dewey's description of the necessary role of a national library: "a center to which the libraries of the whole country can turn for inspiration, guidance, and practical help." Centralized cataloging, interlibrary loan, and a national union catalog were among the services described.[27]

Immediately after the end of the hearings, Putnam supplemented his comments in a letter in which he summarized the testimony of the ALA witnesses. The future Librarian of Congress found that:

> On one point in particular we were very strongly in unison . . . an endeavor should now be made to introduce into the Library the mechanical aids which render the Library more independent of the physical limitations of any one man or set of men; in other words, that the time has come when Mr. Spofford's amazing knowledge of the Library shall be embodied in some form which shall be capable of rendering a service which Mr. Spofford as one man and mortal can not be expected to render.[28]

Putnam was stating, tactfully, that not only was it time for the Library of Congress to modernize, but also its services should be expanded far beyond those offered by the Library under Spofford.

The 1896 hearings marked a turning point in the relations between the Library of Congress and the American library movement. For the first time ALA, albeit cautiously, offered its advice to Congress about the purpose and functions of the Library of Congress. Moreover, Congress listened, for the testimony at the hearings, along with a report filed by Spofford on January 18, 1897, were major influences on the reorganization of the Library that was contained in the legislative appropriations act for FY 1898, approved by President Grover Cleveland on February 19, 1897. The restructuring and expansion of the Library simply could not wait for the report on the hearings held by the Joint Committee on the Library. Because the changes were part of the appropriations act, they became effective on July 1, 1897, the beginning of the new fiscal year.

As urged by Spofford and the ALA witnesses, all phases of the Library's operations were expanded. The size of the staff was increased from 42 to 108, and separate administrative units for copyright, law, cataloging, the general book collections, periodicals, maps, manuscripts, music, and the graphic arts were established. The superintendent of the building and grounds was given a staff of 79. The new law also gave the Librarian of Congress a remarkable degree of autonomy in administering and shaping the institution. During his 32 years in office, and with the consent of the Joint Committee on the Library, Librarian Spofford had informally assumed full responsibility for directing the Library's affairs. This authority formally passed to the office of the Librarian in the 1897 reorganization, for the Librarian was assigned sole responsibility for making the "rules and regulations for the government" of the Library. This included the selection of the staff, which would be appointed "by reason of special aptitude for the work of the Library." The Library thus was left outside the civil service system. The law also required, for the first time, Senate approval of a presidential nominee for the post of Librarian of Congress.[29]

The report of the Joint Committee on the Library on its inquiry was published on March 3, 1897. The committee duly noted that its authority to approve the Library's rules and regulations "would appear to be repealed by the more recent act [February 19, 1897] which places this power in the hands of the Librarian of Congress." For this reason, it did not deem it necessary to report any plan for the "organization, custody, and management" of the Library. It did, however, suggest that funds might be appropriated so that the Library "may be opened at night for the use of the general public."[30]

Congressional debate about the Library of Congress sections of the appropriations bill had been lively. Representative Alexander M. Dockery of the Appropriations Committee was the principal advocate of increased authority for the office of Librarian of Congress, insisting that the Library "should be presided over by some executive officer with authority to appoint and remove his employees." A proponent of the idea of an independent civil service, Dockery worried about the possible influence of politics on the Library: "In organizing this great library in that gorgeous new building, let us not make the grave mistake of also organizing a scramble for 187 offices to be disposed of under the direction and control of the joint committee of the two Houses of Congress, to the detriment of public service." Dockery's insistence on an independent office of Librarian eventually prevailed, but not without disagreement. In the Senate, for example, Wilkinson Call of Florida was unhappy with the possible outcome: "By this bill Congress forever puts it out of their power to control the Library. It now loses its name and function as a Congressional library and becomes a national or Presidential Library, beyond the control of Congress, except by the President's consent."[31]

In truth, in 1896 and early 1897 the development of the Library into a national library quite independent of Congress was precisely what Melvil Dewey, R. R. Bowker, and others in the American Library Association had in mind. In an article titled "The American National Library" in the *Library Journal*, the official ALA organ, Richard R. Bowker asserted: "It is time to recognize in name, the fact that the Library of Congress, so called, is now the library of the nation as well as of Congress; and it should undoubtedly be designated as the National Library." A January 1897 article in the *Library Journal*, contributed anonymously by Edith E. Clarke of the Public Documents

Library in Washington, D.C., called on Congress to "renounce the right, now 96 years old, which it holds in the Library of Congress," and constitute the Library as an executive establishment governed by a board of regents "as the Smithsonian Institution is organized."[32]

Even after the approval of the Legislative Branch Appropriations Act of February 19, 1897, librarians and some congressmen nursed hopes that the Library of Congress might be formally designated as the National Library. For example, on December 6, 1897, Representative Dockery introduced a bill providing (1) that the Library of Congress "shall be known as and styled as the National Library"; (2) that the Librarian of Congress shall be designated "the Director of the National Library"; and (3) that all citizens over the age of 12 and residing in the District of Columbia be entitled "to withdraw books from the national library." A week later the Joint Committee on the Library recommended that the third section of Representative Dockery's bill "be stricken out," but with that change, the bill was approved. No action was ever taken, however.[33]

The pattern was set. From 1896 to the present, Congress has refused to consider seriously either a name change or giving up its jurisdiction over the Library. Nonetheless, it began appropriating steadily increasing sums for the Library's expansion. As a result, during the administrations of Librarians John Russell Young (1897–1899) and Herbert Putnam (1899–1939), the Library of Congress grew into a national library much in the manner advocated by the American Library Association and other library groups—only that national library was under the direct control of the U.S. Congress. Accordingly, the reference and research needs of the U.S. Congress naturally had priority over demands from the Library's other "national" constituencies, including the nation's libraries and librarians.

Expansion into a New Building

On July 1, 1897, the day the reorganization became effective, President William McKinley appointed a new Librarian of Congress to supervise its implementation and the move of the Library from the Capitol into the new building. The new Librarian, John Russell Young, was a personal friend of the president's; he also was a journalist, former diplomat, and a skilled administrator. The Senate, exercising its new authority for the first time, confirmed Young on the day he was nominated. Young's first official act was to name the 72-year-old Spofford Chief Assistant Librarian. The irrepressible Melvil Dewey wrote Young on July 12, encouraging the new appointee and doing his best to influence him:

> Many librarians have expressed themselves strongly against any appointment except of an experienced technical librarian. I have said from the first that I could easily conceive of a strong administration man being put at the head who might be better for the country than any of the professional librarians. I profoundly hope that you are the man needed for the wonderful work that is possible. May I ask you to glance over my testimony before the joint committee last December for what I believe the true idea for the library that ought to lead the world.[34]

In spite of poor health, Young did a remarkable job in the year and a half that he served as Librarian. On November 1, 1897, the new Library of Congress building officially opened. The Library's national stature was greatly enhanced by the monumental structure, which was elaborately decorated and capped with a 23-carat gold-plated dome. Young's principal concerns, however, were organizational. He was flooded with applications for the new positions and he chose well—especially in the leadership positions. His appointments included Thorvald Solberg, a Boston bookdealer and acknowledged copyright expert, to be the first Register of Copyrights; J. C. M. Hanson from the University of Wisconsin as the first head of the new Catalogue Department; and, to assist Hanson, Charles Martel from the Newberry Library.

Young's first annual report, submitted on December 6, 1897, described several major changes that were under way, including an impending reclassification of the collections. He also advocated the transfer of historical manuscripts from the Department of State to the Library of Congress and decried the use of cheap, nondurable paper by publishers, prophetically warning that many of the works coming into the Library "threaten in a few years to crumble into a waste heap, with no value as record."[35]

Young's concept of a national library was similar to that of Spofford, for the need for a comprehensive national collection dominated the new Librarian's thoughts. In February 1898, for example, he sent a letter to U.S. diplomatic and consular representatives throughout the world, asking them to send "to the national library" newspapers, serials, pamphlets, manuscripts, broadsides, "documents illustrative of the history of those various nationalities now coming to our shores to blend into our national life," and many other categories of research materials, broadly summarized as "whatever, in a word, would add to the sum of human knowledge." By the end of 1898, books and documents had arrived from 11 legations and seven consulates.

In his annual report for 1898, Young casually mentioned two developments that, in fact, were of great significance: the first steps in reclassifying the Library's collections, and the compilation of bibliographies specifically for the use of Congress. He pointed out that the new series of bibliographic bulletins was intended to "anticipate the wants of Congress upon the subjects of legislation and hold the resources of the Library ever at the command of those for whom it was founded." The principal bibliographies were separate lists of books relating to the Philippines, Cuba, Nicaragua, Hawaii, and Alaska. The Librarian concluded his report by describing his hopes for the Library:

> It should be our aim to broaden the Library, safeguard its integrity as a library of reference, and bring it home to the people as belonging to them—a part of their heritage—to make it American in the highest sense, seeking whatever illustrates American history—the varied forms of American growth, theology, superstition, commonwealth, building, jurisprudence, peace, and war. And, while accepting this as the chief end of the Library, it is no less incumbent to seek out and gather in the learning and piety of every age. With the considerate care of Congress and a due appreciation of what has been done and what may so readily be done by the American people, there is no reason why the Library of Congress should not rival those noble establishments of the Old World, whose treasures are a people's pride and whose growth is the highest achievement of modern civilization.[36]

Young also inaugurated what today is one of the Library's best-known national activities, library service for the blind. In November of 1897 the Library began a program of daily readings for the blind in a special "pavilion for the blind" complete with its own library. In 1913 Congress directed the American Printing House for the Blind to begin depositing embossed books in the Library, and in 1931 a separate appropriation was authorized for providing "books for the use of adult blind residents of the United States."

A final accomplishment of Librarian Young is worth special mention: He firmly established the tradition of the Library of Congress as an apolitical institution. This achievement is a tribute to his personal integrity and somewhat ironic since Young himself was a political appointee. John Russell Young's career as Librarian was productive, but brief; after a year of serious illness, he died on January 17, 1899.[37]

Putnam and the Development of National Services

The American Library Association apparently was unable to wield any influence in President McKinley's appointment of a successor to Spofford, but after Librarian Young's death ALA undertook a concerted effort to have a professional librarian appointed as Librarian of Congress. On January 23, 1899, Harvard librarian and ALA president William Coolidge Lane wrote President McKinley to urge the appointment of an experienced library administrator since the Library of Congress, as the national library, should "stand at the head of American libraries as the best organized and best equipped of all." Lane also pointed out that, under the right leadership, the Library could "be made a leading factor in the educational and intellectual life of the country" and "exercise an important influence on the progress of the library movement." ALA's candidate was Herbert Putnam, the Boston librarian who testified at the 1896 hearings. The story of how Putnam was nominated is a complicated one, but there is no doubt that without the support of ALA he would not have become Librarian of Congress. William Coolidge Lane not only persuaded President McKinley; it appears that, in the end, he also persuaded Putnam. On March 13, 1899, during the congressional recess, McKinley appointed Herbert Putnam to be the eighth Librarian of Congress. Putnam took the oath of office on April 5 and was confirmed by the Senate, somewhat after the fact, on December 12.[38]

Herbert Putnam was Librarian of Congress from 1899 to 1939, longer than any other Librarian. His administration, particularly in its early years, firmly linked the policies of the Library of Congress with the broader interests of American librarianship. The first experienced librarian to hold the post of Librarian of Congress, Putnam recognized his opportunity and seized it, quickly applying his general knowledge of library methods to the collections and services of the Library of Congress. Three years after he assumed office, the Library of Congress was the leader among American libraries. This turn of events was in accord with Putnam's view of the proper role of the national library—the same view he expressed at the 1896 hearings.

Putnam's decisive actions during the first decade of his administration were appreciated by both the professional library community and the Congress. A few months after taking office, he submitted his first budget request, which called for five new "departments of work not covered by present organization": a reading room for current newspapers and periodicals, a purchasing department, new departments for exchanges and bibliography, and a "reference room" for the Smithsonian collection. He also asked for an increase in the staff from 134 to 230 employees. When a friend doubted that Congress would approve such an ambitious request, Putnam reassured him:

> I believe in Congress. I believe in the men who in Congress are controlling these matters. I believe in their fairness. I believe in their common sense. My experience during the past eight months has confirmed my general belief and has given me a particular confidence. . . . I fully believe that Congress will do whatever is necessary for the Library.[39]

The Librarian was right. On April 17, 1900, President McKinley approved the legislative, executive, and judicial appropriations act for FY 1901, which granted Putnam everything he had requested and even raised the salary of the Librarian of Congress to $6,000 a year.

During the first decade of his administration, Putnam fulfilled the hopes of ALA by inaugurating a host of national library services. There were two innovations, both undertaken in 1901, that greatly influenced American librarianship: an interlibrary loan service and the sale and distribution of Library of Congress printed catalog cards. In announcing the card distribution service, the Librarian stated that "a centralization of cataloguing work, with a corresponding centralization of bibliographic apparatus, has been for a quarter of a century an ambition of the librarians of the United States," and termed the new service "the most significant of our undertakings of this first year of the new century."[40]

According to Putnam, the national library, rather than serving primarily as a great national accumulation of books, should strive above all to serve other libraries. The full dimensions of his national library philosophy were outlined in his July 1901 speech before the annual ALA convention. In it he summarized his opinion of the proper functions of the Library of Congress:

> If there is any way in which our National Library may "reach out" from Washington, it should reach out. Its first duty is, no doubt, as a legislative library, to Congress. Its next is a federal library to aid the executive and judicial department[s] of the government and the scientific undertakings under government auspices. Its next is to that general research which may be carried on at Washington by resident and visiting students and scholars. . . . But this should not be the limit. There should be possible also a service to the country at large: a service to be extended through the libraries which are the local centers of research involving the use of books.[41]

Shortly thereafter, Putnam asked President Theodore Roosevelt to mention the Library of Congress and its potential for truly national service in the president's first state of the union address. In his letter, Putnam explained to Roosevelt that:

> A national library for the United States should mean in some respects much more than a national library in any other country hitherto

meant.... [The] libraries of the United States are organizing their work
with reference to uniformity in methods, to cooperation in processes, to
interchange of service, to the promotion of efficiency in service. They
look to the National Library for standards, for example, for leadership
in all these enterprises. It is now in a position to "standardize" library
methods, to promote cooperation, to aid in the elimination of wasteful
duplication, [and] to promote the interchange of bibliographic service.[42]

The new president agreed to Putnam's request, and in his state of the union
address, delivered on December 3, 1901, he called the Library of Congress "the
one national library of the United States." He then continued:

Already the largest single collection of books on the Western Hemis-
phere, and certain to increase more rapidly than any other through purchase, exchange, and the operation of the copyright law, this library has
a unique opportunity to render to the libraries of this country—to
American scholarship—service of the highest importance.[43]

Putnam had the support, not only of President Roosevelt, but also of Congress. He continued to consult the Joint Committee on the Library and, like
Spofford and Young, continually enhanced his support through appeals to
national pride and patriotism.

The year 1901 ended with another important achievement: Putnam's comprehensive annual report, a 380-page document that described the organization, facilities, collections, and operations of the Library. In the chapter about
the "constitution of the Library" the Librarian states that "the purpose of the
administration is the freest possible use of the books consistent with their
safety; and the widest possible use consistent with the convenience of
Congress." The report is a guide to the best library practice of the day and sets
high standards in almost every aspect of library operations.

The remarkable accomplishments during Putnam's first decade established the nature of the partnership between the Library and American
librarianship and scholarship. The achievements, in addition to interlibrary
loan and the distribution of catalog cards, included: an increase in the direct
appropriation for the Library from approximately $160,000 in FY 1898 to
almost $500,000 in FY 1908; an increase in staff from 134 to nearly 400; an
increase in the size of the book collection from approximately 900,000 volumes to 1,700,000; the creation of over a dozen new divisions and several
new reading rooms; a new emphasis on the compilation and publication of
bibliographies; a greatly expanded acquisitions program for noncopyright
and especially foreign materials; the beginnings of a reference correspondence service; the establishment of a printing plant within the Library; the
resumption and acceleration of the development of a new classification
scheme, as well as the recataloging of the Library's collections; the beginning
of the national union catalog; the publication of the first classification
schedules, the first manuscript catalogs, the first holdings checklists, and the
first union lists; the opening of the Library on Sundays; the transfer, at the
direction of President Theodore Roosevelt, of presidential papers from the
Department of State to the Library; in cooperation with the American Library
Association and the New York State Library, publication of the *ALA Catalog:
8,000 Volumes for a Popular Library*; the publication of historical texts from

the Library's collections; initiation of a program of copying, from foreign archives, manuscripts that related to American history; the first cooperative cataloging efforts with other federal libraries; the acquisition of sizable collections from abroad that today form the basis of the Library's Indic, Russian, and Japanese collections; major steps toward the revision of the U.S. copyright law; and a cooperative effort with the American Library Association that resulted in the publication of the American edition of the Anglo-American cataloging rules.[44]

There were many reasons for Putnam's early success. The political climate was right, and the country was in an expansionist mood. The library movement was eagerly looking to Putnam and the Library of Congress for leadership. The promises that never could be fulfilled when the Library was crammed into its small rooms in the Capitol could now be tested, for there was ample space for expansion—at least for a few years. But the most important reason undoubtedly was Putnam himself. He was in an enviable position and he responded magnificently. He had to be persuaded to take the job, and when he accepted he had the gratitude of both librarians and congressmen. Because of the reorganization act of 1897, he had the authority, power, and independence to operate the Library as he saw fit. He was extremely tactful in his dealings with Congress, patiently explaining all aspects of the Library and skillfully avoiding any partisan entanglements. Herbert Putnam, like Ainsworth Rand Spofford before him, *was* the Library of Congress.

The Legislative Reference Service

The progressive era was the age of efficiency experts and the scientific use of knowledge. One of the many results of the progressive movement was the creation of legislative reference libraries. Specialized library units for legislative reference came into existence in various states, notably Wisconsin, during the early 1900s. By the second decade of the century, the legislative reference movement had reached the national legislature. Before 1911, Putnam maintained that since the Library's principal purpose was service to Congress, a separate administrative unit was unnecessary. On April 6, 1911, however, in a special report on the establishment of legislative reference bureaus, Putnam changed his position and, in typical fashion, took the initiative. After outlining the specific services that a truly scientific and non-partisan legislative reference unit could provide, he noted that the Library of Congress unfortunately could not undertake such an effort without "an enlargement of its present Divisions of Law, Documents, and Bibliography, and in addition the creation of a new division under the title of a Legislative or Congressional Reference Division." After receiving the Librarian's report, the Senate Library Committee asked Putnam for his version of a satisfactory bill for establishing a legislative reference bureau.[45]

In February 1912, the House Committee on the Library held hearings to consider various bills before Congress proposing the establishment of a legislative reference bureau. Witnesses on behalf of the bill included James Bryce, British ambassador to the United States, Frederick A. Cleveland, chairman of President Taft's Commission on Economy and Efficiency, and Charles A. McCarthy of the Wisconsin legislative reference department. The sponsor of the bill, Representative John M. Nelson of Wisconsin, also read several endorsements, including one from Governor Woodrow Wilson of New Jersey. Nelson concluded the hearings by addressing the committee directly:

> I plead for the individual Member of Congress. He needs information and data upon legislation upon which he is to vote; upon bills that he intends to submit upon legislation pending; and I trust that this committee will not urge upon Congress a one-sided bill, one that will simply look after a committee or a party leader; but that we will have an institution here that will look to the collective efficiency, and will enlarge the individual capacity of every Member of the House for legislative service."[46]

A year later, when the Senate held similar hearings, there was general agreement that such a unit would be established within the Library of Congress. Putnam explained that:

> What we do not do, and what a legislative reference division in the Library would do, is to select out of this great collection—now 2,000,000 books and pamphlets—the material that may bear upon one or another of the topics under consideration by Congress or that are likely to be under consideration, or that come up under particular discussions, extracting, digesting, and concentrating material that will bear upon those questions to be set aside, available to Congress or to the individual Member of Congress or a committee of Congress. It requires duplication of material; it requires an approach to the material from a different direction from that which we now approach it.[47]

The establishment of a separate Legislative Reference Service (LRS) within the Library of Congress was authorized with a small appropriation in 1914. In 1915 the functions of the new service were broadened in accordance with new language in the appropriations act: "to gather, classify, and make available in translations, indexes, digests, compilations, and bulletins, and otherwise, data for or bearing upon legislation, and to render such data available to Congress and committees and Members thereof." That year Librarian Putnam reported that the new unit was anticipating questions from Congress concerning the following subjects: "the conservation bills, so-called," the merchant marine, the government of the Philippines, immigration, convict-made goods, railroad securities, federal aid in roadmaking, publicity in campaign contributions, and a national budget system.[48]

The creation of a separate appropriation and administrative unit for legislative reference could be viewed as an indirect acknowledgment of the broad range of national services offered by the Library, insofar that the Congress was forced to create a new organizational unit to respond to its own specialized requirements. However, as Putnam stated in 1913, the legislative reference function was actually a new research service not previously provided. Furthermore, the Library's other administrative units continued to give congressional requests priority.

New Cultural and Scholarly Roles

During the first half of Putnam's administration, lasting roughly from 1899 through World War I, the Librarian had, by and large, the full support of professional librarians and the American Library Association. The next 20 years were not so harmonious, and the Library of Congress and the American library movement drifted apart.

One reason for the separation was that Putnam gave increasing attention to matters that did not directly concern the American library community. The establishment of the Legislative Reference Service is one example. Another was the enhancement of a different type of national role: the Library of Congress as a symbol of American democracy. This role was strengthened in 1921 when the Declaration of Independence and the Constitution of the United States were transferred from the Department of State to the Library and placed on permanent display. Furthermore, in the mid-1920s, through Putnam's efforts, the Library of Congress became a patron of the arts.

In late 1924 Elizabeth Sprague Coolidge offered to give to the Congress a sum of $60,000 for the construction and equipping of an auditorium, connected to the Library, which would be planned for the performance of chamber music. On Putnam's recommendation the offer was accepted. It was followed shortly thereafter by an endowment from Mrs. Coolidge to support the concerts and the Music Division generally, an endowment that led to the creation, on March 3, 1925, of the Library of Congress Trust Fund Board. Through the board the Library, for the first time, could support activities on gift funds, for the board was authorized "to accept, receive, hold, and administer such gifts or bequests of personal property for the benefit of, or in connection with, the Library, its collections, or its service." The Library's first chamber music festival was held in the new Coolidge Auditorium on October 28–30, 1925.

Mrs. Coolidge's generosity was soon supplemented by gifts from others, including James B. Wilbur (for acquisition in photocopy of manuscript material on American history in European archives), Richard R. Bowker (to further the Library's bibliographic service), William Evarts Benjamin (to endow a chair in American history), the Carnegie Corporation (for a chair in the fine arts), and Archer M. Huntington (for a chair of Spanish and Portuguese literature). Gertrude Clarke Whittall donated five Stradivarii instruments to the Library and, in 1936, donated funds to the Trust Fund Board establishing a foundation to maintain the instruments and support concerts in which those instruments would be used.

By the last decade of his administration, Putnam's personal interest in library cooperation and related technical matters had been overshadowed by his concern with the "interpretation" of the collections. The Librarian always had viewed the use of the Library's collections as the prime object of the administration. In the 1896 hearings, for example, he described the national library as, ideally, the library "which stands foremost as a model and example of assisting forward the work of scholarship in the United States."[49] After the establishment of the Library of Congress Trust Fund Board in 1925, he devoted an increasing amount of time to obtaining private funds to support chairs and consultantships for subject specialists who could aid scholars in their use of the collections.

In 1933 Putnam described the purpose of his administration for an anniversary publication prepared by his Harvard class of 1883. That purpose was,

without ignoring the intensive duty to Congress itself and to the other government establishments: (1) to enlarge the collections to a degree and diversity truly comprehensive; (2) to develop an apparatus for the use of them quickly responsive; (3) to widen the service so as to embrace with it the general public of serious investigators; and (4) in whatever ways might be practicable, to render at least the by-products of our operations serviceable to other libraries (of whatever type) in effecting economies in their own administration.

He next described his new efforts to improve the interpretation of the collections, by adding the "human expert" to the apparatus, as "the most significant phase of the evolution of the institution, and one which, if it can be further developed and made permanent, will notably distinguish it."[50] By 1933 Putnam was also concentrating on another internal problem—lack of space. Construction of the badly needed Annex Building, authorized by Congress in 1930, had been delayed. That building, located directly east of the Main Building, would not open until 1939.

In sum, as Putnam focused on other activities, his interest in the role of the Library of Congress as a leader among American libraries lessened. For example, in 1935, in a letter to ALA Secretary Carl H. Milam, the Librarian flatly rejected the notion of locating a federal library bureau in the Library of Congress, contending that the functions of such an agency "would tend to confuse and impede the service to learning which should be the primary duty of our National Library." In Putnam's opinion, the bureau instead "should be associated with one of the executive departments of the government."[51]

Putnam's authoritarian style presented further difficulties. He was a stern administrator, both venerated and feared. Apparently no associate ever called him by his given name, and it appears that there was no one, either inside or outside the Library, who was able to influence him to any significant degree.

Considering all these factors, it is not surprising that Putnam became increasingly isolated from his own staff and from the American library community. By the late 1930s, the Library of Congress was suffering from administrative stagnation, intensified by low staff morale and operational problems such as a large cataloging backlog. These problems were compounded by Putnam's refusal, or inability, to delegate responsibility. The Library's annual report for 1901 lists 16 administrative divisions, each reporting directly to the Librarian. By 1939 there were 35 divisions, each reporting directly to the Librarian. Even Herbert Putnam, with all his gifts, could not successfully oversee 35 diverse units and 1,100 employees. In the late 1930s there were many librarians and politicians who were waiting for Putnam to decide to retire. Apparently even President Franklin D. Roosevelt chose to wait.

In mid-1938 Putnam informed President Roosevelt that he was prepared to step down, and legislation was approved creating the office of Librarian Emeritus. It was nearly a year, however, before a nomination was made. In the meantime, the Library occupied its new Annex Building and Putnam gathered accolades—at least from the scholarly community. For example, in a January 1939 statement addressed to Putnam, the American Council of Learned Societies paid him a special tribute:

> You, and the collaborators and associates whom you have chosen, have made the Library of Congress a national institution, the peer in all respects of its great prototypes, the British Museum and the Bibliothèque Nationale. You have made it an indispensable instrument on

the American continent for the promotion of learning and the increase of knowledge.[52]

Librarian MacLeish Takes Office

One measure of Putnam's success was the change his 40-year term of office brought in the perception of the job of Librarian of Congress. In 1899 the contest was between an ALA candidate, an experienced library administrator, and a relatively unknown Congressman, Representative Samuel Barrows of Massachusetts. In 1939 ALA supported its own executive secretary and a seasoned administrator, Carl H. Milam, for the post, but President Roosevelt instead nominated a well-known national figure, Archibald MacLeish.[53] In President Roosevelt's view, the job required not a professional librarian but "a gentleman and a scholar . . . who in every nation of the world, would be known as such."[54]

In choosing MacLeish, Roosevelt followed the advice of his friend Supreme Court Justice Felix Frankfurter, who informed the President that "only a scholarly man of letters can make a great national library a general place of habitation for scholars." Furthermore, the Library of Congress was "not merely a library and in the immediate future even more so than in the past it will be concerned with problems quite outside the traditional tasks associated with collecting, housing, and circulating books."[55] Roosevelt agreed, and eventually talked MacLeish into taking the job. The nomination was announced at a press conference on June 6, 1939.[56]

ALA was shocked. Not only had Roosevelt ignored its persistent offers of assistance in the search for Putnam's successor, he also had nominated someone with no library experience. Meeting in San Francisco at its annual convention, on June 18 ALA adopted a resolution opposing the nomination because "the Congress and the American people should have as a Librarian . . . one who is not only a gentleman and a scholar but who is also the ablest library administrator available." ALA testified against the nomination in the Senate hearings but to no avail. On June 29, 1939, by a vote of 63 to 8, the Senate confirmed the President's choice, and Archibald MacLeish took the oath of office as the ninth Librarian of Congress on July 10, 1939.[57]

When MacLeish became Librarian, the Library of Congress had a book collection of approximately six million volumes, a staff of about 1.100, including buildings and grounds employees, and, in FY 1939, a direct appropriation of approximately $3 million. Shortly after taking office, the new Librarian tackled the most pressing internal problems left behind by Putnam. Studies were undertaken of the Library's cataloging, acquisitions, personnel, and budget policies. The results were distressing, indicating serious cataloging backlogs, unexpected deficiencies in the collections, professional salaries substantially below those in other government agencies, and an inefficient accounting system. The Librarian's budget requests in early 1940 were based on these studies.

MacLeish asked for substantial increases. The total request was for $4.2 million, and included 287 additional positions. The Librarian explained that this request not only reflected needs deferred until the Annex was completed, but it also was "the first in many years in which the long-existent and long-maturing needs of the various Divisions of the Library, and of the Library as a whole, have been fully presented to the Congress." With regard to the increase requested for the Legislative Reference Service, he explained that he was proceeding on the assumption "that the Congress has a right to scholarly research and counsel in law and history and economics at least as equal to the people who come before committees . . . [and] it is our obligation to present that kind of research and that kind of counsel." Interestingly, this part of his request was denied pending "more experienced and mature study," since, according to the House Appropriations Committee, "if Congress needs the services of research experts along the lines indicated in addition to those that are already found in the federal service, there is a serious question as to whether those experts should be a part of the Library of Congress."[58]

The Appropriations Committee approved an increase of $340,000, barely a third of the Librarian's request, but its report was sympathetic and encouraging. The committee, for example, expressed its pleasure at the "industrious and intelligent manner in which Mr. MacLeish has entered upon his duties." But the committee also set the new Librarian's priorities for him. Since many important needs of the Library had been deferred "due to inadequacy of space and other reasons," the committee felt that "first and foremost in consideration of the needs is the necessity of preventing any further arrearage in the matter of processing material coming into the Library each year . . . and second, the preservation and putting into condition of material already in the Library." To help meet this need, over 50 new positions were given to the processing divisions. In all, the committee approved 130 of the 287 new positions requested by the Librarian.[59]

The Librarian's Committee and Reorganization

In response to the Appropriation Committee's report and to continue the investigations already begun, on April 10, 1940, MacLeish appointed a special Librarian's Committee to analyze the operations of the Library—especially the processing activities. The report of that committee was the catalyst for MacLeish's reorganization, a restructuring that served as the basis of the Library's administrative structure for the next three decades.

The Librarian's Committee consisted of Professor Carleton B. Joeckel, University of Chicago Library School (chairman); Paul North Rice, chief of the Reference Department, New York Public Library; and Andrew D. Osborn, chief of the Serial Division, Harvard College Library. The work of the committee was supported by a grant from the Carnegie Corporation. The Librarian's Committee began its work on April 16, 1940, assisted by the Library's own staff and three individuals from other institutions: Keyes D. Metcalf, director of the Harvard University Library; Francis R. St. John, assistant librarian, Enoch Pratt Free Library; and L. Quincy Mumford, assistant in charge of the preparation unit, New York Public Library. The committee's detailed, 300-page report was submitted to Librarian MacLeish on June 15, 1940.[60]

The major purpose of the committee's effort was to analyze the Library's processing operations and to recommend structural and procedural changes in the existing system. Its final recommendations were in fact much more comprehensive. As explained in the introduction to the report:

> Because of the intimate relationships between the work of the "processing" sector of the Library and the administrative and service

sectors, attention necessarily has been directed also to certain aspects of the structure and operations of the Library as a whole. To this degree, therefore, the Committee has extended the field of its examination beyond its primary assignment.

The report of the Librarian's Committee was organized into nine chapters: Introduction, Organization, Administration, Personnel, the Card Division, the Catalog and Classification Division, the Copyright Office, Special Problems, and Considerations for the Future. Its major conclusion was that "the Library cannot be an efficient operating agency until its organic structure has been thoroughly overhauled," pointing out that "the present organization of the Library is a historical growth in which expediency has been far more important than careful and logical planning." It had been 39 years since a "thorough-going reconsideration" of the Library's organization had taken place. The committee undertook such a reconsideration and advocated a reorganization plan that divided the Library into three major departments [Administration, Acquisition and Preparation, and Reference] and reduced the span of control "at all levels in the hierarchy."[61]

The committee emphasized that the reorganization should be accompanied by a statement of the Library's objectives:

Organization [of the Library] has encountered serious difficulties because of the lack of clearly formulated objectives. The Library has objectives, to be sure, but they appear never to have been stated as a whole in organized form. In general, they must be inferred from what the Library does and from what the various Librarians of Congress have said in certain pronouncements as to the purposes of the Library and the scope of its services [e.g. the Annual Reports of 1869, 1875, 1897, 1907, 1908, and 1928]. Careful analysis of objectives is just beginning in a series of conferences undertaken as a basis for the reclassification of Library personnel by the Civil Service Commission.

As a summary statement on the development of objectives, it may be said that emphasis on various aspects of the work of the Library has fluctuated from period to period. At one time, emphasis was placed on a rather general kind of service; at another, on technical operations in the Library itself and on technical services to the libraries of the nation; at another, on the Library as the Library of Congress. Even the lack of a comprehensive organic act defining the scope of the Library adds to the confusion. [See Herbert Putnam, "The Future of the Library of Congress," in The Library of Tomorrow, ed. by E. M. Danton, Chicago: American Library Association, 1939, pp. 179–191.][62]

In its final chapter, "Considerations for the Future," the Librarian's Committee summarized its most important recommendations, stating them as an eight-point program for the Library of Congress:

1. The Library should be reorganized into three major "departments" (Administration, Acquisition and Preparation, and Reference) and the reorganization should be accompanied by the restatement of definite objectives.
2. The Library's place "in the galaxy of Federal libraries" should be clearly defined, primarily through the organization of a "Federal Library Council" chaired by the Librarian of Congress.

3. The Library needed to put "a new accent on administration." In the technical divisions, for example, administration was at a "low ebb," with high costs, low output, and "appalling arrears."

4. The Library needed to hire more highly qualified personnel, especially in the technical divisions. Reclassification of the staff was imperative and the Library had to "frankly face the possibility of the appointment of its personnel under Civil Service regulations."

5. The Library should "catalog for the Library of Congress," adopting "cataloging methods which meet its own needs without too much concern for what other libraries may think or do." The committee felt that:

> once this basic principle is firmly established, the Library is much more likely to do its own work well. Moreover, it need have little concern about other libraries; they are almost certain to follow with few reservations the practices of the Library of Congress, as they have in the past. (Note: this does not mean that the Library of Congress should disregard cataloging standards. As a large, scholarly library it must maintain standards which would be satisfactory to other libraries throughout the country.) The general result of the adoption of such a policy should be a more sensible attitude toward cataloging techniques. The services of the Library of Congress to other libraries, under such a policy, are likely to increase rather than diminish. The greatest technical contribution the Library of Congress can make to other libraries is to get its own work done promptly and satisfactorily.

6. The Library should make "important and extensive modifications" in its cataloging procedures, adopting standard rules for short cataloging and, in general, speeding up the process. The committee felt that "the time has come at the Library of Congress, as it has in many libraries, when the doctrine of technical perfection in cataloging must be frankly challenged."

7. The Library must make every effort to restore the technical efficiency of its operations. Better planning was needed, along with improved coordination between the processing work of the Copyright Office and that done in the rest of the Library, and the creation of a general plan for the coordinated development of the more than 200 separate catalogs, shelflists, and indexes maintained by various divisions throughout the Library.

8. The Library should develop a program of continuing research directed at solving various internal problems of administration and technique. The list of topics to be investigated included: use of the public catalog, the cataloging of documents, the possibility of printing or reproducing in book form the complete Library of Congress catalog or at least portions of it, the use of a classed catalog, aspects of cooperative and centralized cataloging, improved integration with Copyright Office cataloging procedures, plans for divisional catalogs, a plan for short cataloging, various cost studies, and job analyses of the various kinds of work performed throughout the Library.[63]

Librarian MacLeish's response to the report of the Librarian's Committee was quick and positive. On June 28, 1940, two weeks after receiving the recommendations, he announced that on July 1, or as soon thereafter as possible, three new departments would be established: the Administrative, Processing, and Reference Departments.

The reorganization that resulted took several years to implement; in fact, parts of it were "completed" after MacLeish left office and his associate, Luther H. Evans, had become Librarian of Congress. The fundamental decisions, however, were made between 1939 and 1944. The Administrative Department was created on July 1, 1940, dissolved on June 30, 1943, and then reestablished on February 7, 1946. The new Reference Department's principal functions as described by MacLeish on June 29, 1940, would be (1) reference work throughout the Library; (2) the servicing of books to readers; (3) selection of books for the Library; and (4) the care and custody of the collections. On March 25, 1944, the department was reorganized into three principal services: the Legislative Reference Service, the Public Reference Service, and the Circulation Service. The new Processing Department was organized in late 1940 by L. Quincy Mumford, who assisted the Librarian's Committee and obtained a one-year leave of absence from the New York Public Library for this special assignment. The Legislative Reference Service was given departmental status in 1946. A new Acquisitions Department was established on June 30, 1943, "to provide an administrative organization for the more effective development of the Library's collections." All acquisition, selection, and accessioning functions performed by the Reference and Processing Departments and the Law Library were transferred to the new department. The Acquisitions Department was abolished in August 1947, its functions assumed by the Processing Department. After this consolidation, the basic organization of the Library of Congress into six departments—the Reference, Processing, and Administrative Departments, the Legislative Reference Service, the Law Library, and the Copyright Office, did not change for three decades.[64]

In the October 1944 issue of *Library Quarterly*, Librarian MacLeish described the reorganization, beginning with a description of the Library as he originally found it: "The Library of Congress in 1939 was not so much an organization in its own right as the lengthened shadow of one man—a man of great force, extraordinary abilities, and a personality which left its fortunate impression upon everything he touched. Only a man of Herbert Putnam's remarkable qualities could have administered an institution of the size of the Library of Congress by direct and personal supervision of all its operations, and only if his administration were based upon the intimate familiarities of forty years." He concluded by expressing his hope and belief that the reorganization provided "a sensible, orderly, and manageable structure, strong enough to support the great future of which the Library of Congress is so manifestly capable." Moreover, "whatever else the reorganization of the Library has accomplished it has given, I trust, an increasing number of men and women the sense of participating creatively and responsibly in a work which all of them may well feel proud to share."[65]

The Canons of Selection and Service

By April 1940, when the Librarian's Committee convened, MacLeish and his assistants already were examining the Library's objectives. The committee's observations about the need for stated goals provided stimulus, and the job was done by the end of the year. This first explicit statement of the

Library's objectives, presented in the 1940 annual report, was full of exceptions and qualifications. It also incorporated earlier practices and did not present any new concepts. Nonetheless, the statement was significant as the first attempt to provide the Library with clearly defined goals and as an accurate reflection of the priority accorded the Congress in the Library's operations. The statement was divided into two sections: objectives "with regard to the character of the collections," termed "Canons of Selection," and objectives of the Library viewed "as an agency of research and reference work." The three Canons of Selection were:

1. The Library of Congress should possess in some useful form all bibliothecal materials necessary to the Congress and to the officers of government of the United States in the performance of their duties.
2. The Library of Congress should possess all books and other materials (whether in original or copy) which express and record the life and achievements of the people of the United States.
3. The Library of Congress should possess, in some useful form, the material parts of the records of other societies, past and present, and should accumulate, in original or in copy, full and representative collections of the written records of those societies and peoples whose experience is of most immediate concern to the people of the United States.

In stating these canons, the Librarian of Congress explained that the degree of their implementation was determined by time and money. The Canons of Selection were to apply only to the Library's acquisition of materials by purchase, not to acquisition by gift or by deposit for copyright.[66] The reference and research objectives emphasized the Library's obligation to the Congress. The three objectives were:

1. The Library of Congress undertakes for Members of the Congress any and all research and reference projects bearing upon the Library's collections and required by Members in connection with the performance of their legislative duties.
2. The Library of Congress undertakes for officers and departments of government research projects, appropriate to the Library, which can be executed by reference to its collections, and which the staff of offices and departments are unable to execute.
3. The reference staff and facilities of the Library of Congress are available to members of the public, universities, learned societies and other libraries requiring services which the Library staff is equipped to give and which can be given without interference with services to the Congress and other agencies of the Federal Government.[67]

The first Library of Congress annual report was published in 1866. Since then the most significant reports have been those of 1901 and 1940, issued by Librarians Putnam and MacLeish, respectively. Both Putnam and MacLeish comprehensively outlined the Library's activities and provided the rationale for a new stage in its history. MacLeish, for example, not only stated the Library's objectives; he also explained why, in his view, the Library of Congress served both the Congress and the nation:

By creation and primary responsibility, [it is] the library of the elected representatives of the people of the United States. But Congress long ago extended the use of its library to other officers and offices of the federal government and to the people themselves, placing at the disposition of the users not only the rich collections with which the Library was in time provided, but the skilled services of the scholars, the technicians, and the experts in various fields whose first duty was to make the collections serviceable to Congress.

The Library of Congress thus became what Thomas Jefferson had once called it: "the Library of the United States"—the library of the people's representatives in Congress, the library of the officers of their government and the library of the people themselves. But it became a people's library not in the usual sense of that term, the sense familiar in the so-called public libraries, but in a very special and significant sense. As a consequence of the fact that the Congress extended to the people the use, not of the collections only, *but of the services of scholarship which had been created to make the collections more usefully available to the Congress*, the Library became a *reference* library to the people—A People's Library of Reference.[68]

While his administrative reorganization probably was MacLeish's most significant achievement, it was only one of his accomplishments. He also enhanced the Library's reputation as a major cultural institution, not only because of his own prominence as a poet, but also by inaugurating the first series of poetry readings. He brought many prominent writers and poets to the Library, including war refugees Alexis Saint- Léger Léger and Thomas Mann, and American poet Allen Tate, who served both as poetry consultant and as the first editor of the newly established *Quarterly Journal of Current Acquisitions*. Relationships between the Library and scholarly and literary communities were improved through a new program of resident fellowships for young scholars and the formation of The Fellows of the Library of Congress, a group of prominent writers and poets.

MacLeish, a wartime librarian, quickly became a leading American spokesman for the cause of democracy, a role that helped his relations with the library community. Speaking before the American Library Association on May 31, 1940, he asserted that librarians "must become active and not passive agents of democratic process." The association that had so bitterly opposed his nomination a year earlier applauded vigorously, and relations between the Library of Congress and ALA were on the mend. On May 11, 1942, the Library, ALA, and the Association of Research Libraries (ARL) signed an agreement with Edwards Brothers of Ann Arbor, Michigan, for printing *A Catalog of Books Represented by Library of Congress Printed Cards, 1898–1942*. The project was one that the library associations had tried to develop with Librarian Putnam, but without success. At the June 1942 annual meeting of the association, ALA President Charles H. Brown introduced MacLeish as "a man of whom we librarians are very proud," and the Librarian received a thunderous ovation before delivering his address, which was titled "Toward an Intellectual Offensive."[69]

MacLeish and Luther H. Evans, his Chief Assistant Librarian, inaugurated a variety of advisory procedures, both internally and with individuals outside the Library. A staff *Information Bulletin* was started and a staff advisory committee was created "to provide a mechanism for the sifting and crystallization of employee opinion as to measures which the Library administration might appropriately take for the improvement of the operations of the Library." In April 1942 MacLeish announced the formation of the Librarian's Council, composed of distinguished librarians, scholars, and book collectors, who would make recommendations "for the conduct of our services, the development of our collections, and the initiation and control of bibliographical studies." Weekly meetings with department directors were started and in 1943 the Library administration began holding informal, monthly meetings with the professional staff.[70]

During the war MacLeish had helped Roosevelt in a variety of ways. These activities meant that he served only part-time as Librarian of Congress. In October 1941 the president directed him to assume, in addition to his duties as Librarian, supervision of the government's newly established Office of Facts and Figures. The appointment was controversial, both because of the publications produced by the new office and because the Librarian's additional duties often kept him away from the Library. In June 1942 the Office of Facts and Figures was combined with other agencies to form the Office of War Information, which MacLeish served part-time as an assistant director. The Librarian also drafted speeches for the president and represented the government at various meetings, as in March 1944 when he went to London as a delegate to the Conference of Allied Ministers of Education, a forerunner of the United Nations. MacLeish apparently expressed a wish to leave the Library of Congress as early as the summer of 1943, but he stayed in office until December 19, 1944, when he resigned to become an assistant secretary of state, to be in charge of public and cultural relations.[71]

Librarian Evans Takes Office

The American Library Association played a subdued role in the appointment of MacLeish's successor. Remembering the ill-fated attempts of 1939, the association's leaders did little more than offer advice—even though some individual members made stronger efforts. President Roosevelt, and after his death President Harry S Truman, apparently considered several candidates, in particular Julian Boyd, the scholarly librarian of Princeton University, and Theodore C. Blegen, dean of the graduate school of the University of Minnesota. Roosevelt offered the job to Boyd, who declined, and, in the end, Blegen never was asked. As it turned out, Truman's final choice, Chief Assistant Librarian Luther H. Evans, was probably more acceptable to ALA than either Boyd or Blegen.[72] Even though he was a political scientist by training, Evans certainly was an experienced library administrator. The new Librarian, nominated by President Truman on June 18, 1945, and confirmed by the Senate on June 29, was the first Assistant Librarian since Spofford to become Librarian. When he took the oath of office on June 30, the Library had a book collection of over 7 million volumes, a staff of over 1,200, and an appropriation in FY 1945 of over $4.5 million.

Evans was head of the Historical Records Survey until late 1939 when Librarian MacLeish appointed him director of the Legislative Reference Service. Evans thus gained an appreciation of the Library's legislative role before he was named Chief Assistant Librarian and director of the Reference Department on October 31, 1940. After June 30, 1943, he devoted himself exclusively to his duties as Chief Assistant Librarian.

As the war came to an end, Congress began a determined effort to strengthen its own resources, including the Legislative Reference Service. One of Evans' first acts as Librarian of Congress was to reorganize the service, taking advantage of the increased appropriation given to LRS in FY 1946. In March 1946, the Joint Committee on the Organization of the Congress recommended to the Congress "that the Legislative Reference Service be immediately increased in size and scope more adequately to serve the individual members of Congress and also to provide a pool of experts available for use by the committees of Congress."[73] This is precisely what the Legislative Reorganization Act of 1946, approved by President Truman on August 2, 1946, did. Not only were the responsibilities of LRS greatly expanded, but, as mentioned earlier, it also was given permanent statutory basis as a separate Library department. The act authorized increased appropriations to enable LRS to employ nationally eminent specialists in 19 broad subject fields. It also stipulated that the Joint Committee on the Library would consist of the chairman and four members of the Committee on Rules and Administration of the Senate and the chairman and four members of the Committee on House Administration of the House of Representatives.

Luther Evans had a broad view of the Library of Congress and its responsibilities, a view encouraged by President Truman himself. After his initial interview with the president, Evans reported to a friend that Truman "wants the Library to give service to Congress, but he wants it also to be 'the Library of the United States' and give increased service to the little libraries all over the country."[74]

The new Librarian was not satisfied with expanded services for the Congress. He felt that the end of the war also brought new responsibilities to the entire Library, describing one aspect of its new role in the Washington *Sunday Star* in late 1945:

> For the Library of Congress, as a part of the state, an era has ended; a new era begins. It is necessary to bear in mind the fact that our civilization has been threatened with destruction, and to remember that destruction has been avoided only through an unprecedented mobilization of man's knowledge of himself and his environment. . . . No spot on the earth's surface is any longer alien to the interest of the American people. No particle of knowledge should remain unavailable to them.[75]

Evans and his colleagues continued the assessment of the Library's functions and goals begun under MacLeish and concluded that the time had come for the Library to step forward and exert new leadership. As he explained in his 1946 annual report:

> Of all the circumstances which were present when I assumed the librarianship, one was paramount: the knowledge that henceforth we would live and work in a new world. And for me and for my associates it meant that we must revise and rebuild and reconstitute the Library to resolve for its own part and within the terms of its own duties, the problems which this new world would encounter.[76]

The 1947 Budget Request

The result of the assessment was a detailed plan for a major expansion of all aspects of the Library's activities. Evans' plans were explained in the lengthy budget justification he submitted to the House Subcommittee on

Legislative Branch Appropriations on April 22, 1946. The budget estimates, which were "conceived in the light of what we believe to be the Congressional conception of the role and work of the Library," called for a rapid and comprehensive expansion of the Library and an increase in its appropriation from $5,104,568 in FY 1946 to $9,756,852 for FY 1947. Evans felt that the document

> reflects just about the best knowledge, vision, and judgment we of the Library administration could bring to bear on the problem of the future of the Library of Congress in the first year of my tenure as Librarian. Without wishing to blame Messrs. MacLeish and Putnam for anything for which they would not care to assume responsibility, I think it fair to say that much of the thinking behind the budget proposals, and many of the specific objectives sought by them, were approved by them or developed as a natural consequence of the kind of Library of Congress they dreamed of and worked toward. From what I have learned of their lives and work, which is much less than I hope it will be in a few years, I believe the same could be said in reference to Mr. Spofford and other Librarians of Congress.[77]

The Appropriations Committee, however, refused to accede to Evans' request, recommending an appropriation of $5,859,900, an increase of only $755,332 above FY 1946. The principal reason for not approving the amount requested was disturbing. In its May 1946 report the committee explained that it wanted

> to give attention to the need for a determination as to what the policy of the Library of Congress is going to be in the way of expansion and service to the public and to the Congress. The original purpose in establishing the Library was to serve Congress; however, it would seem that the Library has evolved not only into a Congressional Library but a national and international library as well. It is believed that the responsibility for determining Library policy rests with legislative committees of the Congress charged with the responsibility for operation of the Library and not with the Appropriations Committee whose responsibility it is to appropriate for the projects and activities duly authorized by the Congress. If it is the desire to build and maintain the largest library in the world which, according to testimony, the Library of Congress is at present, that is one matter, and if it should be the policy to maintain a library primarily for the service of Congress, it is quite another matter from the standpoint of fiscal needs.[78]

The Senate Committee on Appropriations recommended a slightly higher sum, $6,172,437, and the final total for the Library in FY 1947, as approved by Harry S Truman on July 1, 1946, was $6,069,967—an increase of $965,399 over the previous year but $3,686,885 less than the request.

The congressional reduction in the Library's budget request put the Library of Congress on the defensive during the Evans administration. In the introduction to his annual report for FY 1946, submitted on November 15, 1946, the Librarian referred to the May subcommittee report and expressed his concern:

> Now years and years ago the Congress had, as we supposed, settled these questions once and for all, and for years and years its Library had developed along lines which successive Congresses had carefully con-

sidered and fully approved. No blame for the unfortunate hiatus can, however, attach to the subcommittee. Responsibility for the present crisis in its affairs is squarely the responsibility of the Library itself. It is as selfishly regrettable as it is functionally natural that an institution dedicated to the enlightenment of the Government and people of the United States should itself remain in shadow. It is a source rather than an object of light. But it is high time that the Library should, for a moment, focus the lamp on its own face and explain to the bewildered onlooker its bony structure and its inherited characteristics.

The Annual Report this year begins, therefore, with an introspective and historical statement, which seeks to explain the status of the Library and endeavors to tell how it got this way. It attempts to relate the activities of a year just past to all the other years it has known.[79]

The "introspective and historical statement" was David C. Mearns' *The Story Up to Now: The Library of Congress 1800–1946*, a brief but delightful history that emphasizes, not surprisingly, the Library's national origins and role.

In the same annual report Evans described the formation of a Library of Congress Planning Committee, composed of distinguished persons representing the Library's users. The committee, the Librarian announced, would "produce a report by mid-January for me to forward to the Congress as a presentation of what is believed to be the best judgment of the country, short of the judgment of the Congress itself, as to what role the Library of Congress ought to play in the national life." The committee's membership, the Librarian noted, "should give it the standing which it merits."[80] The chairman was Keyes D. Metcalf, director of libraries at Harvard University. The members were Herbert Eugene Bolton, historian, University of California; Edward U. Condon, director, National Bureau of Standards; Douglas S. Freeman, author of *Robert E. Lee* and editor of Richmond *News Leader*; Waldo G. Leland, director, American Council of Learned Societies; Wilmarth S. Lewis, book collector, editor, and bibliographer; Carl McFarland, McFarland and Sellers, Washington, D.C.; Kathryn Mier, chairman of the Missouri State Library Commission; Lessing J. Rosenwald, book and print collector; Ralph R. Shaw, librarian, U.S. Department of Agriculture; and Walter L. Wright, Jr., professor of Turkish Language and History, Princeton University.

The Planning Committee Report

The Planning Committee report was submitted to Librarian Evans on March 12, 1947, and published as an appendix to the 1947 annual report. The letter of transmittal evokes the seriousness with which the committee undertook its task:

The Planning Committee, in accordance with your request, has addressed itself to the whole problem of the future of the Library of Congress. This has been done in a spirit of free inquiry. Every important issue has been pursued wherever it might lead, regardless of established policies or points of view of agencies or institutions whose interests might be involved in the findings. The Committee has been convinced that you and your colleagues at the Library of Congress desire a direct, fresh, and unprejudiced examination of the future role of the Library, and your staff has given its support in this spirit. The same fine co-operation has come from representatives of agencies and institutions, both governmental and non-governmental, with whom the Committee has taken counsel or from whom it has requested specific information.

As a result, the Committee has been able in a relatively short time to arrive at its conclusions and to make recommendations concerning the role the Library of Congress should play in the affairs of the nation. The role has been important in the past, but it should be even more important in the future. The Committee has tested tentative drafts of its recommendations by having them discussed in meetings of a considerable number of library and scholarly associations. These discussions have been helpful in bringing out the views of a group much broader than the Committee itself. We are glad to report that the consideration given the recommendations by these groups of librarians and scholars has been followed by practically unanimous support of the Committee's proposals.[81]

In submitting its report, the committee expressed the hope that if approved in its present or in a revised form, the document would "serve as a basis for a Charter for the Library of Congress which will provide the legislative authorization required for the present and proposed activities of the Library."

The committee summarized its recommendations in the introduction to its report:

The Committee has studied carefully the collections and services of the Library and is impressed with what the Library has done and can do for the nation. The Committee is convinced that the actual status of the Library as a National Library should be officially recognized in its name and that it should be designated "The Library of Congress, the National Library of the United States of America."

The Committee believes that the library needs of the Congress and of the other agencies of the Federal Government and of the country at large will be served by further strengthening this institution, and it recommends that the Library undertake additional duties and services, which, as presently constituted, it can neither undertake nor perform, but which are properly the functions of the National Library.

The purpose of a national library is to make the world's accumulation of useful knowledge available for national needs. As the National Library of the United States, the Library of Congress should develop its general resources to a point beyond those in any other library, make its collections known and available to the people of the United States, and supplement the collections and encourage the work of other libraries in the United States. At present the Library is not able to carry on any of these functions satisfactorily. Its collections in many areas are too limited; there are serious arrearages in cataloging and making available material already at hand; and the service of the collection is inadequate in many fields.

The Committee believes that a turning point in the history of the Library of Congress has been reached. If the Library fails to provide the services outlined in this report, the Committee believes that it will be necessary to build elsewhere in the Government and throughout the nation the services which it is recommended that the Library of Congress should provide, and that these services, because of their lack of centralization and of connection with the greatest collection of books and other materials in the nation, will be less satisfactory and more expensive than if they were provided by the Library of Congress. The Committee believes that the nation will find it difficult, if not impossible, to discharge important responsibilities to its citizens and to the world unless the Federal Government is prepared to set up the kinds of library services which are proposed, and the Committee sincerely hopes that the recommendations here presented will be given the most careful consideration by the Congress.[82]

After explaining that it did not consider administrative organization or budget questions in its report, the committee divided its recommendations into two major categories, both directed at the Joint Committee on the Library. In the first, it recommended that the Joint Committee ask the Congress to:

A. Recognize by Resolution that the Library of Congress is in fact the National Library of the United States, and that, whenever its name appears in print on official publications or on its own letterhead, it be stated as "The Library of Congress, the National Library of the United States of America."

B. Recognize the Army Medical Library and the Library of the Department of Agriculture as Libraries giving National Service in a Special Field.

C. Recognize the responsibility of the Librarian of Congress to provide other Federal Agencies with materials that those agencies do not need for frequent use and do not have in their own collections.

D. Establish a council, committee or other organization to coordinate the activities of the Federal libraries. This organization should be empowered, when it believes it to be in the national interest, to propose to the Congress recognition of other libraries in addition to the Army Medical and Department of Agriculture Libraries as Libraries giving National Service in a Special Field, and it should consider as one of its objectives such coordination among the Federal libraries in Washington as will best provide the several Federal agencies with the library materials and services needed to carry on their work efficiently, economically, and without unnecessary duplication.

E. Authorize the Librarian of Congress to establish a National Library Advisory Council to aid him in his relations with research libraries of the nation and to help in his efforts to avoid unnecessary duplication of the expensive library services to scholarship that are handicapping the national library program.[83]

The second category of recommendations requested the Joint Committee to direct the Librarian of Congress to:

A. Take the lead in establishing a National Manuscript Council made up of representatives of national, regional, and local historical organizations and agencies, whose duty it will be to advise as to the preservation and distribution of manuscript material.

B. Explore with such officers as the archivist of the United States and the director of the National Gallery the possibility of transferring from the Library of Congress holdings, which it acquired in the past, but would not acquire today because there are other Federal institutions that are more appropriate custodians for the material.[84]

The remaining sections of the report addressed four principal questions: the Library's name; its services as part of the federal library system; its services to nonfederal libraries, institutions, and individuals; and the Library's acquisitions program.

The committee noted that it had been urged to recommend that the name of the Library be changed to "The National Library" on the ground that, "while it is the Library of Congress, it is also the National Library." It explained that

those making this proposal state that the general public does not understand the present position of the Library as a National Library and that the institution will never be seen in its proper perspective until the name is changed.[85]

The Planning Committee did not accept this point of view and recommended instead that a qualifying subtitle be added whenever the name appeared in print and it be stated "THE LIBRARY OF CONGRESS: The National Library of the United States." It was further recommended, however, "that the Joint Committee on the Library ask the Congress to recognize by resolution that the Library of Congress is, in fact, the National Library of the United States."

The proper role of the Library of Congress as part of the federal library system was outlined in three recommendations:

1. The Library of Congress should undertake for Members of Congress any and all library services, including reference, research, and other types of service involving use of the Library's collections, which are required by Members in the performance of their official duties. There should be no exceptions to this rule. Only a lack of means to provide the necessary space, collections, and skilled staff would justify a failure on the Library's part to meet such demands.

2. The Library of Congress should provide upon request, reference and lending service for Government Agencies. It should furnish the agencies with study rooms, access to the Library's collections, and in special cases should assemble material for their use; but the Library should provide research service and compile for other agencies extensive bibliographies only when the interest in the subject is widespread; when the work has been specifically authorized and financed by the Library's own appropriations; or when the arrangements specified in the next paragraph prevail.

3. The Library of Congress, since it is better prepared to perform extensive bibliographical and reference service and other cooperative library activities than other agencies of the Government, should make use of the authority granted by Section 601 of the Economy Act (47 Stat. 417) to accept transfers of funds which will enable it to undertake extensive bibliographical and reference projects on behalf of other agencies when such projects will result in greater efficiency and economy of effort.[86]

The committee outlined nine services that should be provided "for non-Federal libraries and for individuals who are not Federal employees":

1. A clearing house service, including printed catalogs, the card distribution service, and the union catalog, "through which will be made

available a record of the publications at the disposal of American libraries."

2. Reference service to other libraries, available only "after local holdings have been investigated and found inadequate." The Library, moreover, should accept special responsibility for reference service in subjects relating to the United States, and "should seek to have on its staff competent scholars in this broad field."

3. An interlibrary loan service, which "should be encouraged if the material is not available as readily elsewhere." Materials that should not or cannot be loaned "should be made available by photoduplication at cost."

4. Service to individuals, including service to all persons above the age of sixteen in the reading rooms and reference service by mail and telephone "within reason [and] whenever possible." Individual study rooms or desks should be provided, whenever possible, to investigators "whose work is in the public or scholarly interest."

5. Extension service "to the citizens of the country through State and local libraries and in cooperation with other appropriate Government agencies."

6. Special services made possible by gifts received through the Library of Congress Trust Fund Board Act.

7. A general library service for the blind, performed on a national basis, "in recognition of the Federal Government's responsibility for service to the blind, as acknowledged by the enactment of the Pratt-Smoot Bill in 1931."

8. An exhibition program, including travelling exhibits, necessary because the Library "has an obligation to the people of the United States to display for their benefit the treasures contained in its collections, which reflect our national history and the development of our civilization."

9. An extensive publications program.[87]

Finally, the Planning Committee recommended the creation of the National Library Advisory Council, which would aid the Librarian of Congress "in his relations with the research libraries of the Nation and particularly in his efforts to avoid unnecessary duplication of the costly library services to scholarship that are handicapping the national library program."

In order to perform the services outlined in its report, the Planning Committee urged the Library to develop "a carefully planned acquisitions program which should be a part of a national acquisition program for all libraries in the United States." That national plan "should bring into the country at least one copy of all currently published material of interest for research in all fields." With this in mind, the Library of Congress should:

1. Acquire all the material that it needs in order to provide the best possible service to the Congress, and to supplement the service given to Federal Agencies by other Federal libraries in Washington and elsewhere.

2. Acquire at least one copy of all material of importance in connection with national security, except in the fields of agriculture and medicine (where there should be a copy in the Department of Agriculture

Library or the Army Medical Library) and in such other fields as are covered by other libraries which may be recognized later as giving National Service in a Special Field.

3. Acquire as complete a collection as possible of publications originating in the United States and of all material of interest in connection with the history of the United States, its government and law, its civilization, and its citizens, and their activities.

4. Do its share—and its share should be larger than that of any other library—in the acquisition of at least one copy, to be available somewhere in the country, of all the material of interest to research workers. This material should be divided by subjects and the Library of Congress should accept responsibility for inclusive acquisition in certain subjects as its share in completing the national coverage.

5. Continue to collect extensively in the following fields "where it has already taken responsibility for research collections, either by law or by practice approved by Congress": public documents, legal material, publications of academies and learned societies, books about books, music, audio-visual material, maps, prints, and rare books.

6. The Librarian of Congress should arrange for the establishment of a national research library and a specialized staff for the field of science and technology as part of the Library of Congress.

7. The Library of Congress should collect historical, literary, and scientific manuscripts of national interest, including those of men and organizations that have contributed to the government, the institutions, and the life of the American people as a whole.[88]

The Library of Congress Planning Committee concluded its report by calling upon the Librarian of Congress "to build up the quality of the Library's staff unceasingly," for "men and women of the highest scholarly attainments must be in charge of the Library's collections, otherwise the material cannot be efficiently utilized."

Librarian Evans submitted the report of the Planning Committee to Congress, but no formal action was taken. Nor did the report appear to have any important impact on the Library's ensuing appropriations—or on the congressional perception of the institution. Nonetheless, while the growth of the Library during the Evans administration was not spectacular, it was steady. Between 1945 and 1953 the size of the book collection increased from approximately 7 to 10 million volumes, the staff from about 1,200 to 1,600 employees, and the annual appropriation from the 6 million dollars in FY 1947 to over 9 million dollars in FY 1954.

Other Accomplishments

Even without greatly increased appropriations, the legislative and the national roles of the Library were expanded during the Evans administration. The Legislative Reorganization Act of 1946 was a significant milestone in strengthening direct services to Congress. Librarians were pleased with Evans' concern with "bibliographical control," a phrase that the Librarian reportedly invented.[89] A number of important Library of Congress printed book catalogs were inaugurated and there was a new emphasis on cataloging that led to publication in 1949 of *Rules for Descriptive Cataloging in the*

Library of Congress. Evans also took a special interest in cooperative micro-filming projects with other institutions, the development of the motion picture collection, and services to the scientific and technical community. A new Science Division was established in June 1949. In 1950 the Librarian ex-tended the interlibrary loan service to include microfilm, attempting "to prevent wasteful expenditures by libraries for research materials . . . for which they have only occasional need."[90]

The cultural role of the Library was strengthened as well. Gertrude Clarke Whittall donated additional funds to establish a poetry room and support literary programs, a full-scale exhibits program was launched, chamber music concerts were broadcast nationwide on FM radio for the first time, and recordings of poets reading their own works were offered for sale. The Fellows of the Library of Congress awarded the Bollingen Prize in Poetry to Ezra Pound, an event, that stirred controversy in both literary and con-gressional circles. As a result, in August 1949 the Joint Committee on the Library unanimously recommended that the Library cancel "all arrangements for the giving of prizes and the making of awards." Evans announced the Li-brary's immediate compliance. No permanent harm was inflicted on the Library and its cultural program by the incident, but it did serve to remind the Library and its officers of the need for caution in the institution's multifaceted cultural role. Finally, in 1952 with help from the Joint Com-mittee on the Library, Evans took care of some unfinished business. The Declaration of Independence and the U.S. Constitution, on display since 1921 when Herbert Putnam had them transferred from the Department of State, were transferred to the National Archives. This was a difficult task that reflected credit on the Librarian and the institution.

While some staff members were unhappy with Evans' action in the transfer of the two historical documents, on the whole staff morale was high during the Evans years. The Librarian continued the "participatory" style of the MacLeish/Evans administration, including the staff as much as possible in the management process. Evans himself wrote a column in the weekly *Infor-mation Bulletin,* informing the staff about his schedule, visitors, and major decisions. In 1952 the Federal Personnel Council commended the Library for its application of democratic principles to administrative practices.

Two of Librarian Evans' most significant accomplishments were the expansion of the Library's foreign acquisitions program and the increased involvement of the Library of Congress on the international scene. Both of these developments had their origins in the MacLeish administration and reached fruition during the administration of L. Quincy Mumford (1954–1974), but it was Luther Evans who built the foundation for the Library's international role. This role has not always been a popular one with Congress, as Evans was the first to discover. Nonetheless, it accurately reflected Evans' personal view of the Library of Congress as a worldwide institution, one that should gather materials from everywhere.

As described by Evans, the deficiencies in the Library's foreign collec-tions were amply illustrated during World War II and were of serious conse-quence:

> [The Library's] weather data on the Himalayas had assisted the Air Force to cross the "hump" but the want of early issues of the *Voelkische*

Beobachter prevented the transmission of the first auguries of Naziism, and the failure of satisfactory coverage of the plans of European cities resulted in the destruction of a few great intellectual monuments.

In other words, the lesson which the war has taught us is the lesson that, however large our collections may now be, they are pitifully and tragically small in comparison with the demands of the nation.[91]

This belief, plus Evans' involvement with the activities of international organizations such as UNESCO, provided a stimulus to the development of foreign acquisitions programs, area studies reference units, and bibliographic tools such as the *East European Accessions List* (1951), *the Southern Asia Accessions List* (1952), and the *Monthly List of Russian Accessions* (1952).

By the early 1950s, Evans was heavily involved in UNESCO activities; he also was severely criticized by members of Congress for not spending more of his time at the Library of Congress. In mid-1953 he was selected as the new director general of UNESCO and on July 1, 1953, he submitted his resignation as Librarian of Congress to President Dwight D. Eisenhower.

Librarian Mumford Takes Office

The American Library Association heartily approved of President Eisenhower's nominee as Evans' successor, for he was L. Quincy Mumford, librarian of the Cleveland Public Library and ALA president-elect. Mumford's major competitor for the post apparently was Verner W. Clapp, Evans' Chief Assistant Librarian, but on April 22, 1954, Mumford's name was sent to the Senate. The Cleveland librarian, the first graduate of a professional library school to be nominated, had started his career at New York Public Library. In 1940 he assisted MacLeish's Librarian's Committee in its review of the Library of Congress, remaining at the Library through 1941 on a special one-year tour of duty to serve as the first director of the newly created Processing Department. Mumford's prior knowledge of the Library's operations, along with his support from both ALA and the Ohio congressional delegation, smoothed the way for an easy confirmation, which took place on July 29, 1954. It is interesting to note, however, that the Association of Research Libraries, which had pushed Librarians MacLeish and Evans toward increased support for research and scholarly libraries, took a "wait-and-see" attitude toward the nomination.[92]

When L. Quincy Mumford took office on September 1, 1954, the Library's annual appropriation was approximately $9½ million, its staff numbered 1,500, and the book collections totaled about 10 million volumes. Since relations between Librarian Evans and the Congress had been uneasy, the new Librarian faced a considerable challenge. Eventually he guided the Library of Congress through the greatest period of growth in its history, but not until he had restored good relations and mutual confidence between the Library and the Congress. When Mumford retired in 1974, both the legislative and the national roles had been expanded, the book collection contained over 16 million volumes, and the Library's annual appropriation of $96 million supported 4,250 staff members.

The question of the Library's split personality, its legislative and its national roles, was a pervasive theme during the Mumford administration.

Generally speaking, during the first decade Congress continued to view the Library's national activities with concern and some wariness; in the second decade, Congress approved a considerable expansion of those national services.

Librarian Mumford always moved cautiously in his relations with Congress, respecting a statement of the House of Representatives Appropriations Committee in May 1954:

> The new Librarian should be mindful that the Library is the instrument and the creature of Congress. Its duties historically have been to meet the needs of the Members of Congress first and to limit its services to others to that which can be furnished with the funds and the staff available.[93]

The view of the Senate Committee on Rules and Administration about the Library, as summarized at the conclusion of their hearings on the Mumford nomination, was even more instructive:

> A review of the foregoing memorandum indicates that the Library of Congress, through the circumstances of time and legislation, now operates practically as a free adjunct of the legislative branch of the Government.

Librarian's Powers and Responsibilities

The Librarian of Congress enjoys broad, almost autocratic powers, and has done so with the consent of Congress and by authority of law since 1897, when, by the act of February 19 of that year (29 Stat. 544), he was granted power to establish the Library's rules and regulations.

The Librarian may appoint persons to the Library staff solely on the basis of training, experience, and general fitness for the duties of the various positions. He promulgates administrative and security policies and directs the observance of both.

The Librarian is responsible for the collections of the Library. He oversees the acquisition of regular items for the Library, and is in the best position to recommend to Congress the desirability of legislation to authorize special purchases. Under law, he also provides for the accessibility of the Library collections and facilities, supervises the grounds, and appoints the police force, while prescribing regulations for the protection of the collections, grounds, and facilities.

Congressional Oversight

Of these and other of the Librarian's functions Congress seldom takes notice, save on an intermittent and discursive basis. The Legislative Reorganization Act of 1946, in abolishing the Library Committees of the Senate and House, gave substantive jurisdiction over the Library to the Senate Committee on Rules and Administration and the Committee on House Administration. But these committees rarely intervene in Library affairs and usually only if legislation is required. Since the enactment of the Legislative Reorganization Act only one measure dealing exclusively with Library affairs has cleared the Committee on Rules and Administration and the Congress to become law. Indeed, no regular day-to-day, month-to-month contact exists between the Senate Rules and Administration Committee and the Library of Congress.

The Joint Committee on the Library does enjoy a somewhat closer relationship with the Library, as there have been occasions in the past when the Librarian has solicited the advice and counsel of the joint committee's chairmen and members. But more often than not these have been on items on which the guidance, rather than the decisions, of the joint committee was requested. It was the act of 1897, previously referred to, which took from the joint committee nearly 57 years ago its close hand over Library affairs.

Congressional supervision of the Library is more pratically exercised today by the legislative subcommittees of the House and Senate Appropriations Committees. But such supervision is only part of the responsibility with which the subcommittee members are charged for all legislative branch appropriations. In the past, criticism by these subcommittees has resulted in many improvements in the Library. Valuable as their criticism has been, however, it nevertheless has been periodic and seems to have proceeded more from an annual budgetary review of the Library rather than from any continuous day-to-day interest in Library operations.

The Librarian

The general precedent appears to be established that a Librarian of Congress is appointed for life. Congress may object to his actions and decisions if they run counter to congressional intentions for the Library, and exercise its punitive power of withholding appropriations or changing a Librarian's budget requests. Librarians in the past generally have listened sensitively to congressional criticism. Nevertheless the freedom of action allowed them by law, their prerogatives of independent decisions, and the manner in which they discharge their daily duties leave more to their judgment what is owing to the job than what may be owing to Congress.

Librarians MacLeish and Evans

It would seem that the last two Librarians of Congress were not wholly fitted by background for the post, and in addition were engaged in activities apart from their duties. The question of Mr. Archibald MacLeish's administrative ability and his experience as a librarian was debated in the Senate for 2 days. His successor, Dr. Luther Evans, was criticized by a House committee for extensive absences from the Library on business that had little relation to his duties as Librarian of Congress. There is a conclusion that both showed a supervisory responsibility toward the position of Librarian somewhat short of the successful precedent established by the one who served before them.

The "National" Library

With the completion of the new main building in 1897, and the removal thereto from the Capitol of all but the law collections, the Library began a drift away from Congress. More and more, over the past 50 years, Librarians of Congress, by their acts and their public utterances, have evinced a concept of the Library as a national and international institution. Each Librarian, in turn, has declared that the fundamental responsibility of the Library is to serve Congress. But each also, in turn, has, by extension of services to other governmental agencies and to the general public, insured that the importance of the position of Librarian and the description of the Library of Congress as the "National" Library are accepted by the Nation generally. The Library, despite its close relation to Congress, is widely used locally in the District of Columbia, and nationally rivals the outstanding reputation as a tourist attraction of the British Museum.

Mr. Verner Clapp, acting Librarian, told the Senate Appropriations Legislative Subcommittee on June 23, 1954, that the Library of Congress

> shortly after the middle of the last century * * * became regarded as the National Library of the United States with especial obligations, always subordinate to its continuing and primary obligation to the Congress, to be custodian of private collections for the benefit of the country at large.

Subordinate as the Library may be to the Congress, the primary use of its collections today is by the country at large. It is to be admitted that Congress, in extending the Library's activities by law, has been a factor in making it such a nationwide establishment. Congress justifiably has pride in its Library as the most outstanding library in the world. But it is the same Congress which today stands in second position to the public in use of the Library.

Service to Congress

At present the Legislative Reference Service and the American Law Division are heavily occupied with the requests of Members and committees of Congress. A third division—the Loan Division—does not appear to have measured up to its responsibilities. Improvement in its service to Congress is definitely needed.

Need for Organic Act

Also current is the criticism that the Library has long operated without any real organic act. Since its actual establishment in 1800, it has functioned under a succession of laws—some broad, some specific—which are all in general relation to one another, but which do not provide any solid basis for the definition and limitation of the Library's operations. There appears to be unanimous agreement that the need for such an organic act exists and that there should now be a gathering together of all laws affecting the Library with the idea of restating its duties, its functions, and its aims.

Need for More Selectivity

Unquestionably Congress, in authorizing the Library's acceptance of gifts, by voting special purchases, and by opening the Library's shelves to the Nation's scholars, has broadened the operating base of the Library and given it activities unrelated to the legislative process. There appears some doubt, however, that the program of accessions should be as catholic and diversified as it is. For example, [the] practical value which the great manuscript collections in the Library have for Congress is slight. This does not mean that collections of intrinsic value, when offered, should not have been accepted, or bought when practicable. The scope of the collections, however, has been extended outward to cover many things which, on second glance, would appear to be completely extraneous to a Library of Congress. Furthermore, it does not appear that there has always been a proper selectivity of acquisitions, the tendency being to accept everything. A firm policy for the dumping of unsuitable or outmoded material also seems to be lacking.

Arrearages

The Library's most chronic problem is the ever increasing arrearages of unprocessed materials. Since the copyright law of 1870, much of the Library's space has been occupied with uncataloged or untreated items, many of which have not even been uncrated. In 1941 a head-on attack against this arrearage problem was attempted. In that year the present Librarian-designate, Mr. Mumford, was called in as a processing expert. The new system which he set up, though guaranteeing smooth results, did not make the dent in arrearages expected of it. The accretions of World War II and afterward have increased rather than lessened the Library's problem in this regard.

There is a possibility that much information of value to Congress is contained in the large amount of crated and unprocessed material. It is suggested that, as a temporary expedient, this material be examined, and that any items of possible use to Congress be selected therefrom and made available.

If this whole overall problem is to be finally resolved, new methods and even new personnel might be used in a different attack. Definite methods of selectivity, a broad policy of disposal and junking, and a new emphasis on acquisitions which have greater congressional utility should be considered.

Noncongressional Services

It is apparent that too often the Library seems to be submerged by its own good intentions. A stopping place—a final line—should be set beyond which its public services and those to the executive agencies cannot go. Indeed, a withdrawal of many of those services or their deemphasis appears to be in order.

More than 500 of the some 2,300 temporary and permanent employees are engaged in the preparation of executive-department projects. These projects are done, of course, on a reimbursable basis, and the majority are defense projects keyed to the Library's collections. Even though the Library of Congress has not, in the last year or so, accepted any new agency projects, this type of executive-department work continues. If there are termination dates on such projects, they should be validated at once so that the space and the related services given to these projects might be returned to the basic purposes of the Library.

Security Program

Finally, the personnel security program appears to be successfully joined to the program of the executive agencies, for the protection of the sensitive areas in the Library. There does not seem to be, however, any definite policy which would attempt the rather difficult task of identifying the propaganda content of new accessions to the Library, although this is a subject which could come under study.[94]

In view of such statements, it is hardly surprising that the first years of the Mumford administration were primarily years of consolidation. The Librarian deliberately concentrated on strengthening the Library's own collections and services "because so central is the Library of Congress to the library economy and research efforts of the country that, to the extent that the institution is weak, the whole fabric of library service is weak."[95] But even the gradual expansion of the Library increased its space problems and in 1958, with the book collection numbering over 11 million volumes, an intensive study of the requirements for a third major Library building was begun.

The Committee on the Control and Organization of the Collections

During 1958 an internal committee, the Committee on the Control and Organization of the Collections, developed a series of statements outlining the Library's objectives.

These statements, which emphasized the Library's services, were never formally promulgated; in fact, parts of the committee's work apparently were never completed. Its set of objectives, however, is a useful extension of the reference and research objectives outlined in Librarian MacLeish's 1940 report.

Objectives of the Library of Congress

For over one hundred and fifty years the Library of Congress has served the Congress of the United States. Because of the ever-widening interests and responsibilities of the Congress—its Members and Committees—the Library of Congress has developed collections comprehensive in their scope and almost universal in their subject coverage. The Library of Congress has inevitably achieved a national role and national responsibilities by very virtue of its vast collections and attendant bibliographic resources, and with the encouragement of the Congress itself through enactment of legislation for copyright deposit in the Library of Congress, for the establishment of the Library of Congress as the United States depository in the international exchange of publications, and through legislation for specific acquisitions or through providing for specific functions and services. The Library of Congress has had to recognize that these resources and responsibilities impose obligations to scholarship in its broadest sense, responsibilities which may be served either directly or indirectly through library facilities elsewhere in the nation. The obligation of the Library of Congress to continue its principal services to the Congress, as well as its services to the Government and to scholarship in general, cannot always be realized in equal measure and at all times. A balance among the several objectives and service goals of the Library of Congress is therefore offered in the following statement of policy:

1. Service to Members of Congress:

   The Library of Congress undertakes for Members of Congress any and all library services, including reference, research, and other types of service involving use of the Library's collections, which are required by Members in the performance of their official duties. (Only a lack of means to provide the necessary space, collections, and skilled staff would justify a failure on the Library's part to meet such demands.)

2. Service to Government Agencies:

The Library of Congress will provide for other Government agencies the following library services when required by such agencies in connection with the fulfillment of their official responsibilities: (1) lending service upon request; (2) study rooms and access to the Library's collections; (3) reference, bibliographic, and research service when this service is appropriate to the Library's collections, to the skills and competence of its available staff, and when the service cannot be rendered by the staffs of the Government agencies. The Library will undertake extensive reference, bibliographic, and research projects on behalf of Government agencies only when (a) such projects are particularly dependent upon the utilization of the Library's personal or material resources, (b) the projects have widespread potential interest or usefulness, and (c) there is authorization within the Library's own appropriations or a specific transfer of funds can be made under authority of law. Such projects shall not be undertaken when services to Congress are likely to be impeded or when interference with essential Library operations outweighs the advantages to the Library or the value of the projects.

3. Service to the Public:

The Library of Congress will make available its collections, facilities, and other resources for public use and for the public benefit within the limitations imposed by the Library's primary obligation to provide services to the Congress and to agencies of the Federal Government.

For reference purposes on the premises, the use of the Library is, in general, free without introduction or credentials to any adult inquirer. Reference services by correspondence will also be provided, although inquirers will be referred to local, state and regional libraries whenever these might meet the need. Preference will be given to those inquiries which pertain to the Library's holdings of special materials and to subjects in which its collections and bibliographic resources are especially strong.

The Library extends the use of its collections and its services through interlibrary loan, provision of photocopies at cost, preparation and publication of catalogs and specialized bibliographies, and through cooperation with other institutions in developing and improving library resources and services.

4. Interlibrary Cooperation:

Recognizing the interdependence of libraries, the Library of Congress accepts an obligation to lend its resources to the development and enhancement of library services throughout the nation. By reason of the scope and size of its collections, the usefulness of its bibliographic resources and services, and the varied skills represented in its staff, the

Library of Congress has frequently been called upon to assume special responsibilities in cooperative undertakings for the improvement of library services. The Library is in principle receptive to these requests but recognizes that the demands made upon it will, in all probability, always exceed its capacity to participate. In establishing priorities of interest, the Library will be guided by the importance of individual projects, first, to the furtherance of the Library's primary obligations and, second, to the objectives of libraries generally, as well as the possible impact of a given project on the activities and budget of the Library.

5. Resources of the Library:

In order to carry out its responsibilities to Congress and to the nation, the Library of Congress must maintain, organize, and make available collections adequate to support national service in all fields of knowledge, except that the Library need not form comprehensive collections in special subjects and fields where the existence or development of collections and related services in other libraries is recognized, provided that such recognition involves no risk of impairment of the Library's services to the Congress and to the nation.[96]

The Committee on the Control and Organization of the Collections reached several conclusions about the objectives and needs of the Legislative Reference Service. It felt:

1. The Library [of Congress should] continue to be the Library of Congress with the Legislative Reference Service a part of it, and with service to the Congress continuing to be the Library's first obligation.

2. The Library as a research institution must be geared to deal with important research problems that exploit the high-level competence of researchers and division chiefs who are required to prepare reports and surveys for the Congress and for other agencies of the Government.

Questions:

  a. To what extent should the Library staff undertake research for other Government agencies as a part of its regular work program?

  b. To what degree should the Library of Congress depend upon other libraries in Washington for materials that may be needed for the Congress?

3. There is a need in LRS and in special divisions of the Library for immediate copies of ephemeral materials, some of which will not need to be added to the collections and therefore should not receive regular processing treatment.

4. A highly organized special non-circulating reference collection for the use of the Legislative Reference Service and for general Reference Department needs might prove to be a solution to many problems of availability of material, speed and adequacy of service.

5. The Legislative Reference Service should be as close to the Library's collections as is feasible, especially to the Serial Division, Law Library, and the Public Catalog; there should be direct communication to various areas from which LRS is very far removed.

6. Responsibility for specialized selection and acquisitions recom-

mendations must rest with the researcher, who is familiar with the literature of his field and with the events that will produce documents needed for research in that field.[97]

The Bryant Memorandum

The work of the Committee on the Control and Organization of the Collections proved especially useful in 1962 when the Library prepared a report on its legislative and national roles in response to a memorandum by Douglas W. Bryant, associate director of the Harvard University Library, on "what the Library of Congress does and ought to do for the Government and Nation generally." The memorandum, which was prepared at the request of Senator Claiborne Pell of Rhode Island and introduced by the senator into the *Congressional Record* of May 24, 1962, forced both the Library of Congress and the American library community to reassess the Library's national role and services. An additional salutory effect was the elicitation, in the response from Librarian Mumford, of a cogent and forceful expression of his view of the Library's legislative and national roles.

A member of the Joint Committee on the Library, Senator Pell was familiar with the Library and its various responsibilities. When introducing the Bryant memorandum into the *Congressional Record*, he stated his hope that Mr. Bryant's proposals would be discussed widely because "we have tended to take for granted our Library of Congress—our basic working tool which underlies all our useful scholarship, the responsible work of our Congress, and the very culture of our nation."[98]

In his memorandum, Mr. Bryant began with a description of "the present program of the Library of Congress and related agencies." After observing that although "the major functions of the Library of Congress might have been assigned to three or four separate agencies . . . the results appear to be reasonably satisfactory," he described the major functions: service to Congress, federal libraries, and the nation as a whole, and serving as "a national bibliographic center and the keystone in a national system of research libraries." Finally, he noted that the functions of the Library of Congress, as the national library, were "not confined to the collection, cataloging, and circulation of books; there are many other ways in which it enriches the cultural life of the Capital City and of the Nation as a whole."

After outlining the functions of other federal agencies closely related to the Library of Congress, the Harvard librarian called for new federal programs in five specific areas: research in the application of modern technology to libraries, assistance to underdeveloped countries in creating or strengthening their own national libraries and national bibliographies, a national plan for the preservation of research materials, support for research libraries in the form of grants-in-aid, and a program of fellowships and scholarships to recruit and train professional librarians. He also explained that the emphasis on these new programs "should not be allowed to obscure the importance of improving or extending a number of programs to which the Library of Congress is already committed," citing aspects of the Library's acquisitions, cataloging, bibliographic, loan, and photoduplication services, the appropriation of more funds "to eliminate the current arrears in recording the holdings of American libraries in the National Union Catalog," and observed that "Library of Congress holdings and Library of Congress cataloging will not serve the Nation as effectively as they should until extensive backlogs of uncataloged materials have been incorporated into the regular collections, and the Library has been provided with manpower sufficient to catalog current acquisitions promptly."

A comprehensive federal program was outlined. It included recognition of the Library of Congress as the National Library, and the creation of a National Library Advisory Board in the executive branch or perhaps as an independent agency. Bryant's recommendations about the role of the Library of Congress were made in the context of the proposed new federal program:

> The Federal Government is now participating in research library affairs almost entirely through the Library of Congress, and it is evident that most of the activities that have been proposed here would also directly involve that institution. It should be recognized officially as the National Library (without necessarily changing its name), and its national responsibilities should be stated explicitly enough to make it clear that the Congress will henceforth recognize an obligation to support work that the Library must undertake in order to carry out this mission. Any such legislative statement ought, of course, to be formulated very carefully; the following language is offered only as an indication of the approach that might be desirable:
>
>> The mission of the National Library is to collect, preserve, and disseminate the world's recorded knowledge for the benefit of mankind. It should inform the American people of its holdings and facilitate their use. It should supplement the collections and further the work of other libraries in the United States, taking the lead in efforts to provide American scholarship with library service of the high quality that it deserves and that the national interest requires. It should stimulate and enrich the cultural life of America and its cultural interchanges with other nations.
>
> The proposed legislation should also recognize the special status of the two national research collections for agriculture and medicine, and provide for the possibility of other similar collections in the future.
>
> As in the past, the success of the Library will depend significantly on the interest and understanding of the members of the Joint Committee. In the future it will be even more important that Joint Committee members be legislators genuinely concerned with the well being of research and scholarship through the Nation.
>
> From what has been said already it is evident that, while the Legislative Reference Service of the Library of Congress is appropriately attached to the Legislative Branch of the Government, the Library's other functions—the Copyright Office, services to agencies of the Government generally, and services as the National Library—logically ought to be attached to the Executive. If, however, it was thought that a proposal for transferring the Library of Congress from the Legislative Branch to the Executive would encounter serious practical difficulties, it would not be essential to pursue it.[99]

He concluded with a summary of his views about the Library of Congress and a strong appeal for increased support for all research libraries:

The Library of Congress differs significantly from other governmental agencies. It is a great institution with special responsibilities to its Government, but it also serves individual scholars and other libraries of all kinds throughout the Nation. In addition, it is the major instrument through which the Government participates in research library concerns. Furthermore, the Library of Congress is anomalous because of the historical accident of its attachment to the Legislative Branch of the Government.

Though it would be desirable, it is not essential to transfer the Library of Congress to the Executive; it *is* essential that legislation recognize officially what it ought to do, and that a National Library Board (if not a National Research Library Foundation) be established in the Executive Branch.

The Federal Government must lead, not by imposing a program upon the Nation's research libraries, but by encouraging scholars and librarians to formulate their needs and to plan nationally. Leadership calls, above all, for appointment of the best men available to the Advisory Board and for a Librarian of Congress who is determined to make the Library all that it ought to be, both within the Government and in its role as the leading library of the Nation. The Librarian of Congress must be a man who can administer an extremely diversified and organically complex institution; in addition, he must make important decisions on technological innovations in bibliography profoundly affecting the access of scholars to information, supervise the building up of enormous research collections, exercise imaginative leadership nationally, and take advantage of the Library's unique opportunities for contributing to American cultural life. Even an ideal Librarian would require the support and counsel of a strong Advisory Board.

Appointing a Board and defining a program will accomplish little, however, unless continued support for the Board and its program can be enlisted from the Congress, the numerous nongovernmental institutions that must participate, and from the public generally. The Library of Congress and America's other major research libraries are large and complex; the Nation must make sure that they are also strong enough to keep up with the growing requirements of both government and modern scholarship, and agile enough even to anticipate these demands.[100]

The Reply to the Bryant Memorandum

During the summer of 1962, the Library solicited comments on the Bryant memorandum from scholars and librarians throughout the country. The response, which took the form of a "report," was sent to the Joint Committee on the Library on September 28, 1962. Committee chairman Senator B. Everett Jordan introduced it into the *Congressional Record* of October 2, 1962, and both the memorandum and the report were reproduced in the Library's 1962 *Annual Report.*

In his report on the memorandum, Librarian Mumford pointed out that many of Bryant's recommendations coincided with suggestions made by the Library of Congress Planning Committee in 1947. Under the heading "The Library of Congress as the National Library," Mumford stated his opposition to any alteration in the Library's name:

I have never felt that a change of name was necessary. The Library of Congress is a venerable institution, with a proud history, and to change its name would do unspeakable violence to tradition.

I would be happy, however, to have the Congress recognize the national responsibilities of the Library of Congress in some formal way. This could, if the Congress wishes, be done in a statement introducing the "codification, simplification, and completion" of legislation relating to the Library which I was directed to prepare when I took office in 1954. This codification, which spells out the statutory basis for the many national-library activities of the institution, was submitted to the Joint Committee on the Library but final action on it has not been taken. Such a statement would confirm once and for all the status of the Library.

The Congress, since I have been in office, has recognized the national responsibilities of the Library in a way that matters most—with understanding and consistent support.[101]

He defended the Library's role as "the de facto, if not the de jure national library of the United States," by pointing out that "the Library of Congress today performs more national library functions than any other library in the world." Furthermore, while each of the other national libraries of the world carried out some of the following national library functions, the Library of Congress engaged in all of them:

1. Maintains comprehensive collections, especially evidence of the national heritage, for the use of the Government, the scholarly world, and the public, making it a national center for research.

2. Benefits from official, intergovernmental exchange of publications.

3. Receives through copyright or legal deposit materials for the enrichment of its collections.

4. Receives gifts to the Nation in the form of collections of personal papers, rare books, and other valuable materials and in the form of trust funds and bequests, which enable it not only to enrich the collections but to present cultural programs in such fields as literature, art, and music.

5. Develops a comprehensive classification system, which is widely used by other research institutions, and cataloging codes, which are nationally accepted standards.

6. Serves as a center for cooperative cataloging of books and other forms of material by the Nation's libraries.

7. Provides a national catalog card distribution service.

8. Maintains national union catalogs on cards, which serve as guides to the Nation's research resources in various forms (such as books and manuscripts) and in various fields (such as Hebraica and Slavica), and furnishes information about the location of needed materials to those who cannot personally consult these tools.

9. Publishes in book form a national bibliography, or a major contribution thereto, such as the Library's *National Union Catalog*.

10. Gives reference service on its premises and provides extensive information from and about its collections by mail.

11. Participates in a nationwide interlibrary loan system, which enables it to share collection responsibilities with other libraries and to make research materials generally available, thereby strengthening smaller libraries throughout the country by supplementing their research resources through those of the national library.

12. Has an active bibliographic program and makes the results of it widely available through publication.

13. Administers the national books-for-the-blind program.

14. Presents exhibits selected from the national collections for the education and enjoyment of the general public, and circulates exhibits at home and abroad as evidence of the national history and culture.

15. Experiments and conducts research in the area of library technology.

16. Engages in national and international cooperative bibliographic projects and works with other national libraries and international organizations to achieve standardization of rules in order to increase the accessibility of the materials of knowledge without regard to national boundaries and language barriers.

In the final analysis, I have always felt that on the question of being the national library the substance is more important than the form. It is incongruous, of course, that the Library of Congress has not been so designated while two Federal libraries in special fields—medicine and agriculture—have been officially named national libraries—the National Agricultural Library by administrative action of the Secretary of Agriculture (on the basis of the department's organic act of May 15, 1862) and the National Library of Medicine by action of the Congress (P.L. 410 of the 2d Session of the 78th Congress). Thus it seems only logical that the national status of the Library of Congress, the Government's largest general research library, should also be recognized. Any statement of policy by the Congress or proposed legislation on the subject, should, as Mr. Bryant suggests, take cognizance of the status of the NLM and the NAL. In providing for the designation of other collections as national libraries, very high standards should be set, for the danger is not that appropriate libraries will not be so designated but that some libraries will be when in fact they cannot fulfill the functions. The term "national library" could become a status symbol, the achievement of which would do nothing to advance the cause of research or the health of the library community.[102]

Librarian Mumford next addressed the topic of "the organizational location of the Library of Congress":

In the United States there is no national library system, with a directing agency at the apex and branches spreading downward and outward throughout the country. Given our system of government, with the separation of powers at the national level—and, within the Executive Branch, departmentalized organization—and with the division of powers between the Federal Government and the States, there is little possibility that an administratively logical system, with power and direction flowing from the top to bottom, can be developed. Even if such a system were possible, there is a very real question as to whether it would be desirable in a country as large as ours and with as many diverse interests to serve.

There is no point, consequently, in dwelling on the possibility of a national library system, in the strictest sense, or even of a Federal library system. I do not believe the latter would be possible even if the Library of Congress were renamed the National Library and were transferred to the Executive Branch as an independent agency—and it should not be forgotten that the [Hoover] Commission on the Organization of the Executive Branch of the Government deplored and discouraged the creation of additional independent agencies. The several Executive Departments would be loath to give up the direction of their libraries to such an agency, much less to a National Library that might instead be made a bureau of another department, such as the Department of Health, Education, and Welfare, or of some new agency, such as a Department of Scientific and Cultural Affairs.

Whether in the Executive Branch or the Legislative Branch, the Library of Congress would scarcely be in a position to coordinate the activities of other Federal libraries, except in a very informal way. A Council of Federal Librarians might be established, with or without legislative action, and it might well serve a useful purpose as a channel of information, as the means of improving communications between Federal libraries as to their needs and plans, and as a vehicle for organizing cooperative efforts. The Library of Congress has considered the advisability of taking the initiative in organizing such a Council. Some Federal librarians think, however, that such a Council might be little more than a debating society, dominated by the larger libraries. Its recommedations to Executive departments and agencies might be suspect as special pleading, and its proposals would certainly have to compete for support within each agency with its other departmental needs. Thus its influence is unlikely to be great. Nevertheless, the Library will recanvass the possibilities of such a Council.

What, in short, would be gained by transferring the Library of Congress to the Executive Branch? It would still have to obtain support from the Congress for its activities. In the Executive Branch this means, first, conforming to the President's directive as to the size of the Federal budget, second, adhering to departmental policy as to whether increases in certain areas may be requested, and third, scrutiny and perhaps cuts by the Bureau of the Budget before the budget requests can be submitted to the Congress for consideration. Congress has given many evidences of the pride it takes in the Library that bears its name; is it not, then, reasonable to believe that rather more advantage than disadvantage attaches to the Library's being in the Legislative Branch? I am unwilling to believe that the Congress would refuse appropriations for activities in the national interest just because such action would increase the size of the budget of the Legislative Branch.

It has been argued that the Library (the National Library) needs, and would benefit from, the active interest of the Chief Executive. We certainly do not disagree with this point of view. We welcome Presidential support, but it is not necessary that the Library be in the Executive Branch to receive it.[103]

After citing examples of presidential support for the Library of Congress, Mumford warned:

We ought not to discount the proven value of what one might call the corporate directorship of the Congress, exemplified not only by the special roles of the Joint Committee on the Library and the Subcommittees on Legislative Branch Appropriations, but by an ever-increasing interest on the part of the membership of Congress as a whole in this great cultural institution which bears its name. Thanks to the Library Services Act program, the value of library services is being brought home to Members of Congress in dramatic fashion and they, in turn, are giving enthusiastic and ever-broadening support to such programs. The Library of Congress is likely to reap dividends from this situation in the form of greater understanding of, and support for, similar services on the national scene. Already, a number of bills have been introduced (and a hearing has been held in the House of Representatives) to extend the Library Services Act to meet certain needs of research libraries.

It is interesting to note that the division chiefs and department directors in the Library of Congress greatly value the "academic" freedom they have in the Legislative Branch to develop and carry out programs in the Nation's interest.

I cannot feel, in short, that either history, logic, or expediency dictates the transfer of the Library of Congress to the Executive Branch. In the course of 162 years in the Legislative Branch the Library has become a cultural monument to democracy. No one will argue that it cannot or should not be improved, but the possibility of achieving a greater Library—including making it more useful to the Executive Branch and the Nation—lies, I believe, elsewhere than in uprooting it from its traditional place in the Federal Government.[104]

In summarizing his report, Librarian Mumford acknowledged that Bryant's memorandum "has already served a useful purpose by calling attention to the problems of research libraries throughout the Nation." But, he noted, "it will serve an even broader purpose if it brings understanding of the complexities of these problems, strengthens the determination to find solutions, and rallies support, not only in the Congress, but in the Executive Branch, within the library profession, and among the clientele of research libraries."

The Librarian also responded to many of the specific and implied criticisms of the Library of Congress, asserting that the Library "has not abrogated its leadership in the library world," and that the Library "does not find it hard to function as the national library without the name and without a statutory definition of its mission." Moreover, "the officers of the Library are convinced that the institution can accomplish any program suggested by Mr. Bryant or any assigned to it by legislation just as effectively, if not more so, under its present organization as under any of the alternatives suggested."

Librarian Mumford promised to explore the possibility of creating a Council of Federal Librarians, but emphasized that "the responsibilities of the Library of Congress are so diverse and many of them are of such magnitude that the time has never been and will probably never come when the execution of them could not but be improved." He concluded with a statement that also was a pledge: "While strengthening its traditionally operated programs, [the Library of Congress] is seeking to find radically new and better ways for the organization, storage, and retrieval of information in its vast storehouse of knowledge in order to keep the institution creatively responsive to the Congress and the Government at large, to scholarship and the library community, to the people and to the times."[105]

The Brookings Report and the Response

In November 1963, shortly after the Bryant memorandum controversy, the Brookings Institution published *Federal Departmental Libraries: A Summary Report of a Survey and a Conference*, by Luther H. Evans and others. This report revealed that Librarian Mumford had also been defending the presence of the Library of Congress in the legislative branch against assault from another constituency: the federal library community. Perhaps of greater interest was the disagreement about the legislative and national roles of the Library of Congress between Librarian Mumford and former Librarian Evans.

Evans conducted his survey of federal libraries in FY 1959 and also provided the Brookings Institution with "an appraisal of the functions of departmental libraries and recommendations for improving their performance." The Evans report and findings were submitted to a conference of experts for review and discussion prior to publication. The conference, held on June 22, 1963, made several recommendations. The most significant probably was "that the Library of Congress and the Bureau of the Budget jointly invite appropriate agencies to explore the desirability of establishing a continuing interagency group to advise on the problems of federal libraries." During the conference, however, Librarian Mumford requested permission to "file a disclaimer" on many points in Evans' report pertaining to the Library of Congress. The disclaimer was published as an appendix to the report.[106]

Evans' views about the Library of Congress were summarized in the final chapter of his report, titled "Interlibrary Cooperation." He explained:

> The first step which should be taken, I believe, concerns the Library of Congress. Its role is so multi-faceted and central to library operations throughout the government that I am convinced it should be placed in the Executive branch, where it wouild secure more support and greater financial resources. However, the Legislative Reference Service, the special unit of the Library primarily serving members of Congress, should be excluded from any such transfer.
>
> The present arrangement under which the Library is nominally responsible to Congress throws actual policy guidance largely into the

hands of appropriations subcommittees whose normal compelling motive is to keep down the total amount of money appropriated for the Legislative branch. The Library receives guidance on policy matters from no one but the Librarian of Congress, and there is no one other than the appropriations subcommittees to whom it can turn for counsel.

If the Library of Congress were in the Executive branch, the entire situation would be changed. Its role in relation to departmental libraries could be more clearly defined and perhaps expanded in some respects, and its financial requirements could have the kind of Executive support which gets results. In this situation, many of the problems of federal libraries which have been mentioned previously—ranging from cooperative acquisitions to current and compatible classifications, from common storage arrangements to cooperative bibliographies, union catalogs, and in-service training—could more readily be solved.

Just where the Library should be placed within the Executive requires further study. One possibility deserving consideration is to place it in the General Services Administration. The National Archives evidently functions quite satisfactorily there, and greater cooperation between library and archives services would benefit both these services and the research activities of federal agencies.[107]

Librarian Mumford strongly criticized several aspects of the Evans report, emphasizing that many of the comments about the Library of Congress were "outdated by a decade or more," and concluding that the report did a "disservice" to the Library of Congress and its staff. Perhaps his most pointed observations, however, concerned the Library's place in the governmental structure:

> In several places the report recommends most forcefully that the Library of Congress be transferred to the Executive branch. This recommendation appears to rest primarily on the theory that the Library of Congress would be more adequately supported—and therefore of more utility to the libraries of the government and of the nation, as well as to research workers everywhere—if it were removed from the Legislative branch. Not only is this unwarranted assumption unsupported by any evidence, but the report overlooks evidence to the contrary. It seems to me singularly inconsistent and contradictory that a report which catalogs the deficiencies and describes the plight of federal departmental libraries—which refers to libraries in the Executive branch as having inadequate numbers of inadequately paid personnel and purchasing procedures that are "ensnarled in red tape with resultant inefficiencies and exasperating delays"—should recommend this same situation to the Library of Congress. It is strange indeed to learn that the national library would be better off if it were placed in these circumstances. In this connection, it should be pointed out that the Library of Congress, if transferred to the Executive branch, would still have to obtain support from Congress for its activities; and in the Executive branch this means (1) conforming to the size of the federal budget, (2) adhering to departmental policy on increases, and (3) scrutiny for cuts by the Bureau of the Budget before the budget requests can be submitted to Congress. In the Legislative branch, the Library's budget re-

quests go directly to Congress, which has given many evidences of its pride in the national services of its Library and in its national importance. With regard to the benefits that derive from the active interest of the Chief Executive, it is certainly true that the Library of Congress has benefited in the past from the interest of a number of presidents; and its location in the Legislative branch has never been a bar to their interest.[108]

New National Functions

One answer to critics came in the form of greatly expanded national activities during the 1960s. This increased willingness to assume new national responsibilities was endorsed and supported by both ALA and ARL. The change was symbolized by two events a decade apart. In March 1960 the Library announced that it could not undertake a "cataloging-in-source" program that would enable publishers to print cataloging information in the books themselves; the program could not be justified "in terms of financing, technical considerations, or utility." On June 21, 1971, the Library announced that it had received matching grants of $200,000 each from the National Endowment for the Humanities and the Council on Library Resources, Inc., to support essentially the same program, now called "cataloging-in-publication."[109]

Another major development was the expansion of the Library's overseas acquisitions and cataloging programs. As mentioned earlier, during World War II serious weaknesses were discovered in the Library's foreign-area and foreign-language collections. One corrective measure was the initiation, during the Evans administration, of several cooperative foreign acquisitions programs. The Cold War and then the area studies movement increased demands from government and from scholars for additional foreign research materials. In 1958 the Library of Congress was authorized to acquire books by using U.S.-owned foreign currency under terms of the Agricultural Trade Development and Assistance Act of 1954 (Public Law 480). The first appropriation for this purpose was made in 1961, enabling the Library to establish acquisitions centers in New Delhi and Cairo to purchase publications and distribute them to research libraries throughout the United States.

In 1965 President Lyndon B. Johnson approved the Higher Education Act of 1965. Title IIC of the act had great significance for the Library of Congress, for it authorized the Office of Education to transfer funds to the Library for the purpose of (1) acquiring, insofar as possible, all library materials currently published throughout the world that were of value to scholarship; and (2) providing cataloging information for these materials promptly after receipt. At the annual ALA meeting in 1966, John W. Cronin, director of the Library's Processing Department, pointed out that with the passage of this act

the Congress took two important steps to aid libraries of higher education in the United States: (1) it fully recognized for the first time the importance of granting Federal aid and assistance toward solving the problem of cataloging in this country; and (2) it gave the Library of Congress a clear mandate to provide new and unparalleled services for the benefit of academic and research libraries in this country.[110]

The new effort was christened the National Program for Acquisitions and Cataloging (NPAC), and the first NPAC overseas office opened in London in June 1966. In 1971 NPAC funds were made part of the Library of Congress budget.

The 1947 Planning Committee report, the Bryant memorandum (1962), and the Brookings conference (1963) had recommended the creation of an interagency council to coordinate the activities of federal libraries. In his response to the Bryant memorandum, Librarian Mumford was lukewarm to the idea, agreeing to look into it even though "past experience with such a Council does not promise great accomplishments in terms of coordination." By 1965 the situation and atmosphere had changed, however, for on March 11, 1965, the Federal Library Committee was established. As recommended at the Brookings conference, the Library of Congress, with the cooperation of the U.S. Bureau of the Budget, took the initiative in its creation. The purpose of the new committee was "to improve coordination and planning among research libraries of the Federal Government, so that common problems may be identified, solutions sought and services to the Government and the Nation improved." Committee headquarters were established at the Library of Congress.[111]

New cooperative efforts were undertaken with the National Library of Medicine and the National Agricultural Library. Both of these institutions received their designations as "national" institutions during the years of the Mumford administration. In 1956 President Eisenhower approved an act of Congress that expanded the functions of the Armed Forces Medical Library and designated it the National Library of Medicine. The Librarian of Congress was named an ex officio member of its Board of Regents. In 1962 Secretary of Agriculture Orville Freeman marked the one hundredth anniversary of the library of the Department of Agriculture by designating it as the National Agricultural Library. A step toward the development of a national library "system" in the United States was taken on June 26, 1967, when the directors of the three institutions announced creation of the U.S. National Libraries Task Force on Automation and Other Cooperative Services. The general purpose of the task force was to encourage closer cooperation among the three national libraries in developing national library objectives and services.[112]

Other expansions of the Library's national role in the mid-1960s included new automation efforts, particularly the beginning of the MARC (MAchine-Readable Cataloging) system for distribution of cataloging information in machine-readable form, and the initiation of a preservation program intended to serve as the basis for a national preservation effort.[113]

The reasons for the remarkable growth in the Library's national services during the decade of the 1960s were many, but included greater support by the federal government for all libraries, stronger pressure on the Congress and on the Library of Congress from groups such as ARL, the willingness of the Council on Library Resources, Inc., to support various Library of Congress projects during their initial stages, and internal administrative improvements within the Library. The key, however, probably was increased confidence and trust in the Library and its programs on the part of the Congress. The turning point appears to have been 1961–1963, the period when the first steps were taken toward an expanded foreign acquisitions program and when the Bryant memorandum and Librarian Mumford's reply, along with the need for an additional building, forced serious consideration of the Library's future.

Librarian Mumford also seems to have benefited, at least indirectly, from rumors in early 1961 that newly elected President John F. Kennedy wanted to replace him with a "great humanist in the Archibald MacLeish tradition." Congressmen and librarians rallied to support both the Librarian and the tradition of a nonpartisan librarianship of Congress.[114]

The June 1963 report of the House Committee on Appropriations recommended increases in the Library's budget, urged a third building for the Library as soon as possible, and in general was most supportive of Librarian Mumford. The report also addressed the debate over the Library's legislative and national roles:

> This is a great cultural and research institution and in the committee's view ought to be brought to a good state of accommodation and efficiency at an early date. Although originally conceived and established as the Library of Congress, it is in fact, by reason of many Congressional actions over a long period of years, the national library of the United States and of inestimable value to the nation's library facilities at all levels. . . . There have been suggestions over the years, renewed recently, that the Library of Congress ought to be officially designated as the National Library of the United States and its administration shifted to the Executive Branch. There is a considerable reservoir of feeling in the committee against such a proposition of transfer and, very likely, that feeling would be shared by many members of Congress. . . . As to the matter of designation, it has been said that custom and tradition are stronger than the law. There would, likely, be considerable opposition to a change of the name although there would appear to be merit in a formal designation of the Library as the National Library. There are now two specialized libraries so designated formally—one in the field of agriculture, and the other in the field of medicine. But even so, it could be said to be a distinction without benefit of the substance of much difference.[115]

On October 19, 1965, President Johnson approved a supplemental appropriation act that authorized $75 million for the construction of a third Library of Congress building "to be named, The James Madison Memorial Building and to be located directly south of the Main Library building." Actual construction, however, did not begin until 1971.[116]

Report to the National Advisory Commission

The creation, in 1966, of the National Advisory Commission on Libraries led to further examination of the Library's national role and served as an impetus for further development of national services. Established by President Lyndon B. Johnson on September 2, 1966, the commission's general purpose was to appraise the role and adequacy of the nation's libraries and recommend actions that might be taken by public agencies and private organizations "to ensure an effective, efficient library system for the nation." Librarian Mumford was asked to serve on the commission and promptly accepted the invitation.[117]

At the conclusion of the commission meeting held on May 22, 1967, the Library of Congress was asked to provide a statement "of the Library's view of itself as the National Library of the United States, summarizing some of the points made to the Commission and looking to the future." The response was a paper prepared by the Library's staff titled "The Library of Congress as the National Library: Potentialities for Service." Published in *Libraries at Large* (New York: R. R. Bowker Company, 1969), the paper carries a footnote cautioning the reader that the account "does not pretend to be a blueprint for action," for "it is a vision and not necessarily a prediction of the role of the Library of Congress as the National Library." The vision put forth is a far-reaching one, reflecting careful study and imaginative thinking.

The paper begins with the assumption that the Library of Congress is the de facto national library of the United States assuring that:

> The Library of Congress, within the framework of its responsibilities to the Congress, to the library community at large, and to all the many publics that it serves, is not merely willing and ready but *committed* to play an appropriately central role in the planning and operation of the emerging national library and information network.[118]

After describing various relationships between the Library and the "emerging national library and information network," the Library's organization, and its automation program, the authors described the functions currently being carried out by the Library of Congress in its role as the national library. The premise stated by Librarian Mumford in his reply to the Bryant memorandum is repeated: "Although it is not in name the national library, the Library of Congress performs more typical national-library functions than any other national library," but the list of functions has been expanded and updated.

In its national role, the Library:

1. Collects comprehensively, having collections that reflect the national heritage and are universal in scope, and serves as a national center for research.
2. Benefits from intergovernmental exchange, copyright, and legal deposits.
3. Receives gifts to the nation (personal papers, rare books, gift and trust funds).
4. Administers worldwide acquisitions programs, such as the Public Law 480 Program to acquire foreign materials for other libraries, as well as for LC, and the National Program for Acquisitions and Cataloging, authorized by the Higher Education Act of 1965.
5. Devises and keeps up to date classification and subject-heading systems that serve as national standards.
6. Serves as the national center for cataloging.
7. Has a national catalog-card distribution service, now to include also the distribution of catalog information on magnetic tape.
8. Publishes in book form the national bibliography, the *National Union Catalog*, issued in the early 1950's, with its supplements, including the *National Union Catalog of Manuscript Collections*, which was begun in the early 1960's.
9. Maintains other union catalogs on cards; the *National Union Cata-*

log on cards describing pre-1956 imprints is now being published in 600 volumes of 700 pages each.

10. Gives reference services, in house and by mail, and operates such information "switchboards" as the National Referral Center for Science and Technology.

11. Extends services by participating in interlibrary loan and national and international photoduplication service.

12. Has an active bibliographic and publications program, producing the *Quarterly Journal*, guides, subject directories, area bibliographies, materials relating to children's literature, etc.

13. Administers the National Books-for-the-Blind Program, expanded in 1966 to include library services to all physically handicapped persons unable to use or read conventionally printed material.

14. Presents concerts, exhibits, and literary programs, including extension concerts and loan exhibits, which enrich the cultural life of the nation.

15. Experiments and conducts research in library technology; presently the major program is directed toward the automation of the Library's central bibliographic apparatus, with the aim of developing a national information-transfer system in which libraries all over the country may participate.

16. Conducts a program for the preservation of library materials, planned as the nucleus of a national program to attack the problem of deteriorating paper faced by all libraries.

17. Engages in national and international cooperative programs, such as the development of the Anglo-American Code for descriptive cataloging, in order to promote standardization and to increase accessibility to the materials of knowledge.[119]

The authors next addressed the subjects of the Library's governance and the need for a formally recognized national library:

Without a charter spelling out its responsibilities, but with broad powers and Congressional support, the Library of Congress has been able to undertake all the above national-library functions. There are many other activities the National Library of the United States might well perform, but we have not been able to undertake them. There is a real question whether or not a detailed charter, which so many urge, would have been, or would in the future be, more help than hindrance. If areas of responsibility and relationships within and outside the Government were defined in precise detail, we in the Library of Congress are convinced that a charter would quickly become outdated and would consequently become a serious handicap.

Much of the same may be said of the Library's position as an agency of the Legislative, rather than the Executive Branch of the Federal Government. Looking back over the 169 years of the Library's history, it would be difficult to argue that its freedom of action, its ability to respond whenever a need was strongly felt, would have been any greater, if as great, in the Executive than it has been in the Legislative Branch. The Library of Congress has grown to its present size and eminence not because of where it was placed in the structure of Govern-

ment, but because it has been free to respond to changing times and to
needs as they developed and were expressed by the American people
through their elected representatives in the Congress.

Looking forward, the Library *does* feel that it would be highly beneficial if the Congress gave formal recognition to its dual role as the
Library *of Congress* and as the National Library of the United States,
to which for so many years the Congress has given its tacit consent and
material support. If such recognition is to be fruitful, however, it must
go beyond a mere Congressional resolution. There needs to be a felt
demand from the country strong enough to convince the Congress to
vote, not just for the addition of a subtitle, "The Library of Congress:
The National Library of the United States," but for the funds required
for the full support of national-library as well as of LC functions.
Basically, it is *fiscal support* that the Library needs if it is to sustain and
expand its role as the National Library of the United States. If we had
the necessary money, now that adequate space is in prospect to take care
of the physical needs of the next two decades, there is probably little
in the way of expanded services and activities that we could not undertake.[120]

The major portion of the paper is devoted "to a sketch of some services
and activities that the Library of Congress might expand or undertake if it
were formally recognized as the National Library and supported accordingly." The description is prefaced by a cautionary note:

A basic characteristic of the Library of Congress in the role of *de jure*
National Library of the United States would be that each of the services
and activities performed would have both an internal and an external
component. Also, the Library would be acting formally—as it does at
present informally—in a national setting and on a much larger stage. In
certain functions, The Library of Congress: The National Library would
be the sole agent, the active agency; in others, it would work as a part of,
or with, or through another organization, or organizations, or groups. In
terms of its overall responsibilities, it would, as the National Library,
act not as a Legislative agency but as an independent Federal agency
whose sphere of activity would not be restricted to any one branch but
would embrace all branches of the Government, as indeed its services
now do. In this regard, though it might not have or need to have the title,
it would in fact act as, and be, the national library and information
service agency.

In the following discussion of opportunities and responsibilities for
expanded services and activities that we believe the Library could have
as the National Library, it is of course assumed that the basic Library *of
Congress* function would remain, and that it would remain basic. Although that aspect of the Library's duties was beyond the scope of
inquiry of the National Advisory Commission on Libraries and is therefore not a material consideration in this report, it should be pointed out
that the services and activities of our present Legislative Reference
Service must keep pace in growth not only with the ever-expanding
responsibilities of the Congress but also with the public-service aspects
of the Library.[121]

The description of Library of Congress services and activities that might be expanded was comprehensive. The headings in the description are instructive by themselves:

THE NATIONAL ACQUISITIONS AGENCY

Extend the National Program for Acquisitions and Cataloging to All Countries and All Types of Materials

Acquire Multiple Copies of Foreign Publications

Expand and Modernize the International Exchange Machinery

Acquire Comprehensively and Bring Under Bibliographical Control Federal, State, and Local Government Publications

THE NATIONAL CENTER FOR LIBRARY RESOURCES

Extension of the National Union Catalog

Prepare Guides to the Total Library Resources of the United States

Serve as a National Center for Research, Guidance, and Information on Preservation Problems

THE NATIONAL CATALOGING CENTER

Automate the Catalog-Card Distribution Service

Publish a Current National Union Catalog

A NATIONAL CENTER FOR BIBLIOGRAPHICAL SERVICES

Provide Systematic Bibliographic Coverage of Non-Western Publications

Publish Comprehensive Accessions Lists for All Countries Lacking Adequate Current National Bibliographies

Create New Bibliographic Tools

A NATIONAL CENTER FOR RESEARCH AND TRAINING IN LIBRARY AND INFORMATION SCIENCE

Create a National Technical Processes Service

Create a National Automated System of Subject Controls

Translate the Library's Technical Publications and Bibliographic Tools

Train American Librarians

Train Scholars to Administer Research Collections

Train Foreign Librarians

A NATIONAL CENTER FOR DATA ON SERIALS

A NATIONAL TECHNICAL REPORTS CENTER

THE NATIONAL REFERRAL SERVICE IN ALL FIELDS

THE FOCUS OF A NATIONAL INTERLIBRARY LOAN SYSTEM

A NATIONAL RESEARCH AND INFORMATION CENTER

The United States of America

Other Areas of the World

Center for Science and Technology

A PUBLISHING CENTER

A CENTER FOR PHOTOCOPYING

ADMINISTRATION OF THE UNITED STATES COPYRIGHT LAW

ADMINISTRATION OF THE NATIONAL LIBRARY PROGRAM FOR THE BLIND AND PHYSICALLY HANDICAPPED

A NATIONAL CENTER FOR CULTURAL ACTIVITIES[122]

The paper concluded on a practical note, outlining three "very hard concrete steps" that had to be "mounted and, in some cases, surmounted" before the vision described in the foregoing pages could become a reality:

1. The first requirement for effective implementation of the proposed national library and information service would be not only across-the-board support of such a proposal by the National Advisory Commission on Libraries but also continued support by a permanent commission. This permanent commission's most influential service might well be to provide a voice that would speak in universal accents for the needs of all the people and of "all seasons"—for what is past (and has historical value) as well as for what is (and has great urgency) and what may be (and holds great promise).

2. The next requirement is legislation that would formally recognize the Library of Congress as also the National Library of the United States. The language of such legislation should convey the intent of Congress in a manner so lucid and unequivocal as to command the adherence and support of future Congresses for our dual role. The Joint Committee on the Library, which "considers proposals concerning the management and expansion of the Library of Congress," is the proper Congressional body to take up such legislation and, it is to be hoped, to sponsor it and its objectives with conviction and enthusiasm.

3. Support being in the positive sense the most critical problem of the transition of the Library of Congress from the *de facto* to a *de jure* as the National Library, mammoth efforts must be made to overcome the notion that the price tag on the National Library is an integral part of the price tag for the operation of the Congress of the United States. This notion cannot be overcome solely from Washington, but the voters of America in every county in the country must be made aware of the benefits that accrue to them personally from the National Library. Their sense of pride in such a national treasure must be touched. The library and information community must also be made even more acutely aware of its National Library. And the scholarly world, which realizes its stake in the welfare of the National Library, must also accept its responsibility to mobilize support for it. Until such widespread appreciation and support is evident, the National Library may not be adequately funded.

Direct appropriations, no matter how generous, should not preclude arrangements for gifts, grants, or transfers of funds for specified national objectives. Cooperative arrangements with other Government agencies, foundations, libraries, and library associations would not only have to continue but be considerably expanded.[123]

The Library of Congress in the Federal Establishment

Libraries at Large also contains three background papers submitted to the commission that deal directly with the status of the Library of Congress within the federal establishment: "Research Libraries and the Federal Government" by Charles Blitzer, assistant secretary for history and art, Smithsonian Institution, and Reuben Clark, attorney, Wilmer, Cutler, and Pickering; "A Broad Look at the Federal Government and Libraries," by Richard H. Leach, professor of political science at Duke University; and

"Observations on Government Library Organization and Policy," by Harold Orlans of the Brookings Institution. In general the authors favor stronger federal support for research libraries, increased support for the Library of Congress and, if the Library is not to be made part of the executive branch, at least a formal designation of the institution as the National Library. While each paper discusses the Library of Congress from a different and sometimes critical perspective, the authors also agree that in recent years the Mumford administration had made great progress in expanding the Library's national role. Leach, for example, approvingly quotes a statement made by Thomas P. Brockway, staff director of the American Council of Learned Societies, noting that what Brockway "concluded in 1966 rings even truer in 1968":

> At the moment . . . the Library of Congress is looking and acting like a National Library. None if its intractable problems have been solved, but it is on the move with the active cooperation of ARL [Association of Research Libraries], and its future has new lustre. First, it will, in due course, have the third building it has long needed and pleaded for year after year; and when it is built as a memorial to James Madison the Library of Congress will, for a time at least, have room in which to perform its multifarious duties swiftly and well. Second, as already noted, the Library has accepted responsibility for a national preservation program and for greatly expanded cataloguing operations which will benefit everyone.[124]

The three papers also provide a broad perspective on the problems raised by the dual nature of the Library of Congress, a perspective often lacking in studies initiated by the Library of Congress itself. Blitzer and Clark, for example, while acknowledging that the Library of Congress "is already in effect the National Library," point out that the Library "has been reluctant to seek, as part of its own appropriation, the funds necessary to enable it to serve as a true National Library and has tended instead to rely upon funds from other Federal agencies and from private sources for this purpose." They outlined what seemed to be the ideal solution:

> A single agency of the Federal Government should be given responsibility and authority for all Federal programs directly related to research libraries. Since the Library of Congress (acting as National Library) will inevitably continue to play a major role in this sphere, such a solution would necessarily involve a change in its status.
>
> Following the precedent of the National Museum Act of 1966, a National Library Act could transform the Library of Congress into a true National Library. It could then be explicitly authorized to continue and expand its programs of research and national service to research libraries, to receive both appropriated and private funds for the purpose of making grants to research libraries, and to bear major responsibility for the coordination of all Federal programs affecting libraries. Of course the Library of Congress must, in any event, continue to serve as the legislative library of the United States. To this end, its Legislative Reference Service (perhaps restyled the Legislative Research Service) should build upon its already impressive strength and expertness,

guided by the Joint Congressional Committee on the Library of Congress. In performing its national services, the National Library—which might be known as "The Library of Congress: The National Library of the United States"—should be guided by a strong and distinguished Board of Trustees, composed of both public and private members. The Board of Regents of the Smithsonian Institution, which represents the private sector as well as the three branches of the Federal Government, is a possible model for this Board.

Under this scheme, operating funds for the Legislative Reference Service would remain within the Legislative section of the Federal budget. Funds for national programs, whether performed directly by the National Library or by grants to other libraries, could be appropriated to the Library of Congress in the Executive Branch section of the Federal budget, either as an appropriation to an independent agency or under the category of Appropriations to the President of the United States.[125]

Orlans, who edited the 1963 Brookings Institution volume by Luther H. Evans and others, *Federal Departmental Libraries*, summarized what he found to be the most fundamental criticism of the Library:

> The most important function that LC is not performing is leadership. LC responds rather than initiates; somehow our most indispensable library seems politically and administratively isolated from other major libraries within or outside of government. It is an empire unto itself, benevolent and hospitable, perhaps, but an empire nonetheless, rather than an agency involved in all the normal processes of responsible, and responsive, democratic government.[126]

Orlans strongly favored the transfer of the Library of Congress to the executive branch even though he shared "the general opinion that the Congress will probably not consent to a transfer at this time, regardless of how the pill may be sweetened." Nonetheless, he felt that "a transfer should be pressed to the point at which sympathetic members of each House file a bill and hearings are held," for "only then will responsible, and not hypothetical, judgments be entered on the record." Moreover, "only good would come from the resultant public discussion of LC's national responsibilities." Finally, Orlans felt that the designation of the Library of Congress as "The National Library" by formal congressional action was "long overdue." He suggested new legislation that would create a permanent library commission, give the Library of Congress a board of regents and a subtitle such as "The National Library of the United States" while also defining the responsibilities inherent in that designation.[127]

Leach's analysis of the Library's national role began with the list of national library functions presented by K. W. Humphreys, librarian of the University of Birmingham, in the *UNESCO Bulletin for Libraries*, July–August 1966:

> Fundamental functions of a national library
> Provides the outstanding general collections of the nation's literature, broadly defined to include books, manuscripts, memorabilia, maps, music scores, periodicals, films, etc.
> Serves as the central dépôt legal of the nation to ensure systematic collections of all published material in that nation

Provides as full coverage of foreign literature as possible through
    more systematic method of acquisition
Publishes a current national bibliography and a union list of periodi-
    cal holdings
Serves as a national bibliographical information center
Publishes catalogues of the contents of the library
Exhibits its collections for the information and benefit of the people
    as a whole
Desirable functions of a national library
    Maintains a system of interlibrary loans
    Maintains a manuscript section
    Conducts research into library techniques
Functions of national library service not essentially functions of the
    national library
    Conducts an international book exchange service
    Provides special library services for the blind
    Offers opportunities for training in library service
    Provides assistance to other libraries in services and techniques.[128]

While the Library of Congress, according to Leach, performed most of these functions and "has done so over a considerable period of time," it still "does not in fact occupy the national library position." There were two main reasons why it did not: (1) certain limitations in its own operations held it back from full occupancy of the position; and (2) the Library had to share the role with two other libraries designated as national libraries.

With regard to the first point, Leach, like Orlans, doubted that the Library of Congress could continually exert the leadership role in American library affairs that is expected of a true national library. He cited the difficulties between Librarian Evans and the Congress as the reason for "an unfortunate hiatus in leadership . . . which the present Librarian has only recently been able to bridge over." Moreover, even though the Library "has recently taken the initiative in asserting leadership in such matters as book and library resource preservation, automation and cataloging, bibliographical services, and technical processes research, there is evidence to demonstrate that in other areas it has hesitated to do so without specific congressional authoriza- tion. If this is understandable, and even correct, it is nevertheless unfortunate that it must be so." Since, in Leach's analysis, the Library would probably stay in the legislative branch of government, a more effective means had to be found "to relate either the Library of Congress to the Executive Branch or the Executive agencies to the Library." For "despite the fact that a great deal of communication has developed . . . on an informal basis, the Library of Congress has not sought to push the development further toward a leader- ship position within the Federal Government on behalf of libraries and library problems."[129]

The second point, the existence of three "national" libraries, also hindered the development of uniform federal library policy:

For the most part the three libraries—the Library of Congress, the National Library of Medicine, and the National Agricultural Library— function as separate institutions. Certainly NAL and NLM have no de- sire to do otherwise. The fact that they do operate independently not only militates against the Library of Congress' taking full possession of the national library functions, but also produces a situation involving a good deal of overlap and duplication in scope and coverage, as well as in processes and procedures, on the one hand, and some competition between the three on the other. Some duplication is probably inevitable, inasmuch as the two specialized libraries have a more limited clientele than the Library of Congress, and a certain degree of competition is generally regarded to be healthy. Even so, a useful area of research might be a study of the validity of maintaining three independent national libraries and of the feasibility of alternatives to the existing situation.[130]

The National Commission on Libraries and Information Science

The National Advisory Commission on Libraries submitted its report to President Johnson on October 3, 1968. As might be expected, the commission's recommendations concerning the Library of Congress were brief and less controversial than many of the suggestions in the papers submitted for its consideration. The commission recommended the "recognition and strengthening of the role of the Library of Congress as the National Library of the United States and the establishment of a Board of Advisors" for the Library. It also recommended the creation of a permanent commission, a suggestion that became a reality when, on July 20, 1970, President Richard M. Nixon approved an act of Congress establishing the National Commission on Libraries and Information Science. The Librarian of Congress was designated as an ex officio member of the new commission.[131]

The establishment of a permanent commission was an attempt to provide a national focus on the nation's library and information programs—a focus that no single organization could provide. In July 1975 the commission released a report, *Toward a National Program for Library and Information Services: Goals for Action*, that outlined specific responsibilities for the Library of Congress in its proposed national program. The list of responsibilities was prefaced by the statement that the commission "believes that the Library of Congress should be designated as the National Library" and the acknowledgement that "new legislation may be needed to designate the Library of Congress as having responsibility for integral aspects of the National Program." The commission listed nine areas in which it believed the Library of Congress, as the national library, should accept responsibility:

1. expansion of its lending and lending-management function to that of a national lending library of last resort;
2. expansion of the National Program for Acquisitions and Cataloging;
3. expansion of the Machine-Readable Cataloging program;
4. distribution of bibliographic data through online communication;
5. development of an expanded general reference program to support the national system for bibliographic services;
6. operation of a comprehensive national serials service;
7. establishment of a technical services center to provide training in, and

information about, Library of Congress techniques and processes, with emphasis on automation;

8. development of improved access to state and local publications; and
9. further implementation of the national preservation program.[132]

The Legislative Reorganization Act of 1970

The services of the Library of Congress as a legislative library were also studied during the last decade of the Mumford administration. Furthermore, those legislative services were also strengthened and expanded, primarily through the Legislative Reorganization Act of 1970.

In 1965 the Joint Committee on the Organization of Congress began considering ways in which the Congress could be made more efficient; the services and organization of the Library of Congress, and particularly the Legislative Reference Service, naturally were part of the review. Committee and staff members considered many of the same questions debated by those who wanted the Library of Congress to assume greater responsibilities as the national library. Should the Legislative Reference Service be broken away from the rest of the Library and formally be made part of the Congress itself? Such an action of course would pave the way for the move of the rest of the Library into the executive branch or perhaps for its reconstitution as an independent agency on the model of the Smithsonian Institution.

Congress rejected a complete separation of the legislative and national functions. In its report on the pending legislative reorganization bill, submitted June 17, 1970, the House Committee on Rules recommended increased autonomy for the Legislative Reference Service, which should be renamed the Congressional Research Service (CRS), a closer relationship between CRS and the Congress, and a considerable expansion of the CRS—expecting, for example, the size of its staff to triple by 1975. It also explained why the CRS should remain part of the Library: "As did the Joint Committee on the Organization of the Congress, we considered and rejected a complete divorcement of the Service from the Library. In our judgement, the Library serves as a useful mantle for protecting the Service from partisan pressures. Furthermore, the effectiveness of the CRS will be enhanced by its continued instant access to the Library's collections and administrative support services."[133]

On October 26, 1970, President Nixon approved the Legislative Reorganization Act. The new law changed the name of the Legislative Reference Service to the Congressional Research Service, effective January 3, 1971, and expanded the duties of the service, placing increased emphasis on policy research and analysis and on direct services to both individual members of Congress and congressional committees. To assist CRS in performing its new functions, the act authorized the appointment of senior specialists and specialists in fields other than those specifically listed in the statute, as well as the use of the services of other experts, consultants, and research organizations. In addition, CRS was required to prepare and file a separate annual report with the Congress. The most significant feature of the measure, however, was its clear statement of a new relationship between the legislative and national functions of the Library. Even though Congress rejected any formal separation of the Library's legislative and national functions, it protected itself against any erosion of the legislative services provided by the Library and gave the new CRS maximum independence within the Library. The new law stated that:

1. the Librarian of Congress shall, in every possible way, encourage, assist, and promote the Congressional Research Service in—
   A. rendering to Congress the most effective and efficient service,
   B. responding more expeditiously, effectively, and efficiently, to the special needs of Congress, and
   C. discharging its responsibilities to Congress; and
2. the Librarian of Congress shall grant and accord to the Congressional Research Service complete research independence and the maximum practicable administrative independence consistent with these objectives.[134]

The autonomy of CRS within the Library's administrative structure was emphasized by two further stipulations: The pay level of the director of CRS was raised above that of other Library department heads and the director of CRS was to be appointed by the Librarian of Congress only "after consultation with the Joint Committee on the Library." This directive was the first formal limitation on the authority of the Librarian since 1897.

Mumford's Last Years in Office

The last few years of the Mumford administration were difficult internally, primarily because of problems concerning the lack of growth space and personnel administration. On May 27, 1971, the House Office Building Commission, chaired by Representative Carl Albert, recommended that no further action be taken on the appropriation of funds for the third Library of Congress building until the location of a fourth House Office Building had been determined. The question was settled on June 4 when, in the House debate on the legislative branch appropriation bill for FY 1972, the House rejected by a vote of 69–48 an amendment that would have deleted the recommended appropriation of $71,090,000 for construction of the superstructure of the James Madison Memorial Building.[135] Later in the same month the council of the American Library Association approved a membership resolution that called on the council to inquire into and report on the allegations by a personal member of ALA that the Library of Congress "discriminated on racial grounds in recruitment, training, and promotion practices." On November 9, acting on the instructions of Representative Wayne L. Hays, chairman of the Joint Committee on the Library, Mumford informed ALA that the Library would not present testimony before the association's inquiry team. In the opinion of Representative Hays, "the American Library Association is infringing on and usurping the oversight responsibilities of Congress in making an investigation of an Agency under the exclusive jurisdiction of Congress."[136] Librarian Mumford strongly defended the Library's employment and personnel policies and, in early 1973, approved a new employment opportunity plan that inaugurated a comprehensive affirmative action program for the Library under the provisions of the Equal Employment Opportunity Act of 1972. In mid-1973 he appointed a committee to develop a labor-management system for the Library. The system went into effect in October 1975, after Mumford had left the Library.

On December 31, 1974, after a 20-year career as Librarian of Congress, L. Quincy Mumford retired. At its January 1975 meeting, the Association of Research Libraries recognized Mumford's achievements and expressed its appreciation to him for his two decades of service as Librarian, noting that the job required nothing less than "astute participation in many levels of governmental relationships, a perception of national, public, and professional needs, and a cordial and mutually productive interaction with many professional and business communities."[137]

During the last years of the Mumford administration the Library began making long-range plans concerning its future role in supporting the cataloging and bibliographic needs of the nation's libraries. In the period between Mumford's retirement and the nomination of a successor, Library officials presented these plans to the library community at large.

At the same ARL meeting that paid tribute to Mumford, Processing Department Director William J. Welsh and John C. Rather, chief of the Technical Processes Research Office, discussed the future of catalog control at the Library of Congress. They expressed their hope that an automated system of cataloging control using the MARC data base would be available by 1979. If so, the adoption of the system might be timed to coincide with the move into the James Madison Memorial Building—and would enable the Library to close its card catalog at the same time.[138] On June 9, 1975, at a meeting of the Council for Computerized Networks, Welsh presented a paper entitled "The Library of Congress as the National Bibliographic Center: A Current View From the Processing Department." At this meeting, and at an ARL meeting later in the year, he stated his belief that the Library should serve as the national bibliographic center as libraries moved into the new era of bibliographic control made possible by computerized library networks. The proper role of the Library would be "to develop and maintain standard bibliographic devices that would promote consistency in decentralized input to a comprehensive national data base." He explained that the decentralized input was a requirement in a national system because "the Library of Congress recognizes that it cannot supply 100 percent of the cataloging information that is required nationally."[139]

Librarian Boorstin Takes Office

On June 20, 1975, President Gerald R. Ford nominated historian and author Daniel J. Boorstin, senior historian at the Smithsonian Institution, to be Librarian of Congress. The Senate hearings on the nomination lasted three days. Opposition came from the American Library Association for largely the same reasons ALA had opposed the nomination of Archibald MacLeish to be Librarian of Congress in 1939: The nominee's background, "however distinguished it may be, does not include demonstrated leadership and administrative qualities which constitute basic and essential characteristics necessary in the Librarian of Congress."[140] Opposition also came from the Capital Area Council of Federal Employees, No. 26, AFSCME, AFL-CIO, and two Library of Congress employee organizations. The nomination was strongly supported, however, by a bipartisan group of congressmen including Senators Mark O. Hatfield, Adlai E. Stevenson, and Charles H. Percy; and Representatives Carl

Albert, Speaker of the House of Representatives, and John J. Rhodes, Minority Leader of the House of Representatives.[141]

The Senate hearings on the Boorstin nomination also set the stage for yet another review of the Library's legislative and national responsibilities. Senator Claiborne Pell asked Boorstin if he were familiar with the Bryant memorandum that the senator had sponsored 13 years before, commenting that those recommendations "had real merit" but that Librarian Mumford "was very upset and disturbed" by the memorandum "and had various criticisms." Boorstin replied that he had read the report:

> I think, if I am not mistaken, one of [its] principal recommendations was that the Library of Congress have its name changed and that its legal locale be shifted into the executive branch, and be given the name of The National Library.
>
> I would say, Senator, that I have a great attachment to the name of the Library of Congress and would be sorry to see the name changed.
>
> I also think that its location in the legislative branch is a piece of good fortune for all of us, as scholars, who have benefitted from the generosity of the legislature—and I also would not like to see that change.[142]

In addition, Senator Pell queried the nominee about what steps he might take, upon becoming Librarian of Congress, "to find out what are the major problems of the Library, and what should be done about them?" Boorstin replied that his objective would be "to discover the extent to which the Library is or is not serving its constituents satisfactorily." He would do this by questioning the Congress and would also

> seek the counsel of the other constituencies of the library world, the professional librarians, professional scholars, the general public, the press and other media and also the staff of the Library, not only to see what could be done to improve the morale in the Library, but also to have the advice of the members of the staff as to the possibilities of the Library.[143]

The senator next asked if the nominee had "thought of the idea of setting up a task force that would be charged with the responsibility to make some recommendations, looking for patterns, and report back to you?" Boorstin replied that yes, he had thought of the idea, and while he was unwilling to commit himself with regard to the objectives or membership of such a task force, if it were set up he would consider it his duty to share its recommendations with members of Congress.[144]

In 1975, as in 1939, the Congress readily accepted the nomination of an author and cultural figure and not a professional librarian to head the Library of Congress. Confirmation occurred, without debate, on September 26, 1975, and on November 12, 1975, Daniel J. Boorstin took the oath of office as the twelfth Librarian of Congress.

The Boorstin swearing-in ceremony, held in the Library's Great Hall, emphasized the institution's national character. It was attended by national leaders from both the executive and legislative branches, including President Ford, Vice-President Rockefeller, and Speaker of the House Carl Albert, who administered the oath. Representative Lucien N. Nedzi, chairman of the Joint

Committee on the Library, presided. In introducing the President, Nedzi commented on the Library's dual role:

> As its name reveals, the Library is the Library of the Congress—a fact in which the Congress of the United States takes great pride—and, of equal importance, if not more so, it is a national library that serves all of the people of the United States.[145]

The Task Force on Goals, Organization, and Planning

One of Librarian Boorstin's first official acts was to create, on January 16, 1976, a staff Task Force on Goals, Organization, and Planning, which was charged with the responsibility of carrying out "a full-scale review of the Library and its activities." The Task Force effort was to be supplemented by advice from eight outside advisory groups, each representing one of the Library's principal constituencies. The advisory groups were established through generous grants from several private foundations. The Task Force and advisory groups were given one year to review the Library's services and make recommendations for their improvement.[146] In explaining to the staff why the review was needed, Librarian Boorstin recalled the review initiated by Librarian Archibald MacLeish:

> A third of a century has passed since the Library last undertook a full-scale, comprehensive review. These decades have been full of momentous change. Our nation has suffered the pangs of adjustment after a World War and has been involved in two other wars. In vast territories of the world the free flow of information is obstructed.
>
> We have lived through a technological revolution more intimate and more pervasive than any before. . . . No part of the Library of Congress has been untouched by these transformations. Today hundreds of our staff are engaged in activities never imagined a half-century ago. The traditional activities of our Library—acquisitions, cataloging, helping the nation's libraries, and communicating information to the Congress—have also been reshaped.
>
> At the same time, the size of our Library has multiplied. When Librarian Archibald MacLeish initiated the last full-scale review 37 years ago, the Library had a book collection of some six million volumes, an annual budget of about $4 million, and a staff of 1,000. Today our book collection has at least trebled and we have added whole new types of materials. Our annual budget is $116 million and our staff numbers over 4,600.
>
> During these decades the Library of Congress has been given a vast range of new statutory responsibilities. . . . Plainly the time has come for a review. The arrival of a new Librarian of Congress and the near completion of the Madison Building make such a study especially appropriate now.
>
> Therefore I am now commencing a major review of the Library's goals, organization, and planning. This will require close consultation with the Congress, will draw on the suggestions of our staff, and will reach outside for the constructive criticism and imaginative suggestions of all our constituencies. After full study and careful reflection, our conclusions will, I hope, produce a more effective and efficient Library of

Congress, better adapted to the needs of the Congress and the nation as we enter our third century.... The review will be wide-ranging, free and imaginative. It will start from our primary duty to serve the Congress. It will take account of those changes in technology, in the nation and the world, which affect our usefulness to the Congress and our effectiveness as a national library.[147]

The Librarian outlined the major questions to be considered. These questions, listed below, called for nothing less than a redefinition of the role of the Library of Congress in American life:

1. How well are we serving Congress? How can we better serve the Congress?

2. How well are we serving other Government agencies? How should we be serving them?

3. How well are we serving the nation's libraries? How (within our legal mandate) can we better serve the nation's public libraries, special libraries, research libraries, and other educational institutions?

4. Are our collections as widely and as fully used as they ought to be, by scholars, scientists, historians, lawyers, social scientists, poets, composers, performers, and members of the business community? How can improved administration, the addition of private and foundation resources, and more widely diffused information about our resources increase our usefulness to creative persons? How can we more effectively encourage research and creativity in the interest of the Congress and the nation?

5. How have new technological resources increased our opportunities for service to traditional constituencies and opened avenues of service to new constituencies? What can we do that we are not now doing to serve the blind and physically handicapped, to improve the nation's reading? How can we better serve the media?

6. How has new technology shaped our opportunities and our duty to preserve a full record of American civilization in our time?

7. As the quantity of informational and cultural materials increases, what can we do that we are not now doing to keep the citizen from being overwhelmed by quantity, and to guide the reader and the viewer through the thickening wilderness of printed and graphic matter?

8. In a period of change in technology and in the legal protection of authors and artists, what can the Library of Congress and its Copyright Office do "to promote the progress of science and the useful arts"?

9. In the midst of rapidly changing technology, what can the Library do to preserve and enrich the tradition of the Book?

10. In a world where many governments censor and restrict publication and inhibit free expression, are we doing everything necessary and appropriate to keep knowledge and information freely flowing into our Library from everywhere? Are we doing well all that we can to provide the Congress and the nation with a fully stocked free marketplace of the nation's and the world's knowledge and ideas? What can we do to make our collections more speedily available?[148]

The new Librarian of Congress concluded:

I will work closely with the Task Force and the Task Force advisory groups. We want and need the ideas and suggestions of the whole staff.

An essential part of the job of the Task Force will be to encourage and insure this participation.

Our Library, with the generous support and the enlightened guidance of the Congress, has flourished during a century and three quarters. To establish a Congressional library as a nation's library was itself a bold and democratic New World innovation. Today, in this great Library, we are the heirs of two complementary traditions: the Tradition of Tradition and the Tradition of Change. If, as I confidently expect, we succeed in the review we now undertake, we can set an example of democratic vitality—of how we can draw on the full resources of our past to meet the surprising and exacting demands of the future.[149]

Notes and References

1. U.S., Congress, Senate, *Annals of Congress*, 9th Cong., 1st sess., 1806, 15: 54–55.
2. For descriptions of the Library under Beckley and Magruder, see Edmund Berkeley and Dorothy Smith Berkeley, "The First Librarian of Congress, John Beckley," *LC Quarterly Journal* 32: 83–117 (April 1975), and Martin K. Gordon, "Patrick Magruder: Citizen, Congressman, Librarian of Congress," *LC Quarterly Journal* 32: 155–171 (July 1975).
3. Jefferson to Samuel H. Smith, September 21, 1814, Jefferson Papers, Library of Congress.
4. U.S., Congress, House, *Annals of Congress*, 13th Cong., 3d sess., 1815, 28: 1105–1106. 3 U.S., *Statutes at Large* 195.
5. *National Intelligencer* (Washington, D.C.), October 25, 1815.
6. For an account of Watterston's librarianship, see William Matheson, "George Watterston: Advocate of the National Library," *LC Quarterly Journal* 32: 370–388 (October 1975).
7. U.S., Congress, Joint Committee on the Library, *Report*, 14th Cong., 1st sess., 1816, S. Rept. 26, pp. 6–7.
8. *National Intelligencer* (Washington, D.C.), March 25, 1817.
9. For a description of Meehan's administration and the role of Senator Pearce, see John McDonough, "John Silva Meehan: A Gentleman of Amiable Manners," *LC Quarterly Journal* 33: 3–28 (January 1976).
10. U.S., Congress, Joint Committee on the Library, *Report on the Durazzo Library*, 28th Cong., 1st sess., 1844, H. Rept. 553, p. 2. U.S., Congress, Senate, *Congressional Globe*, 28th Cong., 2d sess., 1845, 14: 105–106.
11. 9 U.S., *Statutes at Large* 102.
12. For a discussion of the Jewett-Henry dispute, see Wilcomb E. Washburn, "Joseph Henry's Conception of the Smithsonian Institution," in *A Cabinet of Curiosities* (Charlottesville: University of Virginia Press, 1967), pp. 106–129.
13. U.S., Congress, House, *Congressional Globe*, 32d Cong., 1st sess., 1851, 24(1): 153–154. 10 U.S., *Statutes at Large* 1. 10 U.S. *Statutes at Large* 3.
14. Benjamin Perley Poore, *Perley's Reminiscences of Sixty Years in the National Metropolis*, vol. 1 (Philadelphia: Hubbard Brothers, 1886), p. 176.

15. U.S., Congress, Joint Committee on the Library, *Report to Accompany Bill S. 456*, 35th Cong., 1st sess., 1857, S. Rept. 328, p. 1.
16. 11 U.S., *Statutes at Large* 253. 11 U.S., *Statutes at Large* 379.
17. Pearce to Lincoln, March 8, 1861, Lincoln Papers, Library of Congress.
18. See David C. Mearns, "The Story Up to Now," *LC Annual Report for 1946* (Washington, D.C.: U.S. Government Printing Office, 1947), pp. 82–87, 94–95. Also Constance Carter, "John Gould Stephenson: Largely Known and Much Liked," *LC Quarterly Journal* 33: 77–91 (April 1976).
19. For a detailed account of Spofford's librarianship, see John Y. Cole, "Ainsworth Rand Spofford: The Valiant and Persistent Librarian of Congress," *LC Quarterly Journal* 33: 93–115 (April 1976).
20. John Y. Cole, "Of Copyright, Men, and a National Library," *LC Quarterly Journal* 28: 128 (April 1971).
21. Ainsworth Rand Spofford, "The Government Library at Washington," *International Review* 5: 769 (November 1878).
22. Cole, "Ainsworth Rand Spofford," pp. 106–107.
23. Fred Israel, ed., *The State of the Union Messages of the Presidents, 1790–1966*, vol. 2 (New York: Chelsea House, 1966), pp. 1354–1355. U.S., Congress, House, *Congressional Record*, 47th Cong., 2d sess., 1882, 14 (1): 221.
24. U.S., Congress, Joint Committee on the Library, *Special Report of the Librarian of Congress*, 54th Cong., 1st sess., 1895, S. Doc. 7, p. 14.
25. U.S., Congress, House, Committee on Appropriations, *Hearings on the Legislative, Executive, and Judicial Appropriation Bill for 1897*, 54th Cong., 2d sess., 1896, pp. 121–122.
26. Ainsworth Rand Spofford, "The Functions of a National Library," in Herbert Small, *Handbook of the New Library of Congress* (Boston: Curtis and Cameron, 1897), p. 123.
27. U.S., Congress, Joint Committee on the Library, *Condition of the Library of Congress*, 54th Cong., 2d sess., 1897, S. Rept. 1573, pp. 139–168, 179–203, 216–218. Hereafter referred to as *Condition of the Library of Congress*.
28. Ibid., p. 228.
29. 29 U.S., *Statutes at Large* 538.
30. *Condition of the Library of Congress*, pp. i–ii.
31. U.S., Congress, House, *Congressional Record*, 54th Cong., 2d sess., 1896, 29(1): 311–319. U.S., Congress, Senate, *Congressional Record*, 54th Cong., 2d sess., 1897, 29(1): 975–977.
32. Richard R. Bowker, "The American National Library," *Library Journal* 21: 357–358 (August 1896). Edith E. Clarke, "A Congressional Library or a National Library?," *Library Journal* 22: 7–9 (January 1897).
33. U.S., Congress, House, 55th Cong., 2d sess., 1897, H. Rept. 34.
34. Dewey to Young, July 12, 1897, Library of Congress Archives.
35. *LC Annual Report for 1897* (Washington, D.C.: U.S. Government Printing Office, 1897), pp. 17–21, 31, 49.
36. *LC Annual Report for 1898* (Washington, D.C.: U.S. Government Printing Office, 1898), pp. 12–13, 22, 46–47.
37. For a description of John Russell Young's career as Librarian of Congress, see John C. Broderick, "John Russell Young: The Internationalist as Librarian," *LC Quarterly Journal* 33: 117–149 (April 1976).

38. Lane to McKinley, quoted in William Coolidge Lane, "The Appointment of a Librarian of Congress," *Library Journal* 24: 99 (March 1899). Thorvald Solberg, "An Unwritten History of the Library of Congress from January 17, 1899 to April 5, 1899," *Library Quarterly* 9: 285–298 (July 1939). Also see John Y. Cole, *For Congress and the Nation: A Chronological History of the Library of Congress* (Washington, D.C.: Library of Congress, 1978), pp. 66–68.
39. Putnam to George Bowerman, January 26, 1900, Library of Congress Archives.
40. *LC Annual Report for 1901* (Washington, D.C.: U.S. Government Printing Office, 1901), pp. 36–37.
41. Herbert Putnam, "What May Be Done for Libraries by the Nation," *Library Journal* 26: C10–C11 (August 1901).
42. Putnam to Roosevelt, October 15, 1901, Theodore Roosevelt Papers, Library of Congress.
43. Israel, *The State of the Union Messages*, p. 2049.
44. The most perceptive accounts of Putnam's career have been written by David C. Mearns. They are "Herbert Putnam: Librarian of the United States," in *An American Library Reader*, selected by John David Marshall (Hamden, Conn.: Shoe String Press, 1961), pp. 362–410; and "Herbert Putnam and His Responsible Eye," in U.S., Library of Congress, *Herbert Putnam, 1861–1955, A Memorial Tribute* (Washington, D.C.: Library of Congress, 1956), pp. 1–52. Also see Edward N. Waters, "Herbert Putnam: The Tallest Little Man in the World," *LC Quarterly Journal* 33: 151–175 (April 1976).
45. U.S., Congress, Senate, Committee on the Library, *Legislative Drafting Bureau and Division*, 62d Cong., 3d sess., 1912, S. Rept. 1271, p. 37. Senate Library Committee to Putnam, April 25, 1911, Library of Congress Archives.
46. U.S., Congress, House, Committee on the Library, *Hearings on Various Bills Proposing the Establishment of a Congressional Reference Bureau*, 62d Cong., 2d sess., 1912, p. 114.
47. U.S., Congress, Senate, Committee on the Library, *Legislative Drafting Bureau and Division*, 62d Cong., 3d sess., 1912, S. Rept. 1271, p. 29.
48. Herbert Putnam, "Legislative Reference for Congress," *American Political Science Review* 9: 544 (August 1915).
49. *Condition of the Library of Congress*, p. 22.
50. Harvard College, Class of 1883, *Fiftieth Anniversary, 1883–1933* (Cambridge, Mass.: Printed for Class, 1933), p. 276.
51. Putnam to Milam, January 31, 1935, Library of Congress Archives.
52. *LC Annual Report for 1939* (Washington, D.C.: U.S. Government Printing Office, 1940), pp. 2–5.
53. Betty Schwartz, "The Role of the American Library Association in the Selection of Archibald MacLeish as Librarian of Congress," *Journal of Library History* 9: 242 (July 1974).
54. This statement was made on June 6, 1939, when Roosevelt announced the nomination. Quoted in Nancy L. Benco, "Archibald MacLeish: The Poet Librarian," *LC Quarterly Journal* 33: 237 (July 1976).
55. Frankfurter to Roosevelt, May 11, 1939, Frankfurter Papers, Library of Congress.

56. Benco, "Archibald MacLeish," p. 237.
57. See Schwartz, "The Role of the American Library Association," pp. 241–251; and Dennis Thomison, "F.D.R., the ALA, and Mr. MacLeish: The Selection of the Librarian of Congress, 1939," Library Quarterly 42: 390–398 (October 1972). The text of the ALA resolution is in U.S., Congress, Senate, Congressional Record, 76th Cong., 1st sess., 1939, 84(8):8216.
58. U.S., Congress, House, Committee on Appropriations, Hearings on the Legislative Branch Appropriation Bill, 1941, 76th Cong., 3d sess., 1940, pp. 2, 3, 93. U.S., Congress, House, Committee on Appropriations, Report, 76th Cong., 3d sess., 1940, H. Rept. 1764, p. 14.
59. Ibid., pp. 10, 15.
60. LC Annual Report for 1940 (Washington, D.C.: U.S. Government Printing Office, 1941), pp. 2–3. U.S., Library of Congress, "Report of the Librarian's Committee to the Librarian of Congress on the Processing Operations in the Library of Congress," by Paul North Rice, Andrew D. Osborn, and Carleton B. Joeckel, chairman, June 15, 1940. Hereafter referred to as "Report of the Librarian's Committee." The report, which is in the Library of Congress Archives, was "declassified" on June 7, 1971.
61. "Report of the Librarian's Committee," pp. 1–2, 8–9, 284–285.
62. Ibid., pp. 11–12.
63. Ibid., pp. 284–293.
64. See the LC Annual Reports for 1940–1948 and Archibald MacLeish, "The Reorganization of the Library of Congress, 1939–44," Library Quarterly 14: 277–315 (October 1944). The MacLeish article was reprinted in the LC Annual Report for 1945 (Washington, D.C.: U.S. Government Printing Office, 1946), pp. 107–142. The reorganization is outlined in Cole, For Congress and the Nation, pp. 105–127.
65. MacLeish, "The Reorganization of the Library of Congress," pp. 279, 315.
66. LC Annual Report for 1940, pp. 24–26.
67. Ibid., pp. 27–29.
68. Ibid., pp. 23–24.
69. ALA Bulletin 36: P38 (September 15, 1942).
70. Cole, For Congress and the Nation, pp. 112–115.
71. Benco, "Archibald MacLeish," pp. 242–243, 247.
72. Betty Milum, "Choosing MacLeish's Successor: The Recurring Debate," Journal of Library History 12: 92–98, 103–109 (Spring 1977).
73. U.S., Congress, Joint Committee on the Organization of the Congress, Organization of the Congress, 79th Cong., 2d sess., 1946, S. Rept. 1011, p. 15.
74. Evans to John C. L. Andreassen, June 17, 1945, Library of Congress Archives. For Evans' career as Librarian, see William J. Sittig, "Luther Evans: Man for a New Age," LC Quarterly Journal 33: 250–267 (July 1976).
75. Sunday Star (Washington, D.C.), December 2, 1945.
76. LC Annual Report for 1946, pp. 230–231.
77. Ibid., p. 307. The entire budget justification is reprinted on pp. 308–447.

78. U.S., Congress, House, Committee on Appropriations, *Legislative Branch Appropriation Bill, 1947,* 79th Cong., 2d sess., 1946, H. Rept. 2040, p. 6.
79. *LC Annual Report for 1946,* p. 12.
80. Ibid., p. 234.
81. "Report of the Library of Congress Planning Committee, March 12, 1947," in *LC Annual Report for 1947* (Washington, D.C.: U.S. Government Printing Office, 1948), p. 101.
82. Ibid., p. 102.
83. Ibid., pp. 102–103.
84. Ibid., p. 103.
85. Ibid.
86. Ibid., pp. 104–105.
87. Ibid., pp. 105–106.
88. Ibid., pp. 106–108.
89. Verner W. Clapp, "Luther H. Evans," *Library Journal* 90: 3388 (September 1, 1965).
90. Sittig, "Luther Evans," pp. 257–263. Library of Congress General Order 1436, Library of Congress Archives.
91. *Sunday Star,* December 2, 1945.
92. Benjamin E. Powell, "Lawrence Quincy Mumford: Twenty Years of Progress," *LC Quarterly Journal* 33: 275–276 (July 1976).
93. U.S., Congress, House, Committee on Appropriations, *Legislative-Judiciary Appropriation Bill, 1955,* 83d Cong., 2d sess., 1954, H. Rept. 1614, p. 4.
94. U.S., Congress, Senate, Committee on Rules and Administration, *Nomination of Lawrence Quincy Mumford to be Librarian of Congress,* 83d Cong., 2d sess., 1954, pp. 144–147.
95. "Report of the Librarian of Congress on the Bryant Memorandum," *LC Annual Report for 1962* (Washington, D.C.: U.S. Government Printing Office, 1963), p. 110.
96. "Statement of the Committee on the Control and Organization of the Collections," 1958, Library of Congress Archives.
97. Ibid.
98. U.S., Congress, Senate, *Congressional Record,* 87th Cong., 2d sess., 1962, 108(7): 9158.
99. Douglas W. Bryant, "Memorandum on the Library of Congress," in *LC Annual Report for 1962,* pp. 92–93.
100. Ibid., p. 94.
101. "Report of the Librarian of Congress on the Bryant Memorandum," *LC Annual Report for 1962,* pp. 95–96.
102. Ibid., pp. 97–98.
103. Ibid., pp. 98–99.
104. Ibid., pp. 99–100.
105. Ibid., p. 111.
106. Luther H. Evans and others, *Federal Departmental Libraries: A Summary Report of a Survey and a Conference,* ed. by Harold Orlans (Washington, D.C.: The Brookings Institution, 1963), pp. v–viii, 144–147.
107. Ibid., pp. 47–48.

108. Ibid., pp. 144–145.
109. *LC Annual Report for 1960* (Washington, D.C.: Library of Congress, 1961), p. 8; *LC Annual Report for 1971* (Washington, D.C.: Library of Congress, 1972), pp. 2–3.
110. John W. Cronin, "Remarks on LC Plans for Implementation of a New Centralized Acquisitions and Cataloging Program under Title IIC, Higher Education Act," *Library Resources and Technical Services* 11: 35 (Winter 1967).
111. *LC Annual Report for 1965* (Washington, D.C.: Library of Congress, 1966), p. 20.
112. *LC Annual Report for 1967* (Washington, D.C.: Library of Congress, 1968), pp. 21–22.
113. Powell, "Lawrence Quincy Mumford," pp. 279–281.
114. Mary McGrory, "Kennedy Gets No Help in Hunt for Librarian," *Washington Star* (Washington, D.C.), January 1, 1961. See speeches by Congressmen Omar Burleson and Fred C. Schwengel in U.S., Congress, House, *Congressional Record*, 87th Cong., 1st sess., 1961, 107(1): 977–982.
115. U.S., Congress, House, Committee on Appropriations, *Legislative Branch Appropriation Bill, 1964*, 88th Cong., 1st sess., 1963, H. Rept. 369, pp. 15–16.
116. 79 U.S., *Statutes at Large* 968. *LC Annual Report for 1971*, p. 1.
117. *LC Annual Report for 1967*, pp. 23–24.
118. Library of Congress Staff, "The Library of Congress as the National Library: Potentialities for Service," in *Libraries at Large: Tradition, Innovation, and the National Interest*, ed. by Douglas M. Knight and E. Shepley Nourse (New York: R. R. Bowker Company, 1969), p. 435.
119. Ibid., pp. 444–445.
120. Ibid., pp. 445–446.
121. Ibid., p. 447.
122. Ibid., pp. 447–463.
123. Ibid., pp. 463–464.
124. Richard H. Leach, "A Broad Look at the Federal Government and Libraries," in *Libraries at Large*, p. 353.
125. Charles Blitzer and Reuben Clark, "Research Libraries and the Federal Government," in *Libraries at Large*, pp. 396–397.
126. Harold Orlans, "Observations on Government Library Organization and Policy," in *Libraries at Large*, pp. 387–388.
127. Ibid., pp. 388–390.
128. Leach, "A Broad Look," pp. 349–350.
129. Ibid., pp. 350–352.
130. Ibid., p. 358.
131. *LC Annual Report for 1969* (Washington, D.C.: Library of Congress, 1970), p. 2, 84 U.S., *Statutes at Large* 440.
132. U.S. National Commission on Libraries and Information Science, *Toward a National Program for Library and Information Services: Goals for Action* (Washington, D.C.: U.S. Government Printing Office, 1975), pp. 67–70.
133. U.S., Congress, House, Committee on Rules, *Report*, 91st Cong., 2d sess., 1970, H. Rept. 1215, pp. 18–20.

134. 84 U.S., *Statutes at Large* 1140.

135. *LC Annual Report for 1971*, p. 1.

136. *LC Annual Report for 1972* (Washington, D.C.: Library of Congress, 1973), pp. 7–8.

137. *LC Information Bulletin* 34: A-35–A-37 (February 14, 1975).

138. Ibid., A-35. Association of Research Libraries, *The Future of Card Catalogs* (Washington, D.C.: Association of Research Libraries, 1975), pp. 6–10, 58–65.

139. *LC Information Bulletin* 34: 265, 267–268 (June 27, 1975). Association of Research Libraries, *The Library of Congress as the National Bibliographic Center* (Washington, D.C.: Association of Research Libraries, 1976), pp. 7–10.

140. U.S., Congress, Senate, Committee on Rules and Administration, *Nomination of Daniel J. Boorstin of the District of Columbia to be Librarian of Congress*, 94th Cong., 1st sess., 1975, p. 142.

141. Ibid., pp. 14–18, 30–34, 165–206.

142. Ibid., pp. 371–372.

143. Ibid., p. 370.

144. Ibid., pp. 370–371.

145. "Text of Remarks Exchanged by President Gerald R. Ford and Daniel J. Boorstin at Swearing In, November 12," *LC Information Bulletin* 34: 458 (November 21, 1975).

146. Statement by the Librarian of Congress, *LC Information Bulletin* 35: A-234 (April 9, 1976).

147. Ibid., p. A-233.

148. Ibid., p. A-234.

149. Ibid.

2

Report of the 1976 Librarian's Task Force on Goals, Organization, and Planning

Transmittal Letter to the Librarian of Congress

January 28, 1977

Dear Sir:

We are pleased to submit to you a report that contains specific recommendations for immediate improvements in the Library of Congress, as well as many ideas that may be useful in the future. Our recommendations emphasize two points: the Library must develop a sense of wholeness that it does not have at present and it must develop a stronger sense of service to all its users.

The development of a Library-wide perspective on the part of management and staff is imperative. The entire Library serves both the Congress and the Nation. Each administrative unit must view itself as an integral part of the Library of Congress, not solely as an individual department or division that serves a special clientele.

The creation of a sense of wholeness and the strengthening of a sense of service will take time. We feel it will result from a sharper definition of the Library's functions and responsibilities, improved planning, the unabashed exercise of leadership, a more clearly defined decision-making process, sensitivity to the needs and demands of the staff, and a greater willingness to consult with individuals and organizations outside the Library.

We share your enthusiasm about the Library and its potential and look forward to working with you in shaping a new Library of Congress.

Sincerely,

The Honorable Daniel J. Boorstin
The Librarian of Congress

John Y. Cole, Chairman
Alan Fern
Beverly Gray
Tao-Tai Hsia
Edward Knight
Lucia Rather
Lawrence S. Robinson
Norman J. Shaffer
Robert D. Stevens
Elizabeth Stroup
Glen A. Zimmerman

Preface

The Task Force on Goals, Organization, and Planning was created on January 16, 1976, by the Librarian of Congress, Daniel J. Boorstin, to carry out a full-scale review of the Library and to recommend changes that would improve the effectiveness and the efficiency of the institution. The Task Force was urged by the Librarian to make its review "wide-ranging, free, and imaginative," and not to be hampered by thoughts of statutory or budgetary restraints. We were asked to seek counsel and solicit ideas from the Library's staff and to listen to the advice and suggestions of outside advisory groups that would be chosen to represent the Library's various constituencies. With this guidance, plus a list of suggested questions for consideration, we began our work.

More than 500 suggestions for improving the Library and its services were sent to the Task Force by the Library's staff. Fourteen subcommittees were created: area studies, automation and reference services, bibliographic access, the bibliographic role of the Library, collection development, the cultural role of the Library, documents, loan and photoduplication services, serials management, services to Congress, services to libraries, services to staff, training and staff development, and the user survey. Over 160 staff members served on these subcommittees. Many other staff members helped with the user survey and assisted the Task Force in countless other ways.

With support from several private foundations, eight outside advisory groups were established: arts, humanities, law, libraries, media, publishers, science and technology, and social sciences. A total of 75 distinguished individuals from the United States, plus four from abroad, served as advisors.

This report is a planning document that cannot be easily summarized. The recommendations represent our distillation and evaluation of the ideas presented by the Library's staff, our subcommittees, and the advisory groups, to which have been added our own insights and opinions. A special cautionary note is necessary. The Librarian asked us to emphasize what the Library *should be* without worrying about budgetary restraints. We have done so, but are fully aware that the implementation of many of our suggestions would require large amounts of money and many additional staff members. Nonetheless, it is our belief, that many of the numbered recommendations in Chapters I–VII represent practical steps the Library could take now without causing undue budgetary or administrative stress.

The Task Force and its subcommittees have conscientiously reviewed and discussed most of the major activities of this exceptionally complex institution, but many of those activities are not mentioned in our recommendations. Our emphasis is on those functions that we would like to see improved and those new services that, if undertaken, will make the Library of Congress more useful in the future.

We are well aware that there are many other parts of the Library where essential work is proceeding efficiently and in a most satisfactory manner. The Library of Congress does many things very well and we assume it will continue to do many things very well. This realization has been a major part of our education.

The 14 subcommittee reports were treated as recommendations and many of the subcommittee recommendations are reflected in this report. In addition, the subcommittee reports contain dozens of excellent ideas that were not incorporated into our recommendations but which, at some time, should be seriously considered by the Library. The eight advisory group reports offer valuable new perspectives on the Library and its services. In addition to their inclusion as part of this report, they have been presented directly to the Librarian.

The Task Force would like to express its gratitude to those staff members who submitted suggestions, to those who visited the Task Force office during the daily "open house" hour to share their thoughts and concerns, and to those who contributed to our effort as subcommittee or advisory group members.

Our special thanks go to the following subcommittee chairmen and co-chairmen who were not Task Force members: Helen W. Dalrymple, Kimberly W. Dobbs, Ronald Gephart, John R. Hébert, John W. Kimball, Louis R. Mortimer, Suzy Platt, Dorothy Pollet, Joseph W. Price, Winston Tabb, and Robert Zich. Mr. Zich also provided valuable assistance as a member of the Task Force staff. In addition, special help was provided by Constance Carter, Janet Chase, Gladys O. Fields, Adrianne Kirkland, Nancy Mitchell, Marlene D. Morrisey, Melissa Trevvett, Susan Tarr, and Christopher Wright. We hope and trust that this endeavor marks a new direction in the affairs of the Library and that our report justifies the confidence placed in the Task Force by the Librarian and by the dedicated staff of the Library of Congress.

The Task Force process has encouraged openness and the frank exchange of opinions throughout the Library. This new atmosphere, as well as the ideas it has engendered, must not be lost.

[Editor's note. A number of administrative changes took place within the Library during 1976 and are mentioned in the Task Force report and several of the advisory group reports (Appendix C). These changes were made by Librarian Boorstin "to strengthen the Library and improve our services," and did not "foreclose or anticipate any recommendations which the Task Force may make" (Library of Congress Information Bulletin 35: 123 [February 27, 1976]). In April the Reference Department was divided into two new departments: the Department of Reader Services and the Research Department. At the same time a new position, Special Assistant for Network Planning, was created in the Librarian's office. In May another new post, Assistant Librarian for Public Education, was established and that officer given responsibility for the Library's exhibits, information, and publication programs. Finally, during the year a special committee chaired by the Assistant Librarian of Congress studied the organization of the Library's automated systems and presented suggestions to the Librarian quite apart from the Task Force, subcommittee, and advisory group recommendations. Three documents referred to in the Task Force report are found in Appendix A: Supplementary Documents. They are: Reference Service in the Library of Congress (Document 1); Area Studies (Document 2); and A Proposal for a Retrospective Bibliography of American History and Culture (Document 3).]

Chapter I: For Congress and the Nation

The Task Force believes that the fundamental question before the Library of Congress at this stage in its history is one of organizational unity. How can the Library of Congress *as a whole* better serve both Congress and the nation? The Library is a national resource without parallel. It is probably the largest library in the world, containing over 18 million volumes and 72 million pieces of research material, and employing nearly 5,000 people. In fiscal year 1977, Congress appropriated over $137 million for its operations. All of these resources must be continually focused and refocused on providing the Congress and the nation with the best library and information services available anywhere. We must dedicate ourselves to making the Library of Congress one of the finest research and cultural institutions in the world.

Service to Congress

The wide-ranging needs of Congress and its committees require a comprehensive Library with world-wide coverage that uses the most modern information technology. Because Congress long ago extended the use of this Library to the public, there has evolved a remarkable ability in the Library to gather knowledge and techniques from everywhere in the world and to share the organized products of this process with its users. In this basic sense, the national and international roles of the Library are inseparable from its most important function—serving as the library of the United States Congress. It is essential that all the users of the Library of Congress, whether on Capitol Hill or elsewhere, appreciate that improving service to Congress means improving service to all.

Recommendation No. 1: that the Library of Congress as a whole focus its total energies and resources on providing Congress with the most effective and responsive service possible.

This heightened effort should have the following goals: improved coordination and cooperation with all the Library's subdivisions in providing Congressional services; a more aggressive program of informing the Congress about the total resources and services of the Library; and a systematic program of orienting the Library's staff to be more aware of the importance of serving Congress well. To help achieve these goals, the Library should establish the position of coordinator of Congressional services.

The principal task of the coordinator would be to provide a new Library-wide focus on Congressional services by directing and monitoring Congressional requests going to departments beyond the Congressional Research Service, organizing badly needed orientation and information programs on the Library's services, and standardizing record-keeping and statistical reporting of all Congressional services. The position should be in the Office of the Librarian, perhaps associated with the Legislative Liaison Office.

Basic Responsibilities of the Library

Recommendation No. 2: that the Library prepare for Congressional action a codification of the laws relating to the Library of Congress and request the inclusion in this legislation of a statement of purposes, privileges and responsibilities similar to the following:

"The purpose of the Library of Congress is to provide to the Congress and its staff any reference, research, advisory, and interpretive services necessary for the performance of its legislative and representative duties. To perform this function, the Library has been granted special privileges not available to other libraries, including the receipt of copyright deposits for addition to the collections, legal provision for the acquisition of federal documents, and special treaty arrangements for the acquisition of foreign documents. These privileges carry with them obligations to serve as a major repository of the record of American civilization and a significant repository of the record of world civilization, to serve as a cultural and educational resource, to make its collections readily available for the purpose of research and scholarship, and to provide reference and information services to all citizens. These privileges also impose upon the Library the responsibility of serving as a national bibliographic center and as a leader of cooperative activities in acquisitions, cataloging, preservation, and reference work. These privileges impose related international responsibilities as well, including keeping knowledge and information flowing freely between the United States and other nations of the world."

Adoption of a statement of purpose, privileges, and responsibilities would be the first step in developing a formal set of policy guidelines that could be used for evaluating the Library's present services. All proposals for new services or activities should be measured against these guidelines. While considering new services, the Library must constantly seek to improve those organic operations concerned with acquisitions, bibliographic control, and the preservation and use of the collections.

The National Role

The Library of Congress is the most comprehensive library in the world, and this, of course, is one of the reasons it is a national treasure. The collections of the Library must retain their comprehensive character, but the Library's present collecting policies should be studied and carefully delineated. The Task Force does not believe that everything should be collected at the Library any more than it believes that everything should be done by the Library in the area of bibliographic control. The Library must do a better job in sharing—collections, information, and people. The Library should emphasize its role as a national clearinghouse and referral center. To do so, it must pay closer attention to the needs of all its users, including Members of Congress, librarians, information specialists, researchers, scholars, and the general public.

> **Recommendation No. 3:** that the Librarian of Congress establish a Board of Advisors to assist the Library in articulating and fulfilling its national responsibilities. The Board should include as members the chairman and vice-chairman of the Congressional Joint Committee on the Library and distinguished representatives from the library and scholarly communities and from the Library's other constituencies.

The Board of Advisors would in no way impinge on the oversight functions now performed by the Congressional Joint Committee on the Library. Nor would it replace other ad hoc advisory boards created by the Library for assistance on specific programs. In fact, the Task Force feels that the Library should consult far more frequently with representative groups from its various constituencies, both professional and scholarly, with regard to its programs.

The Library must increase its involvement in all aspects of national library affairs, especially by exercising greater leadership. The role of a national library leader is a difficult one, for in fulfilling it, the Library of Congress must be simultaneously a leader and a partner. It should assume the responsibility for seeing that essential tasks are performed, but always remember that those tasks might be best performed elsewhere. It must support and work with all the nation's libraries. What Melvil Dewey said before the Joint Committee on the Library in 1896 is still true: the Library of Congress must become "a center to which the libraries of the whole country turn for inspiration, guidance, and practical help which can be rendered so economically and efficiently in no other possible way." To become such a center, the Library must establish new, formal channels of communication between itself and other libraries and encourage suggestions and criticism. It must open its doors even wider.

> **Recommendation No. 4:** that the Library establish an office to coordinate the services offered by the Library of Congress to other libraries, receive comments from those libraries about our services, and act as a continuing liaison between the Library and the library community.

Located in the Office of the Librarian, this national library office would coordinate the Library's activities with the National Library of Medicine, the National Agricultural Library and, through the Federal Library Committee, with all federal libraries. It would serve as a continuing liaison with all major library associations and groups. The office would publicize the Library's services and coordinate a program enabling the Library to share its skills more effectively, perhaps through visiting teams and internships. It would study new ways by which the Library might lower the prices it charges libraries for our products. In particular, it should study the possibility and desirability of changing the 1902 federal statute governing the sale of the

Library's cataloging to outside libraries, agencies, and individuals, with a view toward creating a sliding scale of charges. Finally, the office would help outside librarians get in touch with the appropriate LC department or division.

The Task Force believes that the Library should provide its users with access to its comprehensive resources in all subjects and in as many languages as possible. It should serve as an information center where all citizens can obtain answers or quickly learn where to obtain answers. It should become a center for scholarship and creativity, an institution that stimulates learning, research, and the exchange of ideas. It should make an even greater contribution than at present to the cultural and educational life of the country. In sum, the Library of Congress—already a grand accumulation of the world's knowledge—must become a more *useful* part of the national life. The first step is to make our collections and the skills of our staff more accessible.

Chapter II: Access

Section A: Collection and Information Services

The whole point of library work is to put the needed object—book, periodical, map, recording—or its intellectual substance into the hands of the user. But the Library's readers have told us repeatedly in the user survey that it is here, in providing intellectual and physical access to the collections, that the Library of Congress needs the most improvement. The need is urgent and there is no excuse for delay.

Delivery of Books

Recommendation No. 5: that the Library place among its highest priorities the significant improvement of its basic book delivery service.

The Library *must* have effective book service in its general reading rooms. Additional staff, new management controls, an attractive setting for deck work, a new mode of staffing and supervision, and a new unified organization will provide the first steps toward greater effectiveness.

It is impossible for the Task Force to determine with precision how much of the problem should be attributed to what cause. It is clear, however, that the problem is multifaceted and that the Library must consequently attack it on many fronts. We urge that the Library conduct a thorough study to determine the cause of our "not-on-the-shelf" problem. This must include the location of the items not in place, an analysis of the reasons why they are not in place, and a determination of the exact not-on-the-shelf rate.

It appears that part of the problem is that the number of Library deck attendants per volume of the general collections is less than half the number in comparable organizations, such as the New York Public Library. We urge, therefore, that the Library increase its page staff by at least one-third by 1980. So far as possible, no deck containing normally used collections should be without its page, and no page should be without a supervisor close at hand. Such an expansion seems ideally suited to absorb positions made available because of automation.

We also urge those who administer the stack service to create and use effective management controls. A book that is not-on-the-shelf is virtually lost to the reader. Supervisors should check all not-on-the-shelf reports, and the administrators of the stack service should spot check items reported by supervisors to be not-on-the-shelf. Supervisors should receive regular reports from shelfreaders as to the state of the decks and incorporate this information and figures on not-on-the-shelf accuracy and speed of book delivery into the evaluation of the delivery system.

In addition, we urge the Library to improve materially the work environment of its pages. We recommend that pages receive special orientation and training to make them skilled searchers. We recommend that the Library review its housekeeping program to ensure that the stacks are always clean, and that graffiti in stairwells and elevators do not achieve eternal life. The Library should move with greater speed in placing new fluorescent lights in the decks and control rooms of the Jefferson Building. We recommend the issuance of smocks and the provision of personal lockers for the page staff.

We believe the Library should make far greater use of part-time pages, specifically college students who have demonstrated interest in and knowledge of some part of the general collections to which they would be assigned as pages. The page job is not constituted in a way that permits it to be the first stage in a page "career"; the position should be a "pass-through" for those (usually students) preparing for other careers. Nor should page work be full-time. It seems unreasonable to expect a staff member to spend eight hours a day isolated on a deck performing duties which of necessity are repetitive and boring. The goal of a conscientious part-time page should be a recommendation for a job elsewhere.

We urge the Library to merge the Stack Service Section of the Stack and Reader Division with that portion of the Collections Maintenance Office in charge of shifting the general collections. The work of these two groups is so closely related that the question of where the work of one begins and the other ends has caused controversy for several years. The units must be brought together and made to work harmoniously toward the achievement of neat, orderly, well-serviced decks and well-maintained collections. The new unit should be assisted in its work by a separate team of highly qualified shelfreaders. A team in the Preservation Office would continue surveying the collection for preservation purposes.

We urge finally that this merged unit be called a stacks section and that it be part of a general reading room and information division (for further details see Appendix A, Document 1). The purpose of the new unit would be to focus more sharply the Library's now diffused efforts to serve readers. Splitting the jurisdiction between book delivery and reference service has left many gaps. Bringing together under a single, responsible administration all those who provide services in the general reading rooms will lay the ground work for a concerted effort to improve these vital functions.

Assistance to Readers

Recommendation No. 6: that the Library create a logical system of reader guidance that begins at the door of the Library (or even on Neptune Plaza) and ends in the office of one of our subject or area specialists.

The Library must in turn do a far more effective job in educating readers to exploit the wide range of services available to them. The Library can make a great effort, for instance, to offer special searches and to put non-circulating books in reference collections; it can charge all books taken from the shelves, and in other ways make our collections more accessible to readers, but the effort is wasted if the reader does not know how to exploit these services.

In the main lobbies of the ground floor entrances to the Library of Congress and Jefferson Buildings there should be imaginative and well-designed orientation centers for tourists and readers. An attractive and easily understood system of signs should be developed to lead visitors through the buildings. Just outside the west entrance to the Main Reading Room a staff member at an information station should begin the sorting out of Library visitors: tourists one place, first-time readers another, experienced researchers another. A sign just inside the entrance to the Main Reading Room should direct all first-time readers to a reader advisory office located in the small alcoves adjacent to the entrance of the Main Reading Room. This office should be staffed at all hours with one or more reference librarians. These librarians would assist readers in making the most effective use of the Library's collections, services, and people.

Many readers should receive the next phase of their education about the Library from reference librarians stationed at the Main Reading Room Issue Desk. The Issue Desk should be staffed by both reference librarians and attendants handling matters of book service (for further details, see Appendix A, Document 1).

Another part of the system of reader guidance must be filled by assistants who will teach our readers how to use the Library's data bases and computer terminals. As a first step, the Library should establish a public computer terminal center at the rear of the Main Catalog and put a station within it for a terminal instruction assistant who must be available during all hours of service. Like the page jobs, these positions should be created by conversion of positions no longer needed because of automation. The Library's staff, along with Congressional staff members, also need such training. A small training facility for the use of these staffs should be part of the reader guidance service.

A Single Reference Department

Recommendation No. 7: that the Reader Services and Research Departments be recombined into a single reference department which would have subunits for area studies, special formats, and general reference services.

We believe that the split of the Reference Department in early 1976 has caused confusion and inefficiency in the Library's operations. It has made coordination of acquisitions, processing, and preservation activities unnecessarily complex and has postponed the development of reasonably uniform reference policies and procedures. Finally, the administrative separation of the general book collections (Reader Services Department) from the special collections (Research Department) has created an additional layer of bureaucracy that must be surmounted in our common effort to view the Library's research collection as a single entity. We therefore urge the recombination of the

Research and Reader Services Departments into a single reference department with three administrative subunits, each headed by an assistant director: area studies, special formats, and general reference services.

Subject Specialists

The new reference department should set as a goal the creation of a staff of reference specialists that ultimately would possess a range of expert knowledge embracing all major subjects. We urge that the Library work toward achieving this goal of comprehensive subject coverage by the early 1980's. In 1980, after the move to the James Madison Memorial Building, additional space for those specialists will be available in the Library of Congress Building. Their services, of course, will also supplement the assistance provided to the Congress by the present Library staff.

Area Specialists

Recommendation No. 8: that the Library enlarge its staff of area specialists to encompass all major regions of the world by establishing an American studies division, a European division, and an African division.

The Library requires a full range of area specialists as well as additional subject specialists. We therefore urge that the Library enlarge its staff of area specialists so as to encompass all major areas of the world. Specifically, we see the need for the creation of an American studies division, a European division, and conversion of the African Section to a division.

The American studies division (covering the United States and Canada) could possibly incorporate the bibliographers working on the *Guide to the Study of the United States*, the staff of the Archive of Folk Song, the Local History and Genealogy Room staff, the American Revolution bibliographers, the Children's Book Section, and the American Folklife Center. In 1980, after the move into the Madison Building, the Library should give this division its own reading room where it would serve those needing expert guidance (and an enlarged reference collection) in American history and civilization. The reading room would, of course, require special facilities for listening and viewing. The Library has a special obligation in the field of American studies. The Task Force believes that the focus on American history and culture which an American studies division, with an enlarged staff of Americanists and bibliographers, can achieve would help fill many embarrassing gaps in both our collections and service. Furthermore the existence of this division would help define the tasks and responsibilities of the staffs in other divisions of the Library.

The European division would incorporate the present Slavic and Central European Division and add specialists for each of the major European countries not now covered. Spain and Portugal would continue to be covered by the Latin American, Portuguese, and Spanish Division. The purpose of a European division is once again to fill obvious gaps in our program of collection development and reference service.

The African Section should become a division. The organization of the new division will require careful thought. The report of the area studies subcommittee provides useful background information, along with Document 2 in Appendix A.

The evidence of the report of the subcommittee on area studies, as well as common sense, reveals there to be a natural community among area study divisions. An assistant director is needed to shape their growth and services.

Once the area studies units are brought together, further study should be given to their organization. They should be structured in a manner which will be as useful as possible to the researcher while also recognizing internal Library needs. One danger to be avoided is the development of unwieldy geographic units. One way of organizing area studies units is to be guided by geographic divisions indicated in the composition of the various scholarly area studies associations. With this concept in mind, the following units would evolve: American, African, European, Latin American, Near and Middle Eastern, and Asian. Consideration should also be given to creating separate units for East Asia and Southern Asia. The report of the area studies subcommittee contains many ideas on this subject.

Special Formats

The position of assistant director for special formats should be created to head the subunit containing the special collections of manuscripts, maps, music, prints, photographs, and motion pictures. The assistant director would play an important role in coordinating the Library's cultural programs as well as in reference and bibliographic work in these difficult areas. This officer would have particular responsibility for working with the Assistant Director (Cataloging) in the Processing Department toward achieving a balanced and coordinated program of bibliographic control within the unit, including development of uniform subject headings and cataloging practices.

Within the special format divisions is a subunit which we wish to recognize. It is the performing arts group: the Music Division and Motion Picture Section. The Library should respond to the more prominent place the performing arts now hold in American culture by enlarging the scope of its performing arts operations. Accordingly, it must give the performing arts units the resources needed to support the expansion. We recommend specifically (1) that the Music Division create a dance section with the duty of describing our present holdings in the field and then much enlarging them with tapes, transcriptions, and other materials of documentation; (2) that the Motion Picture Section become a motion picture and television division and serve as the home for all our general films and videotapes; (3) that a theater specialist become one of the first specialists hired in the general expansion of reference service; and (4) that ultimately the Library consider establishing a theater section or division. These ideas are discussed at length in the report of the arts advisory group.

With the exception of the Division for the Blind and Physically Handicapped, we recommend that the remaining units in the new reference department should be put under an assistant director for general reference services. The Division for the Blind and Physically Handicapped, with its specialized national program and a separate annual appropriation in fiscal 1977 of over $20 million should probably have departmental status or the equivalent. The planning office should study this question further and make a recommendation to the Librarian.

For additional details about the proposed reference department, see Appendix A, Document 1.

The Law Library

We recommend strengthening all aspects of the Law Library's activities. In particular, there is a need for improved communication and coordination between the Law Library and other departments. In certain areas of the provision of legal reference and research services to Congress, the responsibilities of the Law Library and the Congressional Research Service are closely related. To ensure that Congress receives the optimum service in these areas, close coordination between the Law Library and the Congressional Research Service is necessary. The Task Force is pleased to see that progress in this relationship has been made during the past year. It would be useful if, in the future, Law Library and CRS division chiefs could meet periodically to discuss matters of mutual concern. In more general terms, the Law Library must be viewed as an integral part of the entire Library of Congress. The acquisitions, automation, cataloging, and preservation programs of the Library of Congress must include the Law Library and its collections to a greater degree than they have in the past. This is particularly true in the area of automation.

The Task Force believes that the vast and comprehensive collections of the Law Library should be made more accessible to libraries in the United States and abroad through an expanded publications program. Particularly useful endeavors would include an expanded series of law and legal literature guides for foreign jurisdictions, a continuing subject index to the *United States Statutes at Large*, and an informal series of guides to research in legal subjects. More scholarly publications based on the unique foreign law collections are needed as well.

Many proposals have been submitted to the Task Force regarding the organization of the Law Library, its leadership role, and its administrative relationship to the other Library departments. The report of the subcommittee on services to Congress lists some of the suggestions and summarizes others. The future direction of the Law Library is a complicated and important question that must be studied further by the planning office and other officials. In addition to organizational questions, the idea of creating a centralized national law center should be studied. This concept has great appeal, but development of such a center should not be undertaken unless the Library commits itself wholeheartedly. The report of the law advisory group contains many ideas about the Library's law services.

A More Rational Pattern of Reference Service

The Law Library and the various units of the new reference department share many central problems. What is needed is greater uniformity in acquisitions, reference practices, and preservation. To help achieve this goal, the Library should create in both the reference department office and Law Library office the position of reference coordinator. The coordinator should survey existing practices throughout each department. The Library needs, for instance, a rational system of hours of service, at a minimum offering Saturday hours for every reading room, with essential services like the Central Charge file available for extended hours.

The coordinators should develop management tools that permit the continuous monitoring of the work of the departments. The work of the user survey should be continued on a routine basis, allowing the Library regularly to sample the thinking of its users as the basis for evaluating policy and performances.

The coordinators should stay in constant contact with each other and with the Congressional Research Service and should anticipate the impact on the reference department or Law Library of new policies or services in other departments. They should make every effort that is compatible with unimpaired good service to Congress toward arranging the exploitation of the CRS reference machine for the benefit of the general reader. Finally, together with the coordinator of Congressional services, they should study ways of improving the services provided to Congress through the Library's various reference centers and book rooms on Capitol Hill. At present these offices are staffed by different Library departments. As suggested by the subcommittee on services to Congress, a more unified administrative structure should be considered.

Improved Reference Tools

Recommendation No. 9: that the Library provide its reference staff with the services, tools, and setting which will permit an enlarged reference program to be truly effective; specifically fast receipt of reference materials, new guides to Library of Congress staff and services, the use in some form of all the Library's data bases and research studies, and new opportunities for professional development.

As a first step, the Library must make plans for the editing and reproduction of the Main Catalog after it is closed (or "frozen"). Sets of the catalog should be placed in all reading rooms and near all computer terminals.

The reference staff must be able to order reference and other titles urgently needed and feel confident that they will in fact arrive and, indeed, arrive promptly. Few reference staff feel this confidence now. Those who do, in the Congressional Research Service and the Division for the Blind and Physically Handicapped, have a special reference collections staff to call on, and this staff has special ordering and processing privileges. We recommend that these divisions serve as a model to all reference divisions that maintain sizeable reference collections.

These special units must have the ability and authority to order titles from local bookstores or in other ways have the materials they request sent directly to them. Once the material arrives, there should be sufficient staff in the reference division to do any needed processing and send any appropriate notice to the central record of holdings.

The reference staff and readers both must have access to the full range of services and expert knowledge which exists in abundance throughout the Library. We urge that the Library produce an expanded series of guides to its various divisions and services, including a comprehensive directory of online data bases available in the Library. We urge the compilation and publication of a directory of subject and language specialists. Information on the Library's specialists should be available online through the National Referral Center. The National Referral Center itself should explicitly broaden its scope to cover all major subject areas. It should drop the words "for Science and

Technology" from its name, and provide information about people and organizations inside and outside the Library, at home and abroad, in every field of human knowledge. Such an expansion in scope would require its moving from the Science and Technology Division into the reference department office.

We recommend that the Library make publicly available the National Referral Center data base, all of its other non-CRS data bases, and products based on the CRS citation file, the legislative status file, and CRS studies or publications, where possible. The Library should seek permission from Congress to do so as necessary. We believe that the Library can make a persuasive case that giving the American people access to selected CRS data bases and studies will not only in no way injure our service to the Congress, but will in fact encourage and improve policy research being carried out elsewhere.

For the Library's readers to receive full benefit from the enlarged corps of specialists, LC staff must be given greater opportunity to develop their professional skills. The staff must be encouraged in their professional development. The Library should seek a level of staffing that permits our specialists to engage in appropriate research as part of their job and that also permits regular attendance at professional meetings. Subject specialists should be rotated into six-month to one year research positions. Additional staffing should permit the periodic assignment of area specialists to the Library's overseas offices. Such rotational assignments would improve the range and effectiveness of our acquisitions and greatly enhance the specialist's knowledge of a subject or area.

Section B: The Researcher in the Library

Once the Library has created an efficient book and information service, it should take steps to attract to the Library those who, using the service, can best exploit our resources.

A Center for Scholarship

Recommendation No. 10: that the Library make itself more hospitable to the scholar and the world of scholarship by enlarging its facilities for study, providing appropriate courses, and offering grants for research in our collections.

We recommend the Library take the steps listed below to attract and better serve the serious researcher.

As soon as feasible, the Library should provide better physical facilities for all its researchers. Specifically, it should return to scholars the study rooms and areas for study facilities originally intended for these uses; provide a journal and new book browsing lounge and a common room; provide suitable seminar rooms and possibly a dining facility.

Jointly with universities, the Library should establish courses that grow naturally from our collections and services. Specifically, the Library should consider holding an annual institute of advanced bibliographic research, lasting perhaps two to three weeks, and aimed at acquainting scholars with the Library's collections and services; offer a course of training for librarians in the administration of research collections; and offer short courses in such subjects as folklore, maps, and copyright where our resources in people or collections are unexcelled.

The Library might wish to solicit private funds to finance scholarships or fellowships for the purpose of research in specific collections in the Library of Congress. The Library could give the scholar great freedom, but require a particular bibliographic task such as the compilation of a desiderata list or an analysis of a collection to fulfill the terms of the grant.

The services described above would make the Library into a leading center for advanced research and scholarship. Such a center would assure the presence in the Library of those best equipped to exploit the vast range of our collections and to make a unique contribution to the life of the institution.

We have outlined, in considerable detail, what seem to us needed steps toward making the Library an effective research institution offering prompt book service, improved access to the collections, and a wide-ranging, well-trained, well-equipped staff. We have suggested the means for drawing to the Library those best equipped to make use of the powerful instrument of research we have sought to construct. If we are able to secure the resources we need to build what has here been outlined, the Library of Congress will be transformed. It will be transformed from a baffling palace of mirrors that researchers sometimes have warned each other against into a thriving center for research without parallel.

Section C: The Researcher Outside the Library

In serving researchers, the Library should exert leadership in opening up the resources of all the world's libraries. It should do so in part by making its own collections available but also by helping to create fast, efficient loan networks in a comprehensive system covering the nation and the world.

An Interlibrary Loan Network

Recommendation No. 11: that the Library of Congress seek the growth of a system of compatible, coordinated, computerized loan networks that cover without overlap every part of the nation and the world.

Computer records should eventually underpin the workings of an international loan system. The computer could sort out and direct requests and keep a record of the number and kind of books loaned by participants. The Library must begin working with the existing networks in developing the needed standards, in providing the research necessary to forge technical links, in piecing together national and international programs and generally in creating a coherent system in which participation will be irresistible.

When, under the new system, a loan request does arrive at the Library, the Library should seek to supply the request by photocopy or telefacsimile whenever feasible. What the researcher usually needs is not the piece itself, but its text. To preserve our collections and keep them on the shelves ready for other users, the Library should supply, when the copyright law permits, the text in photocopy at nominal cost.

To support a greater role for the Library in the world of international scholarship, we urge that it become the initial source of American imprints for foreign libraries that have exhausted the resources of their own national networks. We believe also that the Library should consider (1) establishing an international lending center to speed loan requests from American libraries for items in foreign libraries, indemnifying the libraries as needed; and (2) establishing a photocopy center to copy foreign items for American libraries and borrowed American items for foreign libraries.

To open the Library's own resources for still further use, the Library should change its policy so that it honors loan requests from any requestor who has gone through the loan network even though the person is not engaged in "advanced research leading to publication." Similarly, the Library should make freely available its little-used foreign language material to any American who can read the language of the text. Better management techniques will help us identify this "little-used material."

We recommend that the Library, in cooperation with other research libraries, support the creation of a national periodicals lending library on the model of the British Lending Library. Such an institution is essential in making the journal literature fully available to the American research community.

As a final step in opening up its resources, the Library should better inform the world's researchers and their libraries about our loan and photoduplication services. It should print pamphlets on these and other Library services for distribution to Congressional offices, patrons, and libraries. It should describe changes in policy in a special loan and photoduplication newsletter or in an enlarged *Information Bulletin*. It should prepare an informational packet of films, slides, and tapes, hold workshops, and consider establishing a staff exchange program. It should use the telephone as much as possible, not only to speed service, but to explain problems and clarify our policy.

An essential corollary to opening our resources is the retrieval in good time of loaned items for the use of others. For this purpose, we believe that except for Congressional and staff loans, the Library should require that all the material it loans be used in the borrowing library or office.

Secondly, if a library establishes a pattern of abuse of its loan privilege, the privilege should be withdrawn.

Thirdly, the Library should work with the Congress in arranging to "clear" persons resigning from Congressional offices; those with items on outstanding loan should have their final paycheck attached until they return or replace these items.

Finally, we believe that the Loan Division and the Congressional Research Service must continue to work together in improving our loan services to Congress and eliminating the duplication of effort in certain activities such as searching.

Photocopying Service

Recommendation No. 12: that the Library use appropriated funds to support aspects of its Photoduplication Service.

An important non-loan component in making our resources more widely available is an efficient photocopying service. Our user survey has shown that many patrons believe our service is slow, and, in some categories, expensive. At present, the Photoduplication Service is operated with income derived from the services it provides its customers. We believe that the division should be supported in part by appropriated funds. This "subsidy" should be applied first to speeding the service and second, if possible, to lowering the rate charged the occasional private user for small jobs. The subsidy could either be direct, as by paying the salaries of the photoduplication searching staff, or indirect, as by creating a centralized searching staff to handle the searching now done in the Union Catalog Reference Unit, the Loan Division, and the Photoduplication Service.

In addition, we would like to see the Photoduplication Service consider establishing a modified service. As now, copies of archival quality would be provided whenever required. But when requested, less expensive copies would be provided rapidly for general use. These copies would be clearly labeled "not of archival quality." This would have to be a tightly controlled system, for we do not want the Library's reputation as a leader in the development and enforcement of technical standards to be diminished.

National Telephone Reference Service

As a final element in opening up our resources, we recommend that the Library expand the National Telephone Reference Service to cover all major library networks and all members of the Association of Research Libraries. Once fully established, the service might be used as the nation's broker for pertinent data bases. We might also consider the creation of a national reference data base, consolidating online the hard won information now mainly on 3 × 5 cards husbanded in the files of reference librarians everywhere. For further information see the report of the subcommittee on services to libraries.

We have proposed many devices to improve access to the riches of the Library of Congress and the world's libraries generally. In his charge to the Task Force, Dr. Boorstin asked "Are our collections as widely and as fully used as they ought to be. . . ?" The answer implicit in this chapter, with its many recommendations, is "No, indeed." Our response is founded on the conviction that riches of the magnitude held by the Library of Congress and other libraries of the world place upon their keepers a profound obligation to share them with all. We hope what we have proposed will permit libraries to do just that, and in far greater measure than ever before.

Chapter III: Collection Development

The Task Force believes that the Library of Congress, in its multitudinous activities, often forgets the importance of its collections. They are central to all its endeavors and the institution is not giving them the attention they deserve. While comprehensive in scope, they sometimes are weak in areas where the Library of Congress assumes and declares they are strong. Their physical condition is a matter for continued concern. In our acquisitions and preservation programs, as in so many other areas, a coordinated, Library-wide perspective is needed. The Library should assume an aggressive stance in its collection development activities, committing new positions and additional funds without apology. We must actively survey and evaluate the collections and acquire the needed items. We must see that each important item in our collection is either properly preserved in its original format or that—using advanced technology—a permanent record of its intellectual content is readily available. And we must enter into a new era of resource sharing with the libraries of the nation, providing new leadership in the development of cooperative acquisitions and preservation programs.

A Collection Development Office

Recommendation No. 13: that a collection development office be established and made responsible for selecting materials for the Library's collections, coordinating all recommending activities, soliciting gifts, and making decisions regarding the custody of the Library's various collections. The chief officer of this unit should have primary responsibility for the preparation of the Library's acquisitions budget and should chair the Acquisitions Committee.

The tasks of recommending and selection in the Library of Congress are infinitely more complex than at other large libraries and consequently require a rationale and coherence that will make the best use of the specialized subject and language talents of the staff. An improved mechanism for recommending and selection is urgently needed.

The present system of dispersed responsibility and part-time attention to the recommending function has produced inconsistency and inefficiency. The separation of selection from recommending creates built-in conflicts. Routing large numbers of catalogs to numerous recommending officers is wasteful and leads to delays. Many of the present problems could be alleviated by bringing together in a single office several groups now engaged in the recommending and selection processes.

The Task Force recommends that the required integration of functions be achieved by creating a collection development office consisting of the present Library Resources staff (Research Department), the Selection Office (Processing Department), the acquisition staff in the Public Reference Section (Reader Services Department), some searching staff from the present acquisitions divisions in the Processing Department, and a staff of full-time collection development officers some of whom might be rotated into the office from reference divisions, depending on the needs of individual units. With the decreasing ties between cataloging and acquisitions, particularly in the shared cataloging operation, the office might well be united with the new acquisition division described in Recommendation No. 16. Such a "resources" branch could be located either in one of the existing departments or in a new department.

The collection development officers would work closely with the reference specialists in the divisions, coordinating and supplementing their efforts. The officers would receive intensive briefings on acquisitions policies and, applying their own firsthand knowledge of bibliography and the researcher's need, provide for the growth, shaping, and filling in of the collections that has long been needed. In addition to recommending acquisitions by purchase, gift, or exchange they would review items rejected by selection officers and survey and evaluate the collections in their own special fields.

The Selection Office, which provides a necessary control in the entire process, would retain its independence within the new unit, working closely with recommending officers in discussing mutual problems and forwarding for review by these officers all items it rejects for addition to the collections. Any unresolvable divisions of opinion would be referred to the chief collection development officer for decision.

The collection development office would also initiate a full-scale study of the Library's arrangements regarding the custody of its collections. There are many anomalies to be assessed, as well as questions concerning further centralization or decentralization. Once the principles have been defined by the Library's administration, the collection development office would have responsibility for all decisions regarding the custody of the collections.

Retrospective Acquisitions

Recommendation No. 14: that the Library, through its collection development office, intensify its efforts to acquire retrospective research materials. An expanded program for the solicitation of gifts must be part of this effort.

The staff of the Library of Congress cannot cover every specialization in depth. When needed, the collection development office should engage outside consultants with strong subject specialities to review portions of the collections and assist in the compilation of lists of desiderata. Such outside desiderata lists as well as internally prepared lists resulting from collection surveys, not-on-the-shelf reports, and reader recommendations should be a basis for retrospective acquisitions. (A distinction should be made between those items that should be acquired in the original because of their value as artifacts and those items for which a microform or other copy will serve the purpose equally well.) The Library must aggressively pursue the search for items placed on the desiderata list, secure funds for their purchase, and arrange for prompt processing of those items acquired.

Increased use of desiderata lists and the continuing shortage of funds for retrospective purchases even under current circumstances suggest the need for an increased book budget and new efforts to acquire gift funds for special purchases. Many divisions of the Library have well-developed gift solicitation programs in their special areas with support service provided by the Exchange and Gift Division. The collection development office should be in charge of the Library's gift solicitation program and play a central role in its coordination and enlargement. The Library has the national stature to attract sizeable donations, both of money and collections. The Librarian, by virtue of his position, has a key role to play in an expanded gift program aimed at soliciting funds from private sources and books or manuscripts in private hands. New approaches are needed. The humanities advisory group has suggested, for example, that the Library actively solicit the specialized collections of distinguished scholars who are retiring from their academic careers.

Management of Serials

Recommendation No. 15: that a committee on serials be established to coordinate the management of serials in every part of the Library.

It is essential that the Library staff step back and take a larger view from time to time in an effort to discern any systematic distortion or malfunction that may have developed in the Library's programs. Suggestions from advisory groups and staff members have convinced the Task Force that at least one such distortion exists now and urgently needs righting. Serials and documents have not received the attention and priority that is demanded by their inherent complications and value as information sources. A higher priority should be directed to these materials through a committee on serials composed of the division chiefs, or their representatives, from the Serial Division, Serial Record Division, and other offices with a major interest in serials. The report of the subcommittee on serials management describes the major problems this committee should address.

In particular, the committee must direct its attention to the problem of coordinating the management of serials throughout the Library. The committee should concern itself with the automation of serials processing, a matter which the Task Force regards as one of particular urgency, and with the maintenance and servicing of our serials collections. Without automation the Library will be unable to cope fully with its most urgent acquisitions problem, the claiming of missing issues or parts of serial titles. It is anticipated that automation will take a considerable period of time and as an interim measure we recommend that the Serial Record Division be provided several new positions to serve as a claiming group using manual methods later to be converted to automation.

In the same vein, the Task Force feels that the Compliance Section of the Copyright Office has not fulfilled its true potential as a means of enriching the Library's collections. In part the fault lies in the Library's inability to claim missing issues and in part in the lack of a strong and persistent compliance program. The new copyright law with requirements for prompt deposit and penalties for failure to deposit provides the opportunity to improve and expand the compliance function. The Copyright Office should expand its staff engaged in compliance actions, pursue a more aggressive compliance program, and orient appropriate Library staff members in the compliance provisions of the new law.

Government Documents

Government documents are by their nature among the most difficult publications to acquire, control, and service. This is an area where the Library has unique opportunities because of laws, executive agreements, and special arrangements with state and other governmental agencies. Ideally the Library of Congress should have a comprehensive collection of the documents of all levels of government in the United States and strong collections of international and foreign publications. At a minimum, the Library must have a complete collection of U.S. federal documents.

The Library should take the lead in organizing cooperative efforts in collecting documents and in advocating improvements in their availability, control, and use. It should encourage the development of comprehensive archival sets of state and local documents in appropriate institutions around the nation. It should urge publication and the acquisition of documents in microform when feasible, and improvements in the cataloging rules relating to documents. In particular, it should cooperate with other institutions to assure that all documents find a place in an appropriate American library. It should also serve as a referral center, directing researchers to the library that holds the documents they need.

The Library should consider creating a special documents unit to concentrate on improving service on this troublesome category of material. There is no doubt that a wider range of services could be offered to Congress and other Library users. A core staff of document specialists would provide a focal point that presently does not exist. Ideas about the possible organization of this unit are in the report of the subcommittee on documents.

The Acquisitions Machinery

Recommendation No. 16: that the Library increase the efficiency of its acquisitions machinery even further by merging the Order Division, the Exchange and Gift Division, and the acquisitions unit of the Shared Cataloging Division, then organizing the new unit into geographical subunits.

Under such an organizational plan the principal officer for each area would make decisions on how most expeditiously to bring the Library what has been recommended for acquisition—through purchase, exchange, or gift. Such an arrangement would minimize the duplication of receipts between purchase and gift items and would lead naturally to arrangements for LC's overseas offices to serve as acquisitions centers for exchange and gift as well as for purchased items. The principal officers would of course work closely with the collection development office.

The Task Force is heartened by the vigor recently shown by the Acquisitions Committee. We believe that it would be a healthy step to include on the committee all assistant directors in the reference department. The committee has a number of important tasks before it in the next few years including the redrafting of the now outmoded canons of selection, a reexamination of existing cooperative acquisitions arrangements, reformulating the definition of "retrospective materials" (and securing additional funds for their purchase), organizing a systematic, comprehensive program of acquisition trips abroad, and instituting a periodic inventory of our collections.

The National Program for Acquisitions and Cataloging (NPAC)

Recommendation No. 17: that the NPAC program be extended to cover countries and regions that present difficult problems of acquisitions or cataloging, and that this expansion include new offices to cover Africa, Asia, and Latin America.

The Library of Congress has been favored with resources and mechanisms for the acquisition of United States and foreign materials unmatched by any other library in this nation or in any nation of the world. These large-scale acquisitions programs are the foundation of the Library's collections and should be expanded and improved. The NPAC program, the basis for the Library's international strength, should be extended to countries and regions of Africa, Asia, and Latin America that are not now covered. The Library must continue to discuss this urgent need with the appropriate Congressional committees.

A National Preservation Program

Recommendation No. 18: that the Library of Congress, in cooperation with other research institutions, proceed as rapidly as possible in developing a truly national preservation program to help solve the serious preservation problems facing the nation's libraries.

The Library of Congress and the entire library world must pay more attention to the essential task of preserving the deteriorating materials in their collections. Preservation activities at the Library have been centralized only since the late 1960's, and the preservation function has not yet been fully integrated into all the Library's activities. However, the first steps have been taken in what someday must be a much larger preservation effort. In developing a national program, the Library of Congress should exercise leadership and provide coordination, but the endeavor must be nation-wide and involve many institutions and organizations.

The magnitude of the collection needing immediate preservation makes a set of priorities essential. The Task Force recommends that the preservation of American materials be given highest priority as a matter of both national responsibility and responsibility to the rest of the world. The Library should endorse and encourage the efforts of other nations to preserve their own heritage, for the scope of the problem is so vast that it can be solved with nothing less than an international effort.

The training of conservators is an important part of any national preservation program. This is one activity that must be performed by the Library of Congress, because of its unique technical facilities. The Library should expand its consultant services and reach out to other libraries through a more active publications program that should include both technical and non-technical materials.

Another desirable aspect of a national program is the creation of a central preservation collection for the storage of materials under controlled environmental conditions. The Task Force does not believe that the Library of Congress should necessarily administer this collection, but it should be intimately involved in its planning and development. This collection of the best copies of research materials in original format should include photocopying facilities and should be located in an easily accessible, central site in the United States. We urge the Library to take the initiative in developing plans for such a national preservation collection. If such a collection is established, it might very well be connected with the proposed national lending library for periodicals.

The Library of Congress receives thousands of duplicate volumes each year that should be used to help build a national collection. We propose that the Library establish its own central repository for storing these duplicates. This depot would be, in effect, a staging area; many of the volumes would ultimately be sent to a national collection. This warehouse might also contain extra copies weeded from the collection and serve as the site for preserving copyright deposits not selected for the Library's permanent collections. We believe that the retention and preservation of these copyright deposits is important. However, the Library also should form a knowledgeable working group to assess the value of the deposits and arrange for the transfer to the general collections of items now deemed valuable. The Library of Congress must continue to take full advantage of the unique copyright deposit privilege that has meant so much to its development as a repository of American culture.

Another national role for the Library is to function as a central clearinghouse for information regarding preservation and microreproduction. The Library of Congress must continue and strengthen its microform clearinghouse activities, thus becoming an active center for information about microreproduction and related preservation projects throughout the United States and the world.

The creation of a central repository for all master microforms created by research libraries and others and which meet technical and bibliographic standards is a corollary worth exploring. The collection presently maintained by the Library of Congress could serve as the base. If such a collection is organized, discussions should be undertaken with commercial micropublishers to determine under what conditions they might contribute their archival negatives. If arrangements could be made whereby all master negatives are deposited in a central location, the problem of protecting these important research sources would be partially solved. The Library of Congress, which has good relations with commercial micropublishers, could provide the leadership in this and other cooperative endeavors with the private sector.

In addition, the Library must provide essential leadership in the establishment of technical standards for preservation and microreproduction. The Library must continue its active involvement with other organizations in this vital activity.

Internal Preservation Priorities

Recommendation No. 19: that the Library's preservation committee be revitalized. The committee should develop a clear statement of Library-wide preservation priorities and a strong, well-coordinated system for selecting items for preservation treatment.

A national preservation program must be coordinated with the internal preservation needs of the Library of Congress. A proper balance must be maintained between the Library's national leadership role and its responsibilities to the preservation of its own collections, particularly the day-to-day maintenance activities. In time, of course, the national role of the Library in preservation will benefit the internal operations directly, but until more resources are available the balance must be carefully watched. For this reason, the establishment of subunits within the Preservation Office to administer the two programs is recommended.

The Library must recognize its preservation activities as truly Library-wide functions that have an impact on all of the Library's operations. Careful planning and close internal coordination are required, particularly with regard to the Library's responsibilities for acquisitions, bibliographic control, and reference service. We believe that the Library's preservation activities must be linked more closely with other Library operations and particularly with those of the various reference divisions. The revitalization of the preservation committee is the first and perhaps most important step that should be taken in this direction. The committee should be supported by a secretariat provided by the planning office.

The committee must concern itself with the internal balance between routine preservation operations involving many items and the more costly and time-consuming preservation of individual pieces. We recommend that the Library increase its capability to perform preservation work of a routine nature, both in the Preservation Office and in the custodial divisions (with Preservation Office guidance). Furthermore, a ready repair station is needed for immediate, albeit intermediate repairs. Both these recommendations, of course, require additions to the staff of the Preservation Office.

Chapter IV: Bibliographic Control

Section A: A National Bibliographic System

The Library of Congress must take new measures to provide, in concert with other institutions, systematic bibliographic control of all materials acquired by American libraries. The Library's ultimate goal must be to achieve the researcher's dream of a coordinated, comprehensive, international, machine-readable data base covering materials in all formats—books, films, sound recordings, periodical literature, and unpublished material—fully indexed. As much of this material as possible should be abstracted.

The road is a long one and there is no hope for one institution to go the whole way alone. All of the nation's bibliographic resources, both non-commercial and commercial, must be called on in this endeavor.

At this moment the Library of Congress has an opportunity that will probably be unique in our lifetime. A powerful and revolutionary tool, the computer, may permit libraries to achieve what was until quite recently an impossible dream. The Library of Congress, while continuing to produce traditional catalog products, must now look to full exploitation of the computer in providing libraries and their readers with access to the world's knowledge.

Leadership

Recommendation No. 20: that the Library of Congress take a strong leadership role in the development of a national bibliographic system.

The Library of Congress is uniquely situated to provide leadership in orchestrating a national bibliographic system. The Library already produces a major portion of the fundamental data for such a system and, through its participation in two cooperative programs, CONSER and COMARC, has made a beginning toward a balanced multilateral network.

To speed the development of this network the Task Force recommends that the Library move swiftly to complete conversion of all current cataloging of materials in all formats, languages, and alphabets to machine-readable form.

While current materials have the highest priority, it is essential that the vast reservoir of existing bibliographic data, both in the Library of Congress and across the nation, also be converted to machine-readable form. This immense project will require the fullest cooperation within the entire bibliographic community and may take a lifetime to implement, but through the computer such a project is eventually possible. As a starting point, we enthusiastically support programs for cooperative input, such as COMARC and CONSER, and urge the use of validated records from other institutions such as the Ohio College Library Center. We also recommend strongly that the Library continue to pursue the development of new technology such as optical scanning devices for conversion of existing catalog copy.

The Library should aim particularly at cooperative entry of such problem publications as state documents and should draw into its computerized system the *National Union Catalog of Manuscript Collections* and other specialized catalogs as soon as possible.

The Problem of Subject Analysis

The entire subject approach to cataloging should be reviewed with an eye to providing the researcher with a more efficient and thorough access to the world's literature. Whether through the use of some new technique such as PRECIS or simply through expanded use of existing headings, the Library must endeavor to provide a scheme for subject analysis in greater depth than it is now offering through the MARC cataloging record.

The existing LC subject heading system was developed in an environment of card and book catalogs and for this reason (and economic reasons) in-depth analysis has up to now not been possible. With the advent of automation, new techniques are available which would allow the assignment of multiple subject terms and allow the user to discriminate by combining terms or by differentiating between the major subject terms and the minor terms describing a given work. Systems such as PRECIS or natural language indexing of abstracts, as provided by CIP publishers, should also be studied.

An urgent matter of long standing is the need for a complete K (law) classification schedule. Without it, the bibliographic control of our important law collections will never be satisfactory. We urge the speedy completion of this schedule.

The Library might also consider enriching its cataloging records with new or alternate forms of entry or subject headings for use in special categories of libraries. Some in the public library community have voiced the opinion that the needs of public libraries are often not met by Library of Congress cataloging which, they believe, is directed to the requirements of the research library. The Library should discuss this assertion with a wide sampling of public and other non-research librarians to determine its validity. If it is valid, the Library should develop and arrange the application of alternate forms.

Bibliographic Data Bases

In order to help create a national bibliographic system, we believe the Library must exert leadership not only in automated cataloging, but also in the information business generally. The Library of Congress has been preeminent in the traditional cataloging of books and serial titles. But the conventional catalog has become just one phase in a whole new world of bibliography. Enormous bodies of data can be merged or at least searched through a single tool, the computer terminal.

Every possible effort must be made to insure consistency and comprehensiveness in data bases. We urge the Library to review the repertoire of existing data bases and services, public and commercial, for three purposes: first, to provide libraries with a comprehensive and regularly updated directory of data bases; second, to develop standards and take other actions to avoid any harmful and unnecessary inconsistency or incompatibility of coverage, access language, format, software, or policy; and third, to take advantage of existing data or techniques to avoid duplication of effort as the Library of Congress develops its own programs.

The Library should also review existing services to discover gaps in coverage and encourage professional groups or commercial agencies to fill in these areas. If this fails the Library should itself consider providing such services.

An obvious gap is the lack of a complete retrospective bibliography of American history and culture. We believe that the creation of such a bibliography, while an enormous task, would be a most appropriate undertaking for the Library of Congress. (For details of such a project, see Document 3 in Appendix A.)

Other suggestions from subcommittees, advisory groups, and individuals have identified a need for automated union lists of manuscripts, music, audiovisual and other instructional material, and microforms. An online catalog of microform masters seems an essential component in an effective national preservation program. Persuasive cases have also been made for more extensive computerized coverage of maps, motion pictures, and legal materials, particularly foreign. The possibilities are so great in the legal field that they could provide the basis for a national law center (see the report of the law advisory group).

Standards

Development of a national bibliographic data base built through cooperative endeavor depends on the existence and use of standards—both in the area of bibliographic codes and in the area of computer formats, protocols, etc. The Library is already deeply committed to a leadership role in the development of such standards, but it needs to increase its involvement with groups working in such areas.

Seminars, Workshops, and Other Training

More detailed information about technical processing procedures and techniques used in the Library would be of great value to many libraries because they depend so heavily on LC bibliographic products—cards, book catalogs, tapes, etc. The Library should seek to fill this need by a vigorous public education program. This could take a variety of forms such as workshops and seminars, more individual consultations, visits by teams of LC experts, videotapes, slide sets, and other types of training.

An Office of Bibliography

The Library must create an effective office to undertake its own enlarged program of bibliography and to expand its role in the world of information. We recommend, therefore, the establishment of an office of bibliography. This office should be attached to the reference department office and should oversee the "traditional" bibliographic program of the Library. It should be capable of compiling the guide to the collections of the Library of Congress detailed below, coordinating the compilation of divisional guides, and compiling on-demand and timely bibliographies that cannot be assigned to present divisions.

Within the new bibliography office should be the position of chief bibliographer to exercise final authority on matters of form, work closely with the cataloging committee (see Recommendation No. 21) in shaping uniform or at least compatible rules for cataloging and bibliography, establish a training program in bibliographic citation that is Library-wide, and compile a bibliographic style manual that is definitive and up-to-date.

The office should conduct a study to determine whether standards for bibliographic citations and standards for cataloging could be brought more into line so that in an automated system, where appropriate, the former could be derived from the latter. This would not preclude the production of individual bibliographies in which the citation, where necessary, was restructured to serve the needs of an individual user or group of users. The director of the office would attend meetings of librarians, information scientists, and the information industry; would work toward the establishment of national and international standards (as well as toward the general cooperation of all parties); and would serve as one of the Library's principal advocates in moving toward the "researcher's dream."

Section B: Control of the Library's Collections

It is imperative for the national bibliographic system to include a record of the total holdings of the Library of Congress. The description the Library can now offer is woefully incomplete, however, and must be greatly augmented. At the present time, no Library-wide administrative mechanism exists for developing a coherent approach to the bibliographic control of all these collections.

Because no such mechanism exists, the Library's reference staff has felt it had no effective voice in setting the Processing Department's cataloging priorities or in other decisions on cataloging. Processing Department staff on the other hand have felt themselves pressured and criticized on all sides no matter what they do.

What is required is a mechanism that will give reference needs effective representation and at the same time make clear the good intentions of the Processing Department.

Priorities and Policy Guidance

Recommendation No. 21: that the Library establish a cataloging committee made up of representatives from the Processing Department and all other Library departments.

This committee would periodically review both the priority system and the general practice of cataloging. Those sitting on the committee would be expected to represent their constituencies with, in addition, the processing group voicing the needs of the nation's catalogers, and the reference group voicing the needs of the nation's researchers. All must, of course, be mindful of the needs of the national bibliographic system. We believe that when catalogers and reference staff sit down to talk about difficult cataloging issues, the airing of their desires and problems will not only contribute to the making of sound decisions, but will foster tolerance and good feeling on both sides. The planning office would provide the secretariat for the committee.

Cataloging Unique Collections

Recommendation No. 22: that the Library make every effort to gain the same level of support for cataloging its unique collections as it has received for cataloging the current output of the world's presses.

The Library has done magnificently in gaining support for its national cataloging programs. The Task Force believes similar support should be forthcoming for cataloging collections in the Library that are unique and constitute national resources. The special collections, particularly microforms, pamphlets, older sound recordings, and prints and photographs, should be brought under suitable bibliographic control and the resulting catalogs and subject analyses made available to other institutions. In doing so, optimal use should be made of copyright cataloging for certain categories of materials, such as sound recordings and unpublished music.

A major portion of the Library's collections (primarily the special subject and format collections), which includes much in the Library's possession that is unique or most valuable, has received either no bibliographic control or control so limited and baffling that the material is lost to all but a small public.

Indeed, a great deal of this material is available only through the memory of a member of the staff. In some cases there are current ongoing cataloging programs, but in most cases, these are holdings which have been given limited cataloging control and which are outside the central bibliographic record. The cataloging committee must determine which methods are most appropriate in each instance—tapes, cards, archival control, published bibliographies—and then determine which unit within the Library should be assigned the cataloging job. Once that is decided, the difficult work of establishing priorities must begin—priorities as to staffing as well as to cataloging.

We are well aware that the present cataloging staff would have to be greatly expanded to achieve many of the goals outlined in this section, as well as in this entire chapter. We wish to emphasize that the crying need for catalogers to work on materials in the special collections must be satisfied without injuring the internationally important cataloging process that now exists. We urge the Library to attempt to secure a larger pie, and not to diminish the size of any of its pieces.

If this is impossible within the near future, however, we urge the cataloging committee to review the Library's overall needs and consider a reallocation which would increase the number of catalogers available to bring the special collections under control. An appropriate time for such a realloca- tion (if reallocation seems to be necessary) might be the time when coopera- tive cataloging online has reduced the Library's needs for book and serial catalogers.

In line with our goal of improved bibliographic control of these currently neglected materials, we urge that some form of access to special format and special collection materials (including ephemera) be available (with loca- tion clearly indicated) in the Library's online data bases and possibly the public catalogs. (This will require the coordination of cataloging in the ref- erence department and the Processing Department that is described in Chap- ter II). The reader advisory office will solve part of the problem this recom- mendation addresses, but not all. No reference librarian could master everything necessary to provide readers the detailed description of our entire collections which is required. More than that, special formats fre- quently provide information which even the most experienced librarian or sophisticated researcher might not imagine. In consequence, no format or collection of materials should be excluded automatically from represen- tation in the general public catalogs and data bases. Researchers perceive the public catalog and data bases as being the key to the collections of the Library. We must see to it that in the future the key unlocks many more doors.

A Guide to the Collections

To provide better access to the entire range of our collections, drawing the strands intelligibly together, we recommend the publication of a com- prehensive guide to the Library's collections, possibly following the example of the excellent *Guide to the Research Collections of the New York Public Library* (1975). Such a work would serve as an essential handbook for the reader advisory office, but more importantly would inform the world, par- ticularly scholars contemplating a visit to the Library of Congress, that we have materials in a variety of forms that would be of use. The comprehensive guide should serve as the culmination of a systematic project to compile detailed guides to each special collection, and indeed to our miscellany of card catalogs and data bases. Perhaps the first such guide might cover our major collections of documents not regularly cataloged, including micro- form collections.

The unified approach to the Library's problems which this report envi- sions should find expression here not merely in a Library-wide cataloging committee, but in many other practical ways, large and small.

The pilot program of stationing catalogers in the public catalog area to advise users should be enlarged to permit a flow of two-way exchanges among all the cataloging and reference divisions, including the Congres- sional Reference Division. Such exchanges would allow catalogers to dis- cover how the catalog that they are creating is used, and would provide reference librarians with information that should allow them to utilize the catalogs and data bases more effectively.

We recommend that subject catalogers consult those in the reference di- visions with appropriate expert knowledge when considering new or revised subject headings. Reference specialists should be consulted about subject headings in their fields of specialization. Area specialists, in particular, desire to see that subject headings expressing a world view are adopted by the Library.

Designated officers from the collection development office should regularly review the backlog in the cataloging divisions and earmark important titles for quicker cataloging.

Bibliographic Continuity

Like all quick and fundamental change, the arrival of computerized cataloging has caused a new generation of problems. We applaud the recent creation of the Committee on the Online Catalog to help guide the development of new services. We recommend, however, that the committee publicize its purpose and accomplishments and systematically seek out the views of the reference staff on questions at issue. It is essential that the committee become an open and effective channel known by all reference staff and used by them to help shape the services, products, and priorities of the online computer operations. The report of the subcommittee on automation and reference services contains many good ideas concerning the internal coordination of the Library's computer services.

> **Recommendation No. 23:** that the Library, through the cataloging committee and Committee on the Online Catalog, create a forum to deal with the problems of introducing new technology, and specifically with the issue of computer-card catalog linkages, multiple online cataloging systems, and bringing all cataloging programs into the computerized bibliographic mainstream.

First the two committees, perhaps meeting jointly, must decide whether the Library will require full linkages between the automated and manual bibliographic systems. The general reference staff has in the past held that to neglect these linkages would be to provide an efficiency for catalogers which would be more than offset by inefficiencies caused the acquisitions librarian, bibliographer, reference librarian, and the general public. The Processing Department staff has argued that creating such linkages would require vast expenditures of time and money, and would nullify one of the prime attractions of going over to a new system. It has argued that creating the linkages would imprison catalogers within the "dead hand of the past." The Task Force is not in a position to decide the issue, but we do urge the committees to seek an expert independent assessment which draws on the evidence of both users and producers of catalogs. The committees could employ the Library's research office or have an outside expert conduct the study. Speed is essential if a sound decision is to be made by the time the Library freezes the card catalog.

Secondly, the committees should investigate the question of the correct number of online catalog systems for the Library. The two present systems have diverse strengths and weaknesses. A single system would not be likely to serve efficiently all the needs now served by the two systems viewed in aggregate. The existence of two systems, however, naturally intimidates the new user, causes confusion, and complicates training. Perhaps a single-access language would solve some of the problems. We urge the committee to investigate all ramifications of the issue and put the Library on an examined and rational course.

Finally, the committees should create a phased plan for working all the Library's cataloging and bibliographic products into the computerized mainstream of the Library's central bibliographic record. Copyright cataloging, the *Monthly Checklist of State Publications*, and the *New Serial Titles*, for example, should all participate in and contribute to this central record with its widely shared standards. Such unification seems likely to improve the efficiency of our cataloging operation and facilitate the use of its product. It would also contribute significantly to creation of the national bibliographic system.

Chapter V: The Cultural and Educational Program of the Library

All great libraries are great centers of culture. The Library of Congress is an important force in the cultural and educational life of this nation. Its role of cultural catalyst is one with obvious and exciting possibilities for exploration and development.

The possibilities in fact are so exciting and so far reaching in their consequences that we feel a special responsibility to consider them with sober common sense. Concurrent with any expansion in its cultural and educational program, the Library must devote equal energy and resources to improving the performance of its basic housekeeping duties. These duties are collecting, controlling, describing, and delivering to patrons the materials of scholarship and the arts. Finally, we must test our ideas against certain basic principles.

The principles which should guide the cultural and educational program of the Library are described in the report of the Task Force's subcommittee on the cultural role of the Library. In general these principles are: (1) create a product—exhibit, publication, film, lecture—of the highest excellence; (2) build on the Library's strengths, developing a program that grows organically from collections and services; and (3) without strong reason, avoid programs that directly compete with existing programs outside the Library.

A Unified Program

Recommendation No. 24: that the Library centralize the overall responsibility for cultural and educational programs in a single office advised by a cultural coordinating committee.

The office, located in the Office of the Librarian, should possess a staff large enough to bear the broad responsibility for coordinating all of the Library's cultural and educational programs. It should be responsible for both policy and operations, from the initial decision on the appropriateness and desirability of an activity to organizing the pieces into a coherent event. Working with the office would be a Library-wide coordinating committee composed of representatives from the various offices concerned with the institution's cultural and educational program. The planning office would provide the secretariat for the committee.

The role of the office would be: (1) to consider, with the coordinating committee, all ideas received from the various constituencies represented;

and (2) to shape the overall program of the Library, most especially the coordination of the Library's exhibits, literary, scholarly, and musical programs, and the related publications and publicity. The final step in creating a coherent structure is to name a cultural liaison officer in each appropriate Library unit to work with committee members and generally to serve as a contact point for those organizing the Library's cultural work.

A Diversity of Products

Recommendation No. 25: that the cultural office and committee plan Library events that involve the full range of the Library's collections, and that result in a wide range of subsidiary products such as catalogs, recordings, lectures, concerts, and other related activities.

For example, at the same time an exhibit opens, the Library should offer a series of publications (invariably including a catalog), live programs (e.g., lectures, concerts, symposia, and plays) that pick up and develop the central theme of the exhibit, and specialized exhibits in the divisions which further develop the central theme. Focusing the Library's efforts on major themes will doubtless attract, both to the Library and to the event, greater attention than we receive at present from the public and the media.

As indicated, we should seek to improve both the organization of our cultural programs and their substance. The report of the subcommittee on the cultural role of the Library suggests many possibilities for improvement. Literary programs are an obvious example. The Library could extend its series of live poetry presentations to include other forms of literature. This would be entirely consonant with the Library viewed as a temple to the printed word. Clearly, it would build on a strength of the Library—what other institution can boast of a stronger collection in world literature? A program of book and author forums or critics' roundtables would add significantly to the cultural life of Capitol Hill and Washington.

Authors of short stories, drama, novels, and non-fiction could be invited to the Library to discuss their work and critics could participate and engage in roundtables. All programs would be taped and made available (as should all Library presentations) to the media, schools, and libraries. Transcripts of the tapes would add distinction to the Library's publication list, while the program as a whole would help establish us as a friend to letters and champion of the printed word.

The scope of our musical programs could also be expanded. Our unparalleled recorded sound collection might be tapped to create informal noonday recorded concerts for tourists, staff, and music lovers generally, a beginning toward exploitation of our enormous riches in this field. Such concerts could provide an opportunity for the public to hear recordings from the Library's collections in the context of reminiscences, evaluation, or other presentations by the artist, his associates, noted music critics, or other experts. The schedule could encompass not only folk music, but jazz, classical, band, and other music. Live folk, jazz, or popular music presentations pose more of a problem. Other organizations, particularly the Smithsonian Institution, have entered the field with some force, and the Library should be cautious in approaching this type of activity.

An appropriate extension of the present live concert series would entail encouraging research to identify works in the Library's music collections that are seldom played and that have not been commercially recorded. Such a program could be used to introduce more variety into the repertoires of the groups that play here. These pieces could be recorded in concert and sold by the Library, filling a gap in the recorded repertoire while at the same time exploiting the collections. A similar program, resulting in reprints rather than performances or recordings, might be undertaken in American literature and drama.

Exploitation of our research collections, particularly the special format collections, might take another direction. When appropriate, the Library's exhibits program should include sound, film, or slide presentations in the exhibits themselves, in an accompanying series of live performances or lectures, or during an exhibit opening.

Exhibits and performances might make better use of the space, though limited, now available in the Library. For instance, the Neptune Plaza is an obvious location for lunchtime band, jazz, or brassband concerts. Orientation exhibits might also begin on the Plaza. The courtyards and the Great Hall are also suitable for certain kinds of performances.

The Cultural Message

Recommendation No. 26: that the Library greatly expand its publicity program for all cultural events.

The different nature of each program demands that the publicity vary. For example, while our chamber music concerts regularly fill the house, we do not always receive the recognition we deserve for presenting them. At the same time, many of the poetry programs play to half-filled houses, in part because we have publicized them only to the converted. Each of these problems requires a different solution. All will entail a greater effort to secure publicity through radio and television spots, recorded telephone messages, more imaginative print advertising, or, on occasion, more Barnum-style hoopla.

Publicity takes many forms and one of the most dignified, effective, and suitable for the Library is representation at scholarly meetings. The "exhibit" by the Library at the December 1976 meeting of the American Historical Association should serve as an inspiration to further efforts in that direction. At a minimum, the Library should attractively display its publications (including appropriate phonorecords, facsimiles, and the like) and demonstrate its computer data bases. The exhibits should be staffed by knowledgeable and friendly reference, information, or subject specialists from the Library. In addition to representation at the American Historical Association and the American Library Association, the Library should exhibit at meetings of organizations such as the American Association for State and Local History, the American Political Science Association, the American Studies Association, the American Society for Information Science, the Modern Language Association, the Organization of American Historians, the Oral History Association, the Society of American Archivists, the Special Libraries Association, various area studies organizations, and many others.

When national conventions meet in Washington, the Library should work with local arrangements committees to plan a more effective présence. For example, it could schedule lectures, tours, or panels covering LC collections of special interest to the group.

Publications

Recommendation No. 27: that the Library reassess its entire publication and sales program, refocus the *Information Bulletin* and *Quarterly Journal* to meet specific editorial purposes, consider establishing a Library of Congress Press, and investigate ways to reduce its dependency on the Government Printing Office.

One essential underpinning of a publicity program must be the Library's periodical publications. At present the *Information Bulletin* is a melange of staff news, Library announcements, and professional news for the general library community. The Task Force recommends a separation of these functions and a strengthening of each. We recommend that the Library publish (1) a weekly house organ of a lively, informal character and (2) a fortnightly or monthly publication with technical and cultural news of general interest to the library world. The *Information Bulletin* should cover in greater depth such matters as the meetings of staff organizations, marriages, births, deaths, new Library regulations, facts about insurance programs, and other matters of internal value.

The second, as the external bulletin of the national library, possibly entitled *The National Library Bulletin*, should devote itself to matters of general professional interest. This should be construed much more widely than at present so that, for instance, the new publication should reprint the full text of all major speeches by Library officials and should provide a full calendar of events within the Library, including all professional meetings attended by outside participants. It should contain regular columns detailing new developments in each department of the Library. To support this work, the publication should have sufficient editorial staff to seek out the news and report it in a clear and graceful style.

On the general topic of publications, we recommend that the *Quarterly Journal* focus its efforts more sharply. The editor, in consultation with the Library administration, should clearly state the purpose of the publication and then test articles submitted against this standard. Secondly, we recommend that in its program of book publication the Library adhere closely to the principles communicated at the beginning of this chapter: it should produce works of unvarying excellence and build on strength. A program of excellence in this connection does not mean that "popular" works (i.e., books of general interest) are not appropriate as Library publications. On the contrary. It does mean, however, that the Library must continue to issue works of the highest bibliographic and scholarly standard even though they appeal to a small audience. In addition the Library should publish or join in publishing popular works that bring to a wide audience a knowledge and appreciation of the resources of the institution.

There is one new work that is badly needed: an up-to-date guidebook describing the architectural and artistic splendors of the Library of Congress building.

The Task Force recommends that the Library consider issuing its publications under its own imprint. A Library of Congress Press could establish the Library as a distinctive source for works of scholarly and bibliographic excellence. At the same time the Library should investigate ways to reduce its dependency on the Government Printing Office. High quality printing, rapid publication schedules, and an established imprint could greatly enhance the Library's reputation as a preeminent cultural resource.

The Library's own publications should be at the core of an enlarged sales operation. We recommend that the Library separate the sales operation from the Information Desk, place the operation administratively in the Publications Office, and provide more space for it as soon as practical circumstances permit. The sales area should be close to the heaviest flow of traffic and provided with sales staff who know not only what the Library has published, but also what it will publish. The shop should sell all of the Library's publications (including technical publications), its recordings, facsimiles (issued as part of an enlarged program of facsimile reproductions), reprints, photographic print reproductions and portfolios, greeting cards, and other reproductions of Library material that are valuable in both form and content.

The shop might also sell items produced elsewhere, such as editions or recordings of poets who are reading at the Library, recordings and scores related to musical performances, books or prints of artists on exhibit, and similar items.

New Departures

What has been described to this point is a program fairly closely tied to what the Library is now doing. However, several of the many new departures suggested to the Task Force seem so filled with vitality that we wish to recommend they be considered. All seem fully compatible with the Library's fundamental mission.

Perhaps the most exciting and ambitious of these is the proposal that the Library actively document American civilization. There are many significant events in American culture which are poorly documented and this documentation seldom finds its way into the Library either through copyright or other acquisition channels. Various kinds of dance and theater events happen only once or twice in remote parts of the country, and their existence is forever lost to the history of our culture except for documentation in skimpy reviews and other inadequate descriptive material. We recommend the Library establish an office to survey constantly the cultural happenings around the nation and record or arrange the recording of appropriate events for our film or videotape archive.

The office should also attempt to secure materials which help to document motion pictures and television, such as film outtakes, multiple drafts of scripts, stills, motion picture set designs, corporate records, and most especially censorship records. The office should take the leadership in making certain that all radio and television programs not acquired through existing copyright or gift programs are preserved. Finally, the office should institute an active program of oral history exploiting the presence of the many scholars, artists, and public figures who appear on the Washington scene.

It has also been proposed that the Library commission works in a variety of forms (film, cassette, videotape, prints) based on our holdings or discussing the Library as an institution. An example is a film tracing the history of modern man's knowledge of geography using LC's globe and cartographic collections as a point of departure. A possible extension of such a program would be the creation of a radio and television series based on the Library's collections and produced either in the Library's studio or under its close supervision.

Still other possibilities of merit are the creation of a translation center (see the report of the humanities advisory group) and an LC speakers bureau supplying roving Library representatives and consultants (see the report of the subcommittee on the cultural role of the Library). The Library might reinstate traveling concerts subsidized by LC gift funds and embark on a much enlarged program of workshops, training courses, seminars, and exchange programs to serve the continuing education of librarians. It might also host a much enlarged program of seminars and symposia on a wide range of topics of national and international interest. Such seminars would be of interest to our Congressional, scholarly, and artistic constituencies.

Many of the programs we have suggested would of course require additional money, staff, thought, and effort. Furthermore, they are often aimed at an audience which is not our primary one. They are, however, programs of great consequence. They bring knowledge of our collections to a wide audience. They make the Library a place in which the potential donor can securely place his confidence. Most importantly, they display to the American people the great riches that make up their cultural inheritance.

Chapter VI: Staff Development and Communication

The Task Force strongly endorses Dr. Boorstin's statement of January 28, 1976, viewing it as a continuing challenge to the entire staff of the Library of Congress: "We must increase the sense of our staff's participation in the greatness of our Library. We must improve the working environment in order to make service in the Library a more enriching experience. We must do all in our power to insure that a career of service in the Library of Congress will be not merely a career of service, but also a career of self-fulfillment."

Career Development

Recommendation No. 28: that the Library create a career development section within the Personnel Office to accomplish the goals of enriching the work and developing the potential of its staff.

To enhance the career potential of each staff member, the Library should have a comprehensive career development and career guidance program to assist employees at all levels and to help the organization meet future staffing needs.

This section should study the interrelationship of all LC positions and compile a computerized job information bank. Perhaps, in its first year, the section could be assigned a finite goal (e.g., a cataloging career program) which could be expanded in successive years. The end result would benefit the majority of LC employees, technical and professional, supervisory and non-supervisory alike. The section would write and make available to staff a career development manual, showing the career progressions and lateral moves possible within the Library. The manual would also have information regarding the experience, training, education, and skills required to reach successive steps in any given career ladder.

By visiting the career development section, staff members should be able to learn the requirements of their career goals. Moreover, the section would offer professional career guidance and factual information (about the number, turnover, and requirements of all LC positions), so that staff members can make well-informed decisions on training and careers at the Library.

This section would share with the Affirmative Action Office the responsibility for investigating the relevancy of posted minimum job qualifications for LC positions, since accurate job requirements and promotion standards are essential to a realistic career development program. With the planning and Training offices, this section would share the responsibility for transfers from non-automation to automation jobs. The planning office would keep the career development section aware of changes that will affect LC positions, and the career development section will use its job bank and guidance service to assist staff members desiring careers in the Library's automated future.

Information and Orientation

Recommendation No. 29: that the Library encourage within the institution the freest possible flow of information: information that orients, that educates, and that guides and enhances individual careers.

The Library must provide each staff member with a thorough orientation. The orientation must begin in a systematic way on the first day an employee reports to work. The Personnel Office should conduct on a regular basis a conscientiously prepared new employee orientation which will include a briefing on the Library of Congress, its history, mission, and organization; a Library tour; and a discussion of personnel matters, with distribution of brochures to be read overnight and discussed the next morning. After the morning discussion, the second day should conclude in the afternoon with a briefing by the new employee's supervisor. This briefing should explain the organization and functions of the new employee's work unit and should review and clarify LC personnel policies. The supervisory checklist should be used. A mandatory follow-up checklist should be the basis for a supervisor/employee consultation 30 days after the employee's arrival to make certain that vital information was not lost in the barrage confronting the employee during the first two days.

In addition, each department should be required to develop an orientation program to be presented at least semi-annually to all those it has recently hired. This program should be coordinated with the Library's central orientation by the Personnel Office.

Since orientation assists an employee in finding his way and understanding his purpose within the organization, it should not be the exclusive right of new employees. Information—current, complete, and correct—about the Library and its work is vital to a person's efficient functioning and satisfaction with the job. We therefore urge that the Library continue the orientation and professional education of its general staff by:

1. Opening the professional orientation series to all whose supervisors verify that their jobs require a substantial knowledge of other parts of the Library. Junior, as well as senior staff, should participate in presenting the lectures, leading the discussions, etc.

2. Instituting monthly or bimonthly tours of each department to be given by one or more of its knowledgeable staff members.

Details of the orientation program outlined above may be found in the report of the subcommitee on training and career development.

Management Training

Recommendation No. 30: that the Library offer a management development program to train its supervisors in effective management techniques.

In addition to providing supervisory staff with a sound knowledge of the Library that is constantly enlarged and brought up to date, we recommend they be given special training leading to professional, supervisory, and management development.

A new systematic program should emphasize the teaching of core practical knowledge and skills (e.g., the rules of labor/management and the writing of sound Personnel Action Recommendations or incentive award justifications). This should be obligatory for all Library managers and should be supplemented by a voluntary updating or enlarging of an employee's professional education. Courses should be offered on new reference works, computer systems, and changes in cataloging practices, among other topics. This training program might be enhanced by special purpose newsletters aimed, for instance, at supervisors. The newsletters would serve not only to convey information, but to develop a feeling of community and *esprit*.

Professional Incentives

Participation in LC organizations and activities by staff members from the outlying annexes should be encouraged by fast, efficient communication. Special efforts should be made to see that these staff members receive postings, the LC *Information Bulletin*, and announcements of activities at the main buildings as soon as possible. The extra effort to include staff in outlying annexes must be made if we are to increase their sense of "participation in the greatness of our Library."

Training and education are, of course, not limited to what happens in a training course. Other devices should be created or encouraged. There should be professional roundtables not only for reference staff, but for catalogers (including copyright and special format catalogers), copyright specialists, subject specialists (like American historians), and others. Flourishing roundtables would permit a natural exchange of information among those who possess a common interest or training, but who are often isolated by their dispersal throughout the organization. The Library should establish a professional reading room that is comfortable, attractive, and well stocked with up-to-date journals. It might also offer a small browsing collection of recent professional books.

The Library administration must take full advantage of the skills, enthusiasm, and dedication of the staff. The Library must continue to reward this dedication through a strengthened Incentive Awards Program. Junior as well as senior people should be sent to represent the Library in workshops and professional gatherings.

The existing non-union staff organizations should be encouraged in their work of professional development and communication. Programs which are clearly educational or which in other ways clearly serve the function of staff development should be exempt from rules designed to cover recreational meetings. Such programs should, in addition, be supported by the Library in practical ways: publicity, equipment, official leave, and so forth.

The Library should do more to encourage staff attendance at its evening cultural programs. A minimum number of tickets to each event should be set aside for staff use.

Supervision and Communication

An aspect of communication which has been curiously neglected in the Library is that of conveying to supervisors and managers exactly what the Library needs and expects from them. Such statements should be systematically formulated and should emphasize administrative duties and skills. They should be reflected in position descriptions and used in the selection and evaluation of supervisors.

We wish to emphasize the need for careful selection and development of our managers. They must, of course, be technically competent, but they must also possess imagination, empathy, flexibility, impartiality, clear-sightedness—in brief, a genuine flair for leadership.

Next, a humble but essential thing. All supervisors should be required to meet with the staff members they immediately supervise at least once a month. The meeting should be part of the statistical record, and a failure to hold such meetings should be recorded in evaluations. In the spirit of furthering communication up and down the hierarchy, the Library should seriously consider urging or even requiring that all administrators from division chief through Librarian reserve an hour each week for a staff "open house." This could consist of private interviews, if necessary scheduled first-come-first-served, or periodic group receptions, or whatever experience showed to be most conducive to the free exchange of information.

The Intern Program

The Library's Intern Program has many virtues in developing professional employees. It is able to attract new employees of outstanding potential; foster communication; act as catalyst for needed discussions among staff; bring a little ginger to the organization; forge useful bonds between the Library, library schools, and the library community generally;

and enhance in a significant way the professional education of those in the program.

We also recognize the shortcomings in the program: the frequent dissatisfaction of interns with their placement at the end of the program, the resentment of those not chosen, the disgruntlement of those who disapprove of the special treatment given interns, and the lessened recruitment need owing to the increased ease in the recruitment of outstanding new employees.

The Task Force subcommittee on training and development suggested as an alternative to the Intern Program an attractive program for professional development. In view of the complex, widely ramified and, for the Task Force, somewhat peripheral nature of the subject, we recommend an intense review of the Intern Program by an appropriate ad hoc committee before initiation of the program for 1978–79.

The Personnel Office

Recommendation No. 31: that the Personnel Office be placed in the Office of the Librarian.

The Personnel Office serves a vital function in the work of the Library. Recruiting clearly affects the quality of our service. Technical work in the mechanics of hiring, promotions, leave, retirements, and separations is intimately related to staff morale. The scope of the Personnel Office is Library-wide. These factors have caused many organizations to attach their personnel unit directly to the top administrative office. We believe the Library of Congress should do the same.

The Personnel Office should be encouraged in active recruitment both internally and externally to find people of outstanding potential or demonstrated excellence. The Library should not hesitate to seek qualified applicants for vacant positions, such as rare book conservators and specialists in foreign law, by reaching out nationwide to academic and vocational institutions, to library schools, and to professional organizations. In addition to such efforts to find needed specialists, the Library must attempt to fill each position—subject specialist, deck attendant, cataloger, messenger, and especially managers—with a person who will bring a measure of professionalism to the Library's work; who will accomplish daily duties with skill, pride, and responsibility; who will flourish in the new setting we seek to create; and who will provide a level of service that does honor to one of the world's great treasure-troves.

The program of orientation, education, and career development that we have described should serve to create a sense of staff participation, enrich experience, and make possible a "career of self-fulfillment" in the Library of Congress. We call on the Library's staff, in return, to seize the opportunity we hope will be offered and to set a new standard of excellence in the performance of its duties.

Chapter VII: Planning and Management

The Library of Congress must take immediate steps to improve all aspects of its planning, but especially its long-range, Library-wide planning. The institution requires strong direction of its total program by its top officers. Such central direction is impossible without systematic planning at all levels, systematic program review and evaluation, a more clearly defined decision-making process, and improved communication among the Library's decision-makers. The Library also must develop a variety of mechanisms for incorporating the advice of staff and outsiders into the planning and decision-making process.

Leadership and Communication

In the recent past, Library-wide planning has been impeded by the lack of a truly Library-wide point of view. The unification of the Library and a new focus on long-range planning will improve both morale and effectiveness. It will take strong, sensitive leadership to break down the psychological and procedural barriers between our major organizational units. We must create an atmosphere in which each unit can take pride not only in its own activities but also in its existence as part of the Library of Congress.

Leadership, communication, and morale of course are intimately related. We urge the Librarian and all top administrative officials to be more visible. They should make informal visits to various parts of the Library as often as possible. There is no better way for administrators to keep up-to-date and to improve staff morale at the same time.

A more formal structure is needed to improve communication between top Library officials and division chiefs. We suggest periodic meetings between the Librarian and the chiefs in each department. These should be informal discussion sessions and include as many staff members as possible.

The Planning Office

Recommendation No. 32: that the Library continue on a permanent basis its newly created planning office and that it establish a research office.

The Task Force is pleased with the recent announcement that a planning office is being established on January 28, 1977, the day the Task Force effort ends. The planning office should play a major role in the Library's administrative process. Although it has no authority to make decisions, it has an essential guiding and recommending role to play. It should be concerned not only with long-range planning and program development, but also with appraising the Library's major ongoing programs and their management. In coordination with the Personnel Office, it should continually perform organizational studies and recommend organizational changes to the Librarian. It must work with the Financial Management Office on budget planning and with the Library Environment Resources Office on the planning and allocation of space within the Library's buildings. The head of the planning office should be an ex-officio member of the director's council and all coordinating committees, and his office should provide the secretariat for each of these bodies, performing staff work and preparing summary accounts of the meetings for distribution or publication.

The planning office should assist the national library office and the coordinator of network development in planning and monitoring the Library's national programs. It should work closely with the coordinator of Congressional services, the library research office, and the collection development office. Another responsibility of the head of the planning office should be chairmanship of an informal planning council consisting of planning officers (or executive officers) from each department.

The organization of the Library's automation activities is one topic that must be of immediate concern to the planning office and other Library officials. The Task Force received many recommendations on this subject, most of which are summarized in the report of the subcommittee on automation and reference services. Several organizational changes have been made in the Library's automation activities during the past year, but the scope and importance of the entire automation program makes continuing study imperative. The Task Force believes that this is one instance where the Library would benefit from a study undertaken by an expert from outside the Library.

Long-range space planning must be a topic of immediate concern to the planning office and other Library officials. The Library must work closely with the Architect of the Capitol in planning for the institution's future growth. It is essential that all direct services to Congress, along with the collections that support those services, remain on Capitol Hill. The basic research collections also must remain centralized and on Capitol Hill; their unique value is in their relationship to each other. There are, however, many administrative services that in future years need not be located on Capitol Hill.

A Research Office

A research office is badly needed. The Library of Congress must improve its capability to perform research into technical matters central to its own operations and into library problems generally. For the most part, research at the Library should be decentralized, but there must be a central coordinating office to oversee the entire research program. The research office would serve four important functions: (1) provide information about outside library operations that are relevant to the Library's programs; (2) encourage individual departments or divisions to undertake needed research; (3) coordinate and review, as necessary, all Library of Congress research activities and contracts; and (4) perform research needed by the Library's management.

The Library is deficient in providing its managers with adequate information for decision-making. It needs improved statistics for determining the cost effectiveness of programs and services. It needs Library-wide policies regarding the uses of labor-saving devices such as word processing equipment. Officials at all levels need statistically sound projections about topics such as collection growth, manpower allocations, and the impact of computer technology and other technologies. Internal standards are needed to measure and control work flow. Furthermore, the Library must begin regular assessments of user satisfaction. Such information is essential if the Library of Congress is going to develop a fully integrated, long-range and Library-wide planning process.

Coordinating Committees

Recommendation No. 33: that the Library reorganize its committee system with the goal of creating a more powerful and responsive group of coordinating committees. A director's council should be the capstone of the system.

With few exceptions, committees at the Library of Congress are not functioning particularly well. Committees are needed in the Library to improve communication among operating officials and staff. They should not manage, but coordinate. They facilitate management by permitting line officers to make more informed decisions. The committee system must be constructed with care to ensure that individual committees do not usurp the decision-making responsibilities of operating officials. The key is the concept of committees as coordinating and advisory bodies. Committees should give management a cross-departmental perspective; they should complement, not duplicate, the administrative structure.

The director's council should consist of the Librarian, the Deputy and Assistant Librarians, the head of the planning office, the department directors, plus any other officials invited by the Librarian. As the Library's principal coordinating body, it should meet at least once a month. The planning office should provide the secretariat. The director's council will define the areas in which the committees are to make their contribution and refer topics to appropriate committees.

The number of coordinating committees should be held to a minimum. No committee should have more than 10 members, which means that each member must truly represent the views of others. Dereliction of this duty or a poor attendance record should result in removal from the committee. Each committee should be required to meet at least six times a year. Each should be abolished after two years if not continued by the Librarian or the Deputy Librarian.

Coordinating committees should be created to consider problems that concern more than one unit, but as groups they should not make decisions. The Librarian or the Deputy Librarian should appoint all committee chairmen, who normally will be the responsible operating officers for each appropriate activity. The committee members, chosen on a Library-wide basis by the chairman, will be responsible officers from each administrative unit involved.

At this time, the Task Force feels that the following coordinating committees are necessary: acquisitions, automation, cataloging, cultural activities, online catalog, preservation, and serials.

Coordinating committees should be supported by various departmental committees as well as by interdepartmental staff discussion groups or "roundtables," such as the Reference Roundtable now in existence.

Chapter VIII: Unique Opportunities for Service

Section A: Organizational Opportunities

Historically, discussions of the organization of the Library of Congress often have included proposals to transfer the Library, or parts of the Library, to the executive branch of government.

The Task Force strongly opposes any such moves. We believe that the Library can fulfill the high hopes we have expressed for it only if it remains in the legislative branch. We are in full accord with the view expressed by the eminent librarian S. R. Ranganathan in 1950, on the occasion of the Library's sesquicentennial: "The institution serving as the national library of the United States is perhaps more fortunate than its predecessors in other countries. It has the Congress as its godfather. This stroke of good fortune has made it perhaps the most influential of all the national libraries of the world."

It is true that in a perfectly logical world, the functions of the Library would probably have been divided among two or three different agencies. The Task Force believes, however, that the diverse functions performed by the Library provide the institution with many unique advantages and opportunities.

Proposals to transfer parts of the Library to the executive branch usually focus on the Copyright Office or the Division for the Blind and Physically Handicapped. Again, we would strongly oppose any such action. The Copyright Office, in addition to supplying materials for the collections, provides the Library of Congress and therefore American librarianship with a vital link to the publishing industry and the creative world of authors and artists. This is a relationship to be encouraged and strengthened. The Division for the Blind and Physically Handicapped performs an important and unique national service. It also serves as a model for the rest of the Library in developing and delivering information services. As stated in Chapter II, the Task Force believes that this division probably deserves departmental status or the equivalent.

Our report emphasizes the need for improved coordination and planning so the Library of Congress can provide the best possible service to Congress and the nation. To achieve this goal, we have proposed several organizational changes plus the creation of a variety of planning and coordinating mechanisms. These proposals reflect our general conclusion that the Library's most pressing organizational problem is not its overall administrative structure, but inadequate coordination and communication between existing administrative units.

Here is a partial summary of organizational and related changes recommended in previous chapters:

a new focus on using the resources of the entire Library to improve services to Congress, with a new coordinator of Congressional services serving as the catalyst

the improved coordination of services provided to other libraries through the creation of a national library office

the improvement of book delivery services through a new, unified administrative structure

the establishment of a new reader guidance system which would include a more coherent sign system, a reader advisory office, and the use of computer terminal assistants

the creation of a new reference department that would include new divisions for American studies, Europe, and Africa, a motion picture and television division, and a new dance section in the Music Division the development of a more rational pattern of reference service by establishing reference coordinator positions in the reference department and Law Library

the strengthening of the Library's photoduplication services through increased support from appropriated funds

the creation of a collection development office by merging the selection function, certain recommending activities, and the responsibility for the solicitation of gifts

the establishment of a committee to coordinate serials management

the strengthening of the acquisitions operations by merging the Exchange and Gift Division, the Order Division, and the acquisitions unit of the Shared Cataloging Division

the establishment of an office of bibliography

the establishment of a cataloging committee to review both the cataloging priority system and cataloging practices

the increased use of the cataloging done by the Copyright Office

the creation, through the cataloging committee and the Committee on the Online Catalog, of a forum to deal with new issues raised by the development of computerized cataloging

the centralization of overall responsibility for the Library's cultural and educational programs in a single office that would be advised by a new cultural coordinating committee

the establishment of a career development section in the Personnel Office

the transfer of the Personnel Office to the Office of the Librarian

a new emphasis on Library-wide planning and program review led by the newly created planning office

the establishment of a research office to coordinate and stimulate an expanded research program

with the help of a reorganized committee structure, the clarification of the Library's decision-making process

The planning office should play an essential role in the Library's organizational development. As stated in Chapter VII, systematic planning and program review is essential for a strong, well-managed Library of Congress. Some of the coordinating functions recommended in earlier chapters, such as the national library office, might even be incorporated into the planning office at a later date.

In this report, the Task Force has also recommended studies of several topics, including:

the entire book delivery system, including the "not-on-the-shelf" problem

the organization of the area studies units within the new reference department possible departmental status for the Division for the Blind and Physically Handicapped

the organization and future direction of the Law Library

ways of improving the reference services provided directly to Congress through the Library's reference centers and book rooms on Capitol Hill

the existing arrangements for the custody of the general and specialized research collections

the desirability and possibility of full linkages between the automated and the manual bibliographic system

the creation of a Library of Congress Press and ways of reducing the dependency of the Library's publishing program on the Government Printing Office

the evolving organization of the Library's automation activities

Finally, we wish to emphasize that the purpose of the various coordinators and coordinating bodies we have proposed is not to erode the authority of the Library's officials but to facilitate communication and informed decision-making. The number of coordinators and coordinating bodies must be held to a minimum.

The purpose of the various job rotation plans suggested in the preceding chapters, e.g., rotation between catalogers and reference specialists and the rotation of recommending officers into the collection development office, is to facilitate communication and strengthen internal services. Job rotation, of course, cannot be applied unilaterally. Unless the benefits of a proposed plan are clear to administrators and the employees who will be involved, it should not be undertaken.

Section B: National Opportunities

In a well-functioning Library of Congress, strengthening service to one group of users frequently strengthens service to all.

Improvement in general reader service by means of an improved book delivery system, for instance, will also help the Congressional Research Service to provide quick and thorough research for the benefit of Congress. Our provision for staff experts in all fields and all regions and languages of the world will powerfully supplement the expert knowledge that already is available to Congress. Our program to catalog thoroughly the entire holdings of the Library, giving particular attention to what is unique to our collections, will increase the range of research material available to everyone.

In our program of national and international library leadership, the picture is the same. Benefits and opportunities flow both ways. We have proposed that it is incumbent upon the Library of Congress, as a national library, to:

provide strong leadership in the development of a comprehensive national bibliographic system

assume leadership in creating a national preservation program

enlarge the national telephone reference service and the national referral center assume leadership in creating a systematic loan network and a national periodical lending library

continually seek ways of making the Library's products available at a price within the financial reach of all libraries

establish a systematic outreach program through workshops, internships, and consultant services

continue to provide leadership in the establishment of standards and guidelines

enlarge its role in the cooperative acquisition of foreign materials

Without exception these are cooperative undertakings that require careful planning and close coordination with the libraries and library associations of this nation and the world. Their successful completion will be impossible without cooperation and support from other libraries. As mentioned in Chapter I, the role of the Library of Congress in these endeavors is a delicate one. It must simultaneously be a leader and a partner. It must be a source of information, a clearinghouse, and a referral center. We think that the creation of the national library office will make this difficult task easier.

Each of the endeavors listed is one element in a strong program of national library leadership. In recent years the Congress has shown an increasing appreciation for such leadership, which benefits libraries in every part of the country. Congress itself has a unique opportunity to serve the entire nation through the Library of Congress.

Each of these endeavors should also enrich the Library itself. If the Library of Congress can unify its internal program, if it can work with greater harmony within itself and with the library and information community, it will improve its services to all—to Congress and the Nation.

3

Epilogue

On January 17, 1977, in anticipation of the presentation of the Task Force report on January 28, Librarian Boorstin established—effective January 28—a new Office of Planning and Development. Charles A. Goodrum, Assistant Director for Coordination and Review, Congressional Research Service, was appointed director. The initial assignment of the new Planning Office was to "receive the reports of the Task Force and the eight outside advisory groups and review their recommendations for appropriate action." The office would "evaluate the reports and collect and analyze any additional information as may be required."[1] Working with Librarian Boorstin, Deputy Librarian William J. Welsh, Assistant Librarian Donald Curran, and other senior officials, the new office would "formulate a series of policy statements which will serve as the basis for shaping the future character of the Library's organization and services."

Librarian Boorstin accepted the report of the Task Force on Goals, Organization, and Planning in a ceremony in the Library's Coolidge Auditorium on January 28, 1977. The invited guests included, in addition to senior Library officials, all who had served on Task Force subcommittees and the advisory group chairmen. The eleven Task Force members joined the Librarian on the stage.

In his remarks the Librarian emphasized that the Task Force enterprise was "only a beginning":

> The presentation of the Task Force report today is only one stage of our continuing effort—not the epilogue but only the first scene in the first act of a drama of refreshment and revival for the Library of Congress. Today is a day not when a period is placed—but only a comma—and, of course, with it a parenthesis, an exclamation point, and perhaps also a question mark.[2]

After acknowledging those who had participated in the Task Force effort, Boorstin reminded his audience that he had not seen the final report:

I have felt that much of the purpose of the Task Force report would not be accomplished if it had any hint of ventriloquism. I wanted to be sure that there was no suggestion that what the report was telling me was what I had asked the report to give us. It should be a free form statement of new criticisms and new ideas and that is what I expect to find.[3]

He concluded his remarks by promising that the Task Force report would be "the raw material, the basis of a program for a renaissance of this Library." The Librarian observed:

We have attained some wonderful momentum, which I will not let us lose. Momentum, I would remind you, is a product of a body's mass and its linear velocity. This is an institution of enormous mass—to produce even a little movement requires an unusual amount of linear velocity. That linear velocity, which consists of the willingness and capacity of people to move, is the most precious thing we have. How can we preserve it? First by preserving the spirit of the Task Force and all of the others who have offered their suggestions. . . . The evidence of that linear velocity being continued is that we have already created a Planning Office to which your suggestions continue to be welcome, including, of course, your comments in writing on the report of the Task Force itself. . . . We will be taking measures almost immediately, measures which will grow out of the Task Force recommendations and which I hope will have your support. . . . We will develop a program, a program not just of memoranda but of action, of improvement and of outreach. And also inreach in the improvement of the opportunities in this Library for people to serve it better and with more excitement.[4]

As promised, the Library of Congress began to change in the spring and summer of 1977. As recommended by the Task Force, a new readers' advisory service and computer catalog center were installed. The changes themselves were not nearly as important as the new atmosphere. The June 3, 1977, issue of *Library of Congress Information Bulletin*, while overdramatizing the occasion, accurately reflected the new attitude:

May 24, 1977, is a date which should be recorded in the history of the Library of Congress as the date on which the Library began to implement the ideas and suggestions generated from a year and a half of self-examination and assessment. It is a date when the Library turned from thought to action, and that action may be summarized in one word: "Openings."

Nowhere is this more apparent than in the changes that have taken place in the Main Reading Room in recent days. The books are the same, the physical setting is the same, and the wide diversity of people who use the Library of Congress is still the same. But what has changed is the *way* in which people now use the Library. The Library of Congress is no longer standing, waiting for those with the stamina—and even the temerity—to approach its vast collections. The Library is coming to them.

A phased introduction system has been added to the Library of Congress, one of the steps recommended by the Librarian's Task Force on Goals, Organization, and Planning.[5]

The same issue included the first in a series of articles that might possibly be of greater significance to the Library than any single organizational change. The article, entitled "Change at the Library of Congress," was by Charles A. Goodrum, Director of the Office of Planning and Development. It both described the activities of the new Planning Office and indicated a new approach on the part of the Library's administration. The article is reprinted below.[6]

CHANGE AT THE LIBRARY OF CONGRESS—JUNE 3, 1977

The Office of Planning and Development has now been in existence for 90 days, and with that date, I would like to begin a series of reports covering three things: what the Planning Office has done so far, what it hopes to do next, and what innovations and changes are occurring throughout the Library—completely apart from any Planning Office involvement. In the next few words, I will try to bring matters up-to-date.

Who Is in the Office?

The office consists of four permanent positions, a floating position to be staffed with rotating, detailed personnel, and an administrative support position. At the present, the slots are filled by John Y. Cole, bringing his experience from designing and running the Librarian's Task Force on Goals, Organization, and Planning; Helen Dalrymple, ex-head of the Executive Branch/Public Administration Section of CRS's Government Division; Robert Zich, one of the founders of the Library of Congress Professional Association and the organizer of the Reference Roundtable; and myself, with 28 years in the CRS. The detail position is now filled by Grace Ross who brings her experience from Serials and Shared Cataloging to the unit. Gladys Fields, long-time assistant to two Librarians of Congress, is providing the administrative support.

What Is the Office Doing?

We are trying to accomplish four things simultaneously. First, we are implementing the recommendations of the Task Force on Goals, Organization, and Planning which were forwarded to the Librarian on January 28 of this year. The Task Force made 33 recommendations. Many of these were generalized in statement, but detailed in both the report explanation and the basic Subcommittee and Advisory Group recommendations on which they were based. The 33 thus broke down into over 100 specific suggestions for things to do. The Planning Office has arranged these into three categories: those that are essentially "quick and easy" and represent suggestions on which there is a general consensus; those which will take longer, require more extensive planning and refinement but which are still generally supported; and finally, those that either represent long-range goals or involve serious disagreement between the impacted parties. We have been trying to do the first group immediately. We hope to do the second between Memorial Day and the end of the year, and the third group will be started in the fall expecting them either to be done or consciously rejected by the time we move to the Madison Building.

As noted, we are doing the quick and easy now. Some examples:

1. With the help of almost a dozen affected administrative units, the office has had a role in designing and implementing a new Readers' Advisory Service. The purpose of the service is to make skilled LC reference people available to the visiting scholars and users of the Library facilities *at the point of entry.* Here immediate assistance will be provided to be certain that the visitor is using the most appropriate collection, the proper reading room, or the most efficient retrieval tool *before* he begins his efforts rather than after he has wasted time or been frustrated in his search. Through interview points in the Great Hall, in two new rooms opened at the door to the Main Reading Room, at a station at the issue desk, and in a newly designed and opened computer terminal center, new public assistance staff will reinforce the traditional reference service provided visitors. Ultimate ends: to enhance the use of the special collections and special reading rooms, to make more efficient use of the traditional catalogs and indexes, to prepare the users for the planned 1980 automation and concurrent "freezing" of the card catalog, and, in sum, generally reduce the user frustration level.

2. The office has had a role in bringing the proper people together and implementing a total "re-signing" of the Library. We discovered literally over 600 different signs in the Main Reading Room alone. Beginning at once, the public information graphics in the three buildings will be changed to a uniform, hopefully more logical, sequential system which will tell a visitor/user where he is, what is available there, how to use it, and if he should be somewhere else, how to get there. (Both of the above are per Task Force Recommendation No. 6.)

3. The CRS and the Law Library have traditionally kept precise statistics on the number of Congressional inquiries answered, their type, and the time spent. Congressional assistance rendered by other units has been recorded and controlled in varying degrees via different systems. It is known, for example, that CRS transfers over 20 percent of its received Congressional requests to departments outside the CRS, and that the Law Library receives 12,000 Congressional inquiries directly, but many departments keep no record of incoming or outgoing Congressional calls at all. The Planning Office has had a role in designing and implementing the new Congressional statistical and status reporting system implemented May 1 throughout the Library. (Per Task Force Recommendation No. 1.)

4. The Library loans approximately a quarter of a million volumes a year to local government agencies, embassies, research institutions, and to libraries throughout the country. For example, 1,500 volumes were loaned via airmail to *British* libraries last year. Since these arrangements were built up over nearly a hundred years, the "terms of agreement" were less than uniform. The Planning Office has had a role in working with the appropriate LC units in designing a coherent, well-monitored interlibrary loan system, and implementation has begun. (Per Task Force Recommendation No. 11.)

Task Force recommendations are therefore the first of the Planning

Office's targets. The second category of work is made up of specific projects that are identified by Mr. Boorstin, Bill Welsh, and Don Curran, and assigned to the office for design and implementation. These are proving to be either ideas for new services, new administrative units, or the coordination of ongoing studies being conducted by multiple groups in different departments.

Examples of this type of work are:

1. The Librarian asked the Planning Office to design a Center for the Book. With much help from units throughout the Library, this has been completed. Representative Nedzi has introduced the necessary legislation. Mr. Boorstin has testified, and the bill has been reported out of Committee for floor approval. If this is enacted, plans for staffing, programming, and funding are ready to go.

2. Bill Welsh asked the office to design a Special Events Office, determine necessary staffing, training requirements, potential programming, and administrative relations. This has been done.

3. The auditor of the Library has completed a vastly detailed inventory of all book and material storage located in the 12 rented facilities off Capitol Hill. Don Curran has assigned the Planning Office the task of coordinating the following queries: (1) how were the materials acquired in the first place and why?; (2) which of the materials should be retained and moved into the Madison Building?; (3) which materials should be discarded and if so, to whom should they be offered before destruction?; and (4) what changes must be made in our acquisitions policies to be certain that the desirable materials of this nature continue to be secured, but the materials deemed marginal do not continue to be received nor are similar publications of like nature permitted to accumulate in the future.

The third category of work in which the Planning Office is involved might be characterized as the "Why don't they ever do anything about. . . ?" questions. There are certain awesomely broad and complicated matters that have frustrated staff and users of the Library for decades. It is possible that in the past, given the resources and the cross-pulls of our three audiences—the Congressional, scholarly, and library worlds—these questions were unsolvable. We hope to see if a resolution's time may not have come. Until proved differently, the Planning Office hopes to face up to some of these cosmic frustrations and try to get a few cleared out in our own time. Examples: the not-on-shelf, why-can't-you-get-a-book-at-the-Library-of-Congress problem. (I will discuss this in detail in a few weeks); the why is a book cataloged once by Copyright, again by Processing, and again by the special collection staff where it comes to rest problem; the why is it that when a single unit automates, it works reasonably well (Card Distribution, CRS-SCORPIO, MARC), but when any attempt is made to rationalize these into an intelligent whole it all comes to a grinding, paralyzed stop problem. And similar targets of fascinating challenge.

The final category of Planning Office activity is far less dramatic, but we hope of equal, potential usefulness: statistical analysis. We hope to do extensive examinations of trends, slopes, long-range implications. Which of our services seem to be of the greatest usefulness? Are our staffing and space resources being allocated to the areas that seem to give us the greatest return? Indeed are the statistics we're keeping really the ones we most want and need?

To date we have completed about 20 fairly substantial projects, and about that many minor ones. About 75 percent of our recommendations have been implemented and are going forward, 15 percent are being revised or are under continued study, and 10 percent have been flatly rejected or indefinitely postponed. We are only now beginning to do anything in the fourth (statistical) area described above.

I have tried to note in this report *who* we are and *what* we're doing. Next week I will try to explain *how* we are trying to do it. I want to discuss how the Planning Office is supposed to relate to the individual departments and divisions, and how we're trying to structure the whole thing so that not only does everyone know what we're doing but how everyone can help us do it properly—mainly how to get your suggestions to us before a change gets etched in steel and becomes a *fait accompli.*

The second Goodrum article, in the *Library of Congress Information Bulletin* of June 17, 1977, and in the unique Goodrum style, included a list of certain Task Force recommendations and their status with regard to implementation. The entire article is reproduced below.[7]

CHANGE AT THE LIBRARY OF CONGRESS—JUNE 17, 1977

On June 3, I started a short report on the work of the Planning Office noting that we were trying to accomplish four things: the implementation of the Task Force recommendations, the design of new programs and administrative units at the specific direction of the three senior Library officers, the resolution of some of the long-time, multi-part problems of the Library, and the analysis of current Library statistics to see if we can identify new and significant trends among our user-audiences, our products, the collections, et cetera.

Ignoring the fourth activity for the moment (trend analysis), I would like to explain *how* we are trying to do the innovation and implementation involved in the first three.

And let me interrupt myself at once to note something about change and innovation at the Library in general, at this specific time. I have been writing about LC and its history for 25 years now, and I can say with considerable conviction *not for nearly a century* have we had such an opportunity for creating new uses for the institution, trying new services, correcting old errors and imprecisions. Note the astonishing vector of forces which have crossed here at the same time—all at the point onto which you and I have stumbled.

1. We have a new Librarian who is eager to enlarge the role of the institution. A nationally recognized scholar himself, he knows how libraries and research institutions are used and he appreciates the skills of highly trained people who are necessary to make them work. He senses the historical moment of another surge in enhancing the Library's support to Congress and widening the Library's place on the national scene. In only the first two years of Putnam and 18 months of MacLeish has a Librarian pressed the need for innovation and change so firmly.

2. At this precise moment, we have inherited a second in command, Bill Welsh, who brings 30 years of experience within the Library and a well-known, accumulated fury against administrative clumsiness, outdated, over-detailed rules and procedures, and general bureaucratic nonsense which he has resisted for years in the Processing Department. He also brings a much-respected reputation for sensitivity to individuals, and a demonstrated belief in the use of greater staff participation through the Library's programs.

3. Look at the people in the Front Office of your own department—look at your division chiefs. At no time in the past 50 years have there been so many new incumbents in the managerial positions throughout the Library. At every level from Section heads to Mahogany Row we have people recently arrived in their posts. We have experienced administrators suddenly responsible for quite new programs, often radically different from their past assignments. This represents an astonishing opportunity to try new things and test new goals and procedures without the knee-jerk reaction of long-time bureaucrats having to justify past decisions and defend traditional turf.

4. The coming shift to the Madison Building will move—literally—every staff member on the Library's payroll. With the possible exception of a few elevator operators and special police, I can identify no one who will be working at the same location 36 months from now that he or she is today. Likewise, in 36 months we will have moved tens of millions of pieces of research material. The possibilities for realigning our interdivisional relationships, smoothing out workflows, improving access to high-use materials and displacement of low, are absolutely unique—a once in a century chance to do it right.

5. Finally, the collections of the Library as a research tool are on the threshold of dramatic change in the way they are retrieved, controlled, and analyzed: as of 1980, the card catalog, traditional index to the Library for 80 years, will be frozen and thereafter all access and control of new acquisitions will be by computer. But "access and control" will be all pervasive—charge records, use statistics, multiple retrieval terms—even the books themselves will carry bar codes for automated scanning (the latter, in fact, within a matter of months). The point again: our approaches to our research tools are new, unprecedented, wide-open. How we shape them suddenly is back in our hands to use them as we see fit, not simply "how it's always been."

Obviously the Planning Office has only a splinter involvement in all this coming change. The overwhelming activity will come at the section and division level. What is vastly important here is for each of us—every member of the staff—to look around us and ask: We've got the best opportunity we've had in a hundred years to *do it right*—what can we do in my unit, in the next 12 months, to bring it off? What can we correct now while we have the chance? If we blow this one, we've got no one to blame but ourselves. I plead with you to think about it.

To return to the Planning Office's part in this innovation: We, too, are acutely sensitive to the need for speed. This is the worst possible time for endless committee meetings searching for gray consensus. To avoid this, we invented a written device which we call "Reconnaissances." Each "Recon" has six parts. When the Planning Office is ready to explore the potential for a new service or develop a new administrative unit, the topic is assigned to a principal planning assistant. The assistant then discusses the idea broadly with everyone he or she thinks may have some ideas on the matter, researches both the library files of memos, Task Force reports, and Task Force letters, and searches the printed literature when it seems appropriate. From all these sources, the planning assistant distills out what he or she believes to be the best possible way of making the suggestion real.

They then write a Reconnaissance. Part I states the recommended action; *what* is recommended. Part II justifies it; explains *why* it is desirable. Part III states the amount of resources which will be required to do it properly in terms of staff, space, and money to run it (beyond personnel costs) in the future; *how much* the idea will cost. Part IV enumerates the LC administrative units which will be affected if the innovation were to come to pass; *who* will be impacted. Part V describes the steps needed to bring it off; *how* to do it. And Part VI is worst case planning, what damage would be done if "everything went wrong."

Once the Recon is completed, it is reviewed by all five members of the Planning Office, changes made, and when approved by myself goes forward to the Messrs. Boorstin, Welsh, and Curran. They decide yes or no; now or later. If they say, "go ahead and explore it," we go back to the impacted departments and divisions and say, "All right, it's time to take this seriously, how do you want it changed to make it work in the best possible way?"

From this comes the rewrites, the refinements, and the caveats which shape the suggestion toward the best possible statement. The Cataloging Committee Recon, for example, was revised four times before all parties could agree, but having a hard-edged recommendation at the outset provides a target for reaction and does seem to hasten resolution.

Once the Reconnaissance has general endorsement, it goes back to the three Librarians and they decide *when* it should go forward and *who* should be responsible for its implementation.

To date the following Recons have been developed.

Reconnaissance	Present Status of Recommendation
1. Center for the Book	Approved and proceeding
2. LC as a Center for Advanced Research and Scholarship	Approved and proceeding
3. Reader Advisory Service	Approved and proceeding
4. A Cataloging Committee	Approved and proceeding
5. Compilation of Statistics on LC Services to Congress	Approved and proceeding
6. An Academic Liaison Office	Approved, implementation deferred
7. A Statement of Mission and Purpose	Awaiting approval

8. Use of the General Collections	Approved and proceeding
9. Interlibrary loans in LC	Approved and proceeding
10. A Library Liaison Office	Approved, implementation deferred
11. An Attractive, Coherent Sign System	Approved and proceeding
12. Special Events Officer	Awaiting approval
13. Visitors and Public Tours Center	Awaiting approval
14. Book Storage	In process
15. Ticket Distribution for Concerts	Awaiting approval
16. An Inventory of LC Book and Periodical Collections	In process
17. A Collection Development and Bibliography Office	In process
18. Serials Claiming	In process
19. Administrative Location of the American Television and Radio Archives	Awaiting approval
20. A Serials Committee	Awaiting approval
21. A Research Office	In process
22. Training of Descriptive Catalogers	In process
23. Restructuring the Public Services and Administrative Support Units of the Library	In process
24. Boards of Advisors	In process
25. Performing Arts in the Library of Congress	In process
26. Staffing the Information and Reference Services of the Library	In process

I am trying to keep these reports to 1,500 words-or-so, so I will stop at this point and pick up the final aspects of the Recon approach (how we decide *what* should be explored and how the *communications* feedback in developing the recommendations is supposed to work) in another issue.

By late summer of 1977, a basic reorganization plan had been formulated. The plan, still in a formative stage, was presented to the staff through another of Mr. Goodrum's articles, this one published in the *Library of Congress Information Bulletin* of August 19, 1977. The entire article is reproduced on pp. 142–146.[8]

CHANGE AT THE LIBRARY OF CONGRESS—AUGUST 19, 1977

Let's talk about reorganization.

Ever since Daniel Boorstin's arrival and the creation of his Task Force on Goals, Organization, and Planning, the Library has brooded over the question, "Is he going to reorganize the place?" Five different plans have now slid together and an answer is possible: Not totally, but in some areas, definitely yes. Will there be new units and realignment of old ones? Very much so. Many.

A new organization chart has been developing through the past six months, and a copy is attached to this report. [This chart is reproduced on pages 144 and 145.] The chart and the organizational changes it represents are at this point simply possibilities to be talked about. A lot of mixes have been discarded as having some merit but not yielding enough improvements to make it worth the shock of change. A number more are definitely good and useful but impossible even to consider until we have the space of the Madison Building in hand and our displaced units are brought back into contiguity again. The structure as shown on the charts can thus be considered discussable, even, do-able, within present constraints of space and personnel. Last Thursday, the Librarian explained his plans at a meeting of departmental officers, and the draft reorganization has been presented to the leadership of all the recognized labor organizations of the Library. We are now going into the discussion period. No formal actions will take place before mid-October at the earliest, but it is time to begin to go from the general, over-all theory and purpose to the finer-grained examination of individual programs and units. The next two months are the weeks for the latter. Now, let's look at the chart and let me point up some of the thinking which went into it.

First, its antecedents. You will immediately recognize that the "reorganization" is really a combination of five different plans from as many different sources.

1. The Center for the Book and the Council of Scholars tied to the Librarian's Office at the top are organizational entities created to carry out Mr. Boorstin's hopes for closer ties with the Library's audiences, and greater emphasis on the shaping and strengthening of the Library's collections.

2. The Copyright changes picture the restructuring of that department as worked out by Barbara Ringer and a series of staff committees who designed a sweeping readjustment in the weeks following the passage of the Revision Act. The obvious purpose was to restructure the office to cope with the new responsibilities and added volume due to hit the office January 1, 1978. More, better, faster.

3. You will note major change in the area of service to the scholarly public. The majority of these readjustments and new entities stem from recommendations of the Librarian's Task Force. They might be generalized as lifting use of the collections to the levels we have traditionally accorded acquiring the collections and processing them.

4. With the exception of a recommendation to move the selection officer to the Librarian's Office, there are no changes within the Pro-

cessing Department. Not only was it recently reorganized by Bill Welsh, but the next real need for reexamination will fall when total automation appears in the Madison, with its resultant impact on processing work flows. The title change simply brings the department into conformity with similar missions in other libraries. The structure as shown for the Congressional Research Service incorporates the changes made or proposed by Gil Gude and addresses the concerns of the House Commission on Information and Facilities.

5. Adjustments in the administrative area of the Library reflect Bill Welsh's and Don Curran's continuing efforts to reduce span of control and sharpen administrative responsibilities among the managerial family.

The Planning Office has made a few suggestions to bridge, smooth out, and implement the recommendations of the other elements, and thus the Boorstin-Ringer Task Force-House-Gude-Curran-Welsh-Planning Office suggestions add up to the printed chart.

What was the general philosophy behind the changes? Essentially it was two-fold: to express clearly and firmly the four great missions of the Library, and then to bring together the appropriate personnel and skills to accomplish these missions with the greatest efficiency, effectiveness, and sensitivity. Obviously each organizational element in the Library contributes to the support of the others but the thrust of the organization is to cluster the major units which carry out the stated missions and strengthen the way they serve their audiences. (Or to get out of the language of the textbook: low walls, fewer units, clearer, sharper responsibilities, and the right people meeting around action tables once a week instead of putting memos in bottles and flinging them out to sea.)

What are the four missions of the Library perceived to be?

To provide information and policy analysis to the Congress.

To support the artistic-creative sector of the nation and protect its product

To support the nation's libraries and help them secure bibliographic control over the world's publishing

To serve the nation's scholarly-research audience and provide it with free and open access to the sources of knowledge it needs to do its work

The bureaucratic chart symbolizes the philosopher's leap from what ought to be to what is—high philosophy to the nitty-gritty. This is not the time nor is there space here to explain each element of change, but let me highlight a few details.

1. The four missions are displayed across the base, clustered into the people who are serving the specific audiences. The traditional "Administrative Department" is lifted up so it expresses not a purpose of the Library to administrate as an end, but the means by which the Librarian supports the programs to which he and the institution are committed.

2. The Center for the Book and the Council of Scholars are entities by which the Librarian hopes to bring in outside scholars and spe-

THE LIBRARY

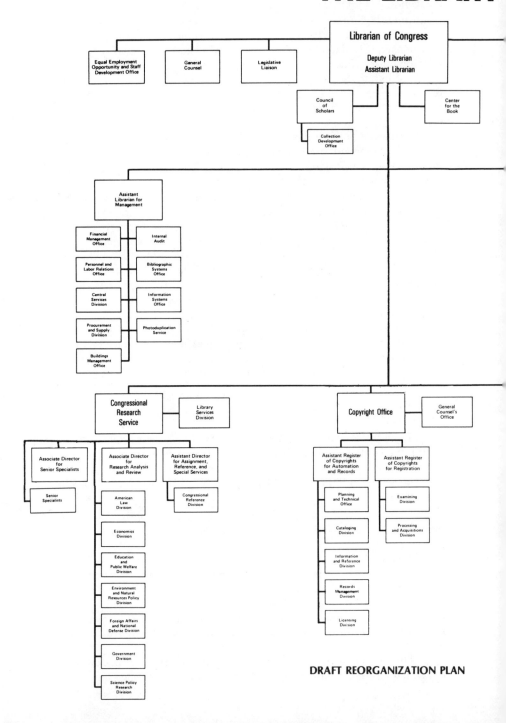

DRAFT REORGANIZATION PLAN

OF CONGRESS

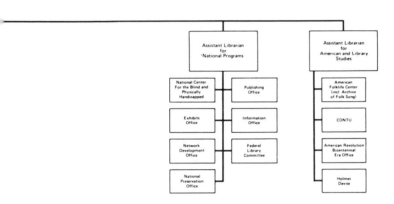

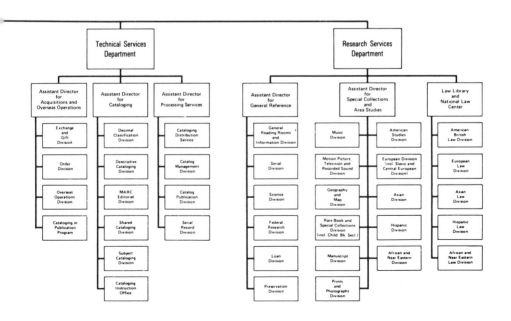

cialists to serve as a bridge between the Library's users and the Library's staff. They will be visiting specialists studying our devices for storing knowledge—the book, tape, film, computer, disc, and they will help us shape our collections so they are cost effective, balanced, and responsive to the need of the particular audience involved. (If you can only get and process a certain portion of the world's knowledge, which portion should that be?)

The council will bring in some two dozen representatives from such fields as law, fine arts, government, business, science, Latin-American studies, and Orientalia, who will in turn be supported by the new Collection Development Office which will convert the council's recommendations into action. The office will contain senior officers representing each of the four mission departments to be certain that the basic programs are fully served.

3. You will note a new Assistant Librarian for National Programs. This officer will bring together the programs that speak for the Library outside the walls plus several of those mandated by Congress through special legislation. In this configuration, these will be tied more closely to the Librarian for direction and support. The Librarian's hopes for dramatic expansion of LC publishing, traveling exhibits, and increased LC involvement in professional organizations fall in this area of activities.

4. The new Research Services Department brings together the elements which the Librarian believes are essential to strong, enhanced, responsive service to the scholarly and research worlds. The units placed under an Assistant Director for General Reference are those that meet the public, respond to the majority of visiting scholars, bring the general materials of the Library to the user either in person, through outside loan, or via microform, photocopy, telecopier, and so on. You will notice the joining of the reading room staffs with the stack personnel and the incorporation of the preservation units.

The special materials and area studies divisions are linked into a single unit awaiting the move to the Madison Building when all the elements can be expanded into Mr. Boorstin's plan for an encyclopedia of professional skills, a spectrum of expert subject support to visiting scholars. A new (and long-discussed) African and Near Eastern Division falls into this area, as well as the new American Television and Radio Archive.

The third area of the Research Services Department is the new, expanded National Law Center and Law Library, called for by so many professional and advisory groups.

These are only the larger adjustments pictured by the chart. There are obviously many smaller changes that will be discussed in the coming weeks. For the moment, I am up to my promised 1,500-word limit for these reports, so we will pick up details and elaborations in subsequent columns.

In September 1977 the Planning Office began a series of meetings with members of the staff to discuss the proposed reorganization. Changes were made and a final plan was expected by early 1978. In the meantime, the

Planning Office began a series of meetings and Mr. Goodrum began a series of *Information Bulletin* columns concerning the Library's "not-on-the-shelf" problem.[9] Their purpose was in full accordance with the spirit of the Task Force: "The Library of Congress—already a grand accumulation of the world's knowledge—must become a more *useful* part of the national life. The first step is to make our collections and the skills of our staff more accessible."[10]

Notes

1. U.S., Library of Congress, *Library of Congress Information Bulletin*, January 21, 1977, pp. 25–26.
2. Remarks of Librarian of Congress Daniel J. Boorstin in accepting the report of the Task Force on Goals, Organization, and Planning, January 28, 1977, Coolidge Auditorium, Library of Congress. Transcribed from tape recording. Library of Congress Archives.
3. Ibid.
4. Ibid.
5. *Library of Congress Information Bulletin* 36: 361 (June 3, 1977).
6. Ibid., pp. 374–376.
7. Ibid., June 17, 1977, pp. 428–430.
8. Ibid., August 19, 1977, pp. 568A–568D.
9. Ibid., October 7, 1977, pp. 698–700; October 14, 1977, pp. 711–712; October 21, 1977, pp. 725–726.
10. U.S., Library of Congress, "Report of the Task Force on Goals, Organization, and Planning" (Washington, D.C.: Library of Congress, 1977), p. 6.

Appendix A:
Supplementary Documents

The three documents in this appendix are referred to in the Task Force report (Chapter 2). Each is a background paper that the Task Force used in developing its recommendations. They are: Reference Service in the Library of Congress (Document 1); Area Studies (Document 2); and A Proposal for a Retrospective Bibliography of American History and Culture (Document 3).

1. Reference Service in the Library of Congress

This document will first propose a logical system of guiding readers in the Library of Congress and second suggest a logical organization of staff for this purpose. It supplements and amplifies information in the Task Force report. It should be emphasized that these ideas are offered in a *spirit of experimentation*. The proposals comprise a first attempt at an improved reference service. If tried, the changes proposed will no doubt require adjustment.

Much of the work of reader guidance should fall to the staff of a reference section (incorporating the Public Reference Section and the reader services function of the Stack and Reader Division), an information section (incorporating part of the Information Office staff, part of the Telephone Inquiry Unit, part of the Reference Correspondence Section, and possibly, the tour guides), and a stacks section (incorporating the Stacks Section of the Stack and Reader Division and those responsible for shifting the general collections who are now in the Collections Maintenance Office in the Preservation Office).

The system of reader guidance should begin at the door of the Library (or even the Neptune Plaza) and end in the office of one of our subject or area specialists.

In the main lobbies at the basement entrances to the Library of Congress and Jefferson Building and just outside the main entrance to the Main Reading Room should be an information station with an attractive, conspicious sign and an assistant who would begin sorting out of Library visitors: tourists in one place, first-time readers another, experienced researchers another. The information assistant should come from a new information section (see below) and should rotate each day between serving at the various public information posts and responding to telephone and letter inquiries sent them by the general inquiries unit (which is also described below). These assistants and a sign just inside the main entrance to the Main Reading Room would direct all first-time readers to the reader advisory office. The office should be located in the small alcoves just inside the main entrance to the Main Reading Room and be staffed at all hours with one or more reference librarians. Here the librarian would interview the reader in depth to discover the purpose of the visit. The librarian would give readers appropriate literature (from an array which should be greatly expanded), refer them to offices and specialists who could help them further, assign special study facilities and passes, if suitable, and in general teach the first steps in making effective use of the Library's collections, services, and people.

Many readers should receive the next phase of their Library education from reference librarians stationed at the Main Reading Room issue desk. The issue desk should be divided in two: attendants handling matters of book service (receipt of call slips, book delivery, and reserve books) should fill the half of the desk containing the pneumatic tubes. Reference librarians should fill the other half; in addition, one librarian should sit at a desk by the gate facing the main entrance to the room. Large, clear, attractive signs should mark the two areas. Deck attendants should rotate into the positions that provide help with book service. This would acquaint them more closely with the consequence and importance of their work. Reference librarians from an augmented Public Reference staff should provide the service in the other half, and the senior reference librarian on duty at the desk should be the floor supervisor for the entire issue desk operation. The reference librarians should, as mentioned, be part of an enlarged pool of reference specialists who would work a varied schedule; one or two hours per day in the reader advisory office, one or two at the issue desk, one or two in Alcoves 4 and 5, and one or two at a secluded desk working on written up telephone inquiries, letters, or special assignments. The staff of reference specialists should be enlarged so as ultimately to possess a range of expert knowledge that embraces all major subjects.

The Library should work toward achieving the goal of comprehensive subject coverage by the early 1980s. In 1980, with much new space available in the Library of Congress Building, these specialists in their increased number would be able to spend half-time in their own offices near the reading room where, amidst an expanded reference collection, they could offer to readers referred to them the thorough, detailed guidance in research which many of our present specialists have yearned to be able to give and which our readers so very much need.

Offering a full range of subject specialists fills, of course, just part of the need. Another part must be filled by terminal assistants near each public collection of computer terminals to teach our readers how to use the Library's data bases. As a first step, the Library should establish a public computer terminal center at the rear of the Main Catalog and put a station within it for a terminal instruction assistant who must be available all of our hours of opening. These positions should be created by conversion of positions no longer needed because of automation.

Finally, the Library requires a full range of area specialists who also, if possible, should be situated reasonably near the Main Reading Room. The Library should enlarge its staff of area specialists so as to encompass all major regions of the world. Specifically, the Library should establish an American studies division and a European division, and convert the African Section to a division. The American Studies division should incorporate possibly the bibliographers working on the *Guide to the Study of the United States*, the staff of the Archive of Folk Song, the Local History and Genealogy Room staff, the American Revolution bibliographers, the Children's Book Section, and the American Folklife Center. In 1980, the Library should give this division its own reading room where it would serve those needing expert guidance and an enlarged reference collection in American history and civilization. The focus on American history and culture which an American studies division, with an enlarged staff of Americanists and bibliographers, can achieve will help fill many embarrassing gaps in both our collections and service.

The European division would incorporate the present Slavic Division and add specialists for each of the major European countries not now covered. Spain and Portugal would continue to be covered by the Latin American, Portuguese, and Spanish Division. The purpose of a European division is once again to fill obvious gaps in our program of collection development and reference service. Finally, the African Section deserves the status of a division.

The system of reader guidance described above should be supported by a new organization of staff. The Task Force has recommended the uniting of the Reader Services and Research Departments into a new reference department. The new department would have three main branches: one for area studies divisions, one for special format divisions, and one for the remaining reference divisions. Each sub-unit should have its own assistant director who would report to the director of the reference department. The assistant directors would speak with one voice for their divisions and give coherent shape to the divisions' programs and services.

The various units of the new reference department and the Law Library would share many central problems. What is needed is greater uniformity in acquisitions, reference practices, and preservation. To achieve this goal, the Library should create in both the reference department office and Law Library Office the position of reference coordinator. The coordinator should survey existing practices throughout each department. The Library needs, for instance, a rational system of hours of service, at a minimum offering Saturday hours for every reading room, with essential services like the Central Charge File available for extended hours.

The coordinators should develop management tools that permit the continuous monitoring of the work of the departments. The work of the user survey should be continued on a regular basis, allowing the Library regularly to sample the thinking of its users as the basis for evaluating policy and performance.

The coordinator's office should contain central inquiries units. In the new reference department, this office might be started with those now in the Telephone Inquiry Unit, the Reference Correspondence Section, and the desk staff of the Information Office who do not become part of the new information section. There could be a rotation between those in the section and unit. The unit would model itself in many respects on the Inquiries Unit of the Congressional Research Service. It should serve as the logging and distribution point for all reference queries, not directed to a specific office, that come to the Library by letter or telephone. This would include press and government agency calls. The unit would send queries to the information section and, for queries needing advanced knowledge for their reply, to the specialists in other sections and divisions. The staff should rotate between receiving and routing telephone queries, and routing reference correspondence. The unit would record deadlines and ensure that they are met. The unit should ultimately computerize its log, thus permitting an automatic and routine check on speed of service.

The coordinators should stay in constant contact with each other and with the Congressional Research Service and should anticipate the impact on the reference department or Law Library of new policies or services in other departments. They should make every effort that is compatible with unimpaired good service to Congress toward arranging the exploitation of the CRS reference machine for the benefit of the general reader. Finally, together with the coordinator of Congressional services, they should study ways of improving the services provided to Congress through the Library's various reference centers and book rooms on Capitol Hill. At present these offices are staffed by different Library departments. As suggested by the subcommittee on services to Congress, a more unified administrative structure should be considered.

The system of reader guidance and library organization proposed here should at the same time increase the efficiency with which readers can use the Library and the efficiency with which the Library can help them. It will give the Library coherence in its service and organization. It will permit us to perform our duty in a way commensurate with our position as one of the great research centers of the world.

2. Area Studies

The Task Force recommended that the Library enlarge its staff of area specialists to encompass all major regions of the world by establishing an American studies division, a European division, and an African division. These divisions, along with the other area studies units now in the Research Department (the Latin American, Spanish, and Portuguese Division and the Orientalia Division) would form one branch in a new reference department. An assistant director for area studies would direct their activities.

A possible organization of the American studies division is described in the Task Force report. The European division would be formed by an expansion of the present Slavic and Central European Division. The creation of the European division, as stated, is necessary to fill obvious gaps in the Library's program of collection development and reference services.

The African Section, which was established in 1960, is now in the General Reference and Bibliography Division in the Reader Services Department.

It is responsible for coverage of sub-Saharan Africa, an area encompassing 45 nations and several dependencies. The disparity in organizational level between African studies and other area studies in the Library of Congress has been recognized for years by other libraries, scholarly associations, and the individual scholars. It should be corrected by giving the Library's African studies unit divisional status. The elevation of the African Section to a division and its combination with the other area studies divisions in a single department would give the Library's area studies program a new unity and impetus.

The organization of a new African division is a complicated question that requires further study. One important consideration is that the Near East Section of the Orientalia Division now has responsibility for coverage of North Africa. Several alternatives should be considered, including the creation of a separate division covering sub-Saharan Africa, the creation of a separate division with responsibility for North Africa, the creation of a separate division with responsibility for North Africa as well as the sub-Saharan region, and the combination of the present African and Near East Sections.

As indicated in the Task Force report, once the various area studies units are grouped together in a single department, the organizational and the jurisdictional responsibilities of all the units must be reviewed. The report of the subcommittee on area studies contains additional recommendations, along with a minority report. In addition, the subcommittee gathered statements from all the Library's area studies units concerning the following aspects of their respective operations: organization, present deficiencies, alternative organizational possibilities, and future objectives. These statements, which constitute a volume of over 200 pages, must be carefully reviewed as the Library embarks on an effort to improve the effectiveness of its entire area studies program.

3. A Proposal for a Retrospective Bibliography of American History and Culture

The Task Force recommended that the creation of a retrospective bibliography of American history and culture would be an appropriate undertaking for the Library of Congress. This document provides additional details concerning the proposed project.

As the participants at the Conference at Belmont of the Joint Committee on Bibliographical Services to History recognized in May 1967, the proliferation of books and serials in the field of American history and culture has overwhelmed the researcher and created an information crisis the proportions of which can only increase. The Library's experience in answering bibliographic requests repeatedly demonstrates the inadequacy of research tools in current use. There are no comprehensive guides to American historical literature published before 1902. The best available series for twentieth-century publications, Griffin's and Masterson's *Writings on American History*, is not only cumbersome to use but contains serious chronological gaps. Few fields are covered by such special bibliographies as Nevins, Robertson, and Wiley's *Civil War Books*. The prospects for future improvement in bibliographic services, moreover, are not encouraging. Recent attempts to cope with the outpouring of historical literature— Carrollton Press' NEXUS data base, ABC-CLIO's *America: History and Life,* and the American Historical Association's new *Writings on American History*—deal almost exclusively with selected serials and contain restricted subject, name, or key-word indexes that limit their usefulness. Although Xerox University Microfilm's *Comprehensive Dissertation Index, 1861–1972* for all fields of knowledge is helpful if the author or title is known, its key-word index is simply inadequate for the task of comprehensive research in broad subject areas.

Given the bibliographic restraints under which historical researchers now labor, it is incumbent upon the Library to assume its proper role as the nation's bibliographic center in American history and culture. Historical organizations have long urged the Library to undertake this responsibility. The Library's holdings of printed primary sources, monographs, doctoral dissertations, and serials are more comprehensive than any in the country and are continually supplemented by copyright deposit, purchase, gift, and exchange. For over 50 years the collections served as the basis for the early *Writings on American History* and hundreds of specialized compilations which were reproduced and distributed by the former Division of Bibliography. Even though LC's bibliographic services to the scholarly community and the general public were curtailed by administrative changes and lack of funds during the Second World War, a number of large-scale efforts have preserved and even modified our earlier tradition. The experience gained in the General Reference and Bibliography Division during the past 20 years in collecting entries for two major bibliographic projects, the *Guide to the Study of the United States* and its supplements and *Revolutionary America,* has given us an unparalleled overview of the production of recent and retrospective historical literature. For the *Guide* nearly a quarter of a million LC proof cards are now being reviewed each year in an effort to select for inclusion in the second supplement the most likely monographic works published between 1966 and 1975 in the broad field of American studies. In the case of *Revolutionary America* hundreds of thousands of LC catalog cards representing works in early American history have been reviewed, hundreds of published bibliographies compared with the accumulating files, and over a thousand historical serials searched volume by volume for literature on the period. While the *Guide* second supplement will contain approximately 3,000 fully annotated entries, the Revolutionary bibliography will include nearly 20,000 titles and 5,000 annotations. In each case the preparation of entries has proceeded from a thorough bibliographic review.

It appears that the techniques and procedures employed and the insights gained during the compilation of the *Guide,* its supplements, and *Revolutionary America* are applicable to several bibliographic programs that should be given serious consideration. The most ambitious and far-reaching of these is (1) to establish at the Library a computer-based bibliographic center for Americana and (2) to publish a comprehensive set of annotated retrospective bibliographies in American history. These two projects would be conducted simultaneously by the same staff. In the first instance search teams would amass an inclusive data base of citations to an estimated 850,000 printed primary sources, monographs (including rare books), doctoral dissertations, serials, atlases, and printed maps on the full range of American history from the age of exploration to the fourth quarter of the twentieth century. Once completed retrospectively, new additions would continually be made by specialists reviewing current literature. The Library would then be in a position to provide Congress, other libraries, scholars, and the general public with comprehensive, computer printout bibliographies on thousands of subjects. Bibliographies could be obtained, for example, on rare books and maps relating to early colonization, on doctoral dissertations treating the Federalist period, on historically related articles published in the *North American Review* between 1815 and 1890, or on monographs on the Potsdam Conference. For more general use in libraries and in teaching, nine selective letterpress bibliographies, similar in design and format to *Revolutionary America*, would be compiled to cover the other chronological periods of American history such as the Jacksonian era or the Populist-Progressive period. Collectively, these bibliographies would contain nearly 250,000 entries and would serve approximately the same ends as the Oxford bibliographies of British history. As the annotations for these works are completed and edited, they can be added to the computer data base to make the comprehensive printout bibliographies more useful. Similarly, the data base would be invaluable in compiling the supplements to the selective letterpress bibliographies that would be issued at ten-year intervals to meet the continuing needs of students and libraries.

One estimate is that it would require a staff of 12 working over a 13-year period to produce a 250,000-entry, multivolume bibliography of U.S. history and culture. At current grades and salaries this portion of the project would cost approximately $2,665,000 or about $205,000 annually, not including publication expenses. Calculating the cost of converting the bibliographic entries into a machine-readable data bank is beyond our present capabilities. Conversations with other specialists in the Library, however, lead us to believe that the development of a comprehensive 850,000-title data base prior to the production of the letter-press bibliographies would increase the staff to approximately 35 subject specialists, searchers, and clerks and raise the cost of the entire project to about $5,845,000 over the 13-year period or an average of nearly $450,000 a year. This figure does not include the expense of developing a specialized thesaurus and computer program or the cost of computer storage and retrieval.

Providing inclusive bibliographic service to Congress and the American people concerning our national heritage will be expensive. But improved bibliographic access can revolutionize the work habits of students and scholars, measurably increasing the quality of historical investigation and revision. Because the scholarly community has no agency or institution capable of developing, sponsoring, or administering a national bibliographic program, it is imperative that it be centralized. Certainly, the trend in automation is toward national and regional information centers capable of distributing bibliographic data through on-line communication. Many large-scale information systems in the United States are presently funded by the federal government, the best known being the Medical Literature Analysis and Retrieval System (MEDLARS) operated by the National Library of Medicine, which issues such recurring MEDLARS-based bibliographies as *Index Medicus* (an annual compilation of over 25,000 articles from 2,400 world medical journals) and the *Bibliography of the History of Medicine.* By the same token, the Library of Congress, because of its experienced staff, comprehensive collections, and technological capabilities, is now the de facto national center for the study of Americana and should accordingly assume its proper responsibility for the dissemination of bibliographic information. Where other than at the Library of Congress are there historians, librarians, and computer specialists within the same administrative framework who can address themselves to the full range of problems that must be solved if order and consistency are ever to be imposed upon the near chaos of American historical bibliography?

Appendix B: Selected Subcommittee Reports

The Task Force had 14 subcommittees: area studies, automation and reference services, bibliographic access, the bibliographic role of the Library, collection development, the cultural role of the Library, documents, loan and photoduplication services, serials management, services to Congress, services to libraries, services to staff, training and staff development, and the user survey. The roster of subcommittee members, which includes over 160 Library of Congress staff members, is in Appendix D.

Only two of the 14 subcommittee reports are presented in this volume: services to Congress and services to libraries. The chairpersons of the subcommittees were Helen W. Dalrymple and Lucia J. Rather, respectively. It is unfortunate that there is not space to include the other subcommittee reports, for each addresses an aspect of the Library's national role. The report of the subcommittee on the cultural role of the Library, for example, concludes that the Library of Congress, "building on the firm foundation provided by Congress and carefully considering both the wealth of [its] collections and its unique position as the nation's principal library," should play "a vigorous role in the nation's cultural life." That role, according to the subcommittee, encompasses four basic responsibilities: cultural leader on the national and international levels, catalyst for cultural development, educator through cultural activities, and custodian of cultural artifacts. The subcommittee's report presents 117 recommendations.

All 14 subcommittees submitted reports to the Task Force in mid-1976. These reports were considered recommendations to the Task Force. As explained in the preface to the Task Force report, the subcommittee reports contain untold numbers of excellent ideas that could not be incorporated into the Task Force's final recommendations. The subcommittee material, which counting supplementary documents totals over 2,000 typewritten pages, is available in the Library of Congress Archives. In addition, descriptions of Task Force, subcommittee, and advisory group meetings were published as appendixes to the *Library of Congress Information Bulletin* as the work progressed. Accounts are found in the 1976 issues of February 13 (A96–98), February 20 (A112–113), March 12 (A175–176), April 9 (A232–234), May 21 (A293–294), July 16 (A417–418), August 13 (A471–473), September 3 (A521–524), September 24 (A595–598), October 29 (A672–674), and December 10 (A765–768). In 1977, the January 14 (A23–24) and February 4 (A100–104) issues of the *Information Bulletin* describe the conclusion of the Task Force effort.

Report of the Subcommittee on Services to Congress

The Subcommittee on Services to Congress took as its charter the two fundamental questions asked by Dr. Daniel J. Boorstin, Librarian of Congress, in elaborating on the need for a complete review of the Library of Congress and its activities. These were: "How well are we serving the Congress? How can we better serve the Congress?"

The report that follows is the product of many hours of study and discussion on the part of the 11-member Subcommittee on Services to Congress. It points out the principal problem areas in providing improved services to Congress; we hope it will give the Task Force some good ideas to recommend to the Librarian. We appreciate the opportunity we have had to work with the Task Force in developing these recommendations. A cautionary note: the recommendations in the report do not appear in any order of priority; rather, they were inserted in logical order as the various topics were discussed.

Communications with Congress

The Subcommittee's discussion and evaluation of the principal findings drawn from the various surveys and recommendations form the basis for the observations and proposals that follow. The Subcommittee also considered two recently issued Congressional publications: *Information Resources and Services Available from the Library of Congress and the Congressional Research Service*, issued by the House Commission on Information and Facilities (known as the "Fuqua Commission") on June 14, 1976, and *Library of Congress Information Resources and Services for the U.S. House of Representatives*, issued by the Ad Hoc Subcommittee on Computers, Committee on House Administration (the so-called "Rose Report") on April 27, 1976.

The surveys of staff in the various Library of Congress departments revealed many areas where the need to improve services to Congress was clearly perceived. Although the range of suggested improvements was quite broad, several common themes appeared as the central issues around which the various individual suggestions tended to group themselves. For example, there is a common feeling, especially in the Congressional Research Service, Research and Reader Services Departments, and Law Library, that the members of Congress and their staffs are in need of a much better and more comprehensive education about the Library and the services it can provide. This expanded information program could include such elements as issuance of a special informational brochure on Library-wide services to Congress, intensified substantive public relations efforts directed at Congress from the Office of the Librarian, and more detailed on-the-spot orientation facilities specifically designed for the benefit of Congressional staff. At the same time, the Subcommittee is well aware of the dangers inherent in reaching out to the Congress. Expectations will be raised; the Library's profile will become much more visible. What is needed is a rational, commonsense explanation of the capabilities of the Library's staff and the services they are equipped to provide the Congress. A "Madison Avenue" hard-sell approach would obviously be totally inappropriate.

> **Recommendation:** That the Library embark on a systematic program of informing the Congress about the resources of the Library, the capabilities and expertise of its staff, and the services they can provide. (Other recommendations dealing with specific components of this kind of a program will be found later in this report.)

Communications with Staff and Between Departments

In a parallel fashion, many staff members surveyed—especially those from CRS—felt that the Library's staff in general was insufficiently aware of the Library's statutory obligation to serve Congress as its "Number One Client." The recurrent suggestion, accordingly, was that a program should be established to raise the consciousness of the Library's staff as a whole as to the particular needs of Congress together with increasing their understanding of and orientation toward dealing with Congressional requests. As a corollary, it was felt that the CRS staff should receive more intensive orientation about the kinds of services available to Congress from other departments of the Library.

Another motif that appeared in staff comments and suggestions was that there should be far better coordination and cooperation between the Congressional Research Service and the LC departments in every phase of their service to Congress. More will be said on these points in later sections of this report.

> **Recommendation:** That the Library undertake a systematic and continuous program of orientation, training, or retraining of Library employees so that they are made more aware of the importance of serving Congress well; and that the Library do everything it can to encourage better cooperation and coordination between CRS and the other LC departments in providing services to Congress.

Statistical Reporting Needs

Because of their fundamental roles in providing services to Congress, CRS and the Law Library regularly compile statistics on their activities. However, the Subcommittee found that the Library as a whole prepares little if any statistical data on the variety of services to its "Number One Client." There appears to be no general policy or guidelines on the kinds of statistics to be kept for all departments to follow. For the most part, statistics are of a random sort and reflect no consistent philosophy. For example, in the Processing Department, only the Exchange and Gift Division and the Order Division perform any regular services for the Congress. Both divisions keep some records of these activities—as it happens, of telephone calls received from Congressional offices. The Exchange and Gift Division, which recorded 556 calls in FY 1975 and 474 in FY 1976, reports these statistics weekly to the Assistant Director (Acquisitions and Overseas Operations) of the Processing Department. No report, however, is made of the Congressional visitors who come to the Division daily to examine and select duplicates for their offices or the use of constituent libraries. The Order Division reports Congressional telephone calls (28 calls in FY 1976, nearly all of which concerned book prices) to the Department of Research for inclusion in the latter's annual statistics. And Loan Division, which has extensive contacts with the Congress through the loaning of materials from the Library's collections, bases its statistics on the *number of items* being loaned, not on the number of Congressional requests it is responding to. The emphasis here is clearly on keeping track of the Library's materials rather than of the services provided to the Congressional client.

Where statistics on Congressional services *are* collected, then more emphasis seems to be placed on the form (telephone, letter, in-person visit) rather than on the substance of the request (what kind of information/research was needed) and the amount of time it required.

While this Subcommittee is acutely aware of the extreme complexity of statistical reporting already being conducted by the various departments and their constituent divisions, it does believe that the Task Force should examine the matter of reporting statistics on Congressional activities very thoroughly with a view to identifying those aspects of activity that should be regularly reported in statistical form. As a note of caution, the Subcommittee feels that any new statistical policy regarding Congressional services should recognize the need for simplicity and relevance, since the existing statistical work load is so great. Special care must be taken to assure that the data gathered reflect significant activity, and this is particularly true in departments whose role is peripheral in direct services to the Congress.

> **Recommendation:** That the Task Force consider the feasibility and desirability of requiring all LC departments to report statistics on their services to Congress annually to the Librarian in a simple and consistent manner. Basic elements in such a reporting system would be date of receipt of inquiry, requesting office (Member or committee name), purpose (official/legislative, staff, constituent), kind (telephone, letter, in-person), description of data requested, amount of time required to answer it, and division or section which provided the final response. Such statistics as are collected should assist the Librarian in preparing budget justifications for the annual Congressional appropriations process.

Administrative Priorities

One general item which the Subcommittee could not agree on was the matter of giving "services to Congress" top priority in all internal administrative operations of the Library. This would mean that personnel actions for LC employees dealing with the Congress would have to be processed before all others; that the broad category of "Congressional services" would have first call on supplies and equipment, on book and periodical orders, and on access to the computer; and that units of the Library serving the Congress would have top priority in terms of limited space on Capitol Hill.

While the Subcommittee felt that this might be a good idea in theory, its practical application might cause more problems than it would solve. A much more worthwhile objective, it would seem, would be to try to upgrade all administrative support services throughout the Library: for example, to provide adequate supplies and equipment to all LC personnel, to process all personnel actions expeditiously, and to expand computer services where appropriate. On the very complicated and difficult questions of space, there is no doubt that the Library administration, which is committed to service to Congress, is cognizant of the importance of keeping vital Congressional services in the Library as geographically close to its important customers as possible.

On this point, it is interesting to note that being physically near the House and the Senate was rated by CRS researchers on the CRS questionnaire as one of the most important factors in the CRS working environment conducive to developing close and productive working relationships with Congressional staff.

Heightening the Profile of the Library

As was mentioned earlier in the report, one of the recurrent themes which the Subcommittee found in the course of its investigations was the need for the Library to undertake a greater educational effort vis-à-vis the Congress. What is needed is a systematic and comprehensive approach to telling the Congress what services the Library can provide its Members, committees, and staffs.

For example, a brochure similar to "CRS Services to Congress," explaining all LC services available to Congress, would be most useful. Brochures are available in the Library now to describe particular services to readers, to the public, and to special clientele (such as "Services of the Law Library"); however, there is no comparable guide for the services provided to the Congress by the entire Library. Perhaps what is needed is a brochure for each department; however, some departments offer few direct services to Congress. [It should be noted here that a brochure on the Library's services to Congress will be distributed to the 95th Congress.]

The Subcommittee also discussed the idea of expanding and personalizing the existing tour services of the Library for Members of Congress and their constituents. Special times during the day could be set aside for Congressional tours, and special LC tour cards could be provided to all Congressional offices. This kind of arrangement now exists for tours of the FBI, the State Department, and the White House.

Another innovative service the Subcommittee discussed was the establishment of a reception center for Members, staff, and constituents, so that when they come to the Library there is some particular place set aside for them to be greeted and to be given an orientation to the Library. As part of this reception center, an innovative service that could be made available is a self-initiating slide display illustrating the services available to Members and staff, and, along with such a presentation, a checklist that the individual could fill out after watching the slide display to indicate areas of special interest in which a follow-up briefing was desired.

This kind of a presentation could also be packaged in such a way that it could be sent to Congressional offices for viewing or could be used by a Library staff member when making a presentation in a Congressional office.

[CRS has recently let a contract for a slide presentation that is comprised of four ten-minute modules describing the services which CRS provides to the Congress. This could perhaps form the core of the self-initiating display the Subcommittee is recommending; one or two modules explaining the various services offered throughout the Library, such as audiovisual services, assistance with files organization, and so forth, could simply be added to it. The CRS slide display presently being developed is not a self-initiating one; it is designed to be operated by a member of the staff so that questions could be raised spontaneously. It is, however, conceived as a presentation that can be packaged as a portable unit for use in Congressional offices.]

> **Recommendation:** That the Task Force give urgent consideration to recommending a greatly stepped-up program of public relations with the Congress. Some elements of an improved communications program were listed above: (1) a brochure describing Congressional services available from the Library; (2) a wallet-sized card giving important LC phone numbers; (3) a self-initiating slide display explaining LC services; (4) a "Congressional visitors" reception center; and (5) an expanded LC tour program. Undoubtedly, many other steps along these lines could be taken. . . .
>
> With regard to CRS, for example, the Service could probably profit from a more systematic program of liaison with the Congress at the highest management levels of the department. A two-fold purpose would be served here: The Congress would get a better idea of the unique reference and search capabilities available in CRS; and CRS management would get some valuable feedback from its users as to how well it is really meeting the needs of Congress.

Coordination of Services to Congress

Results of the Subcommittee's staff surveys and the group's recognition of the need to improve the Library's service to Congress led it to consider organizational changes. The Subcommittee generally agreed that the Library should reaffirm its commitment to priority service for Congress. Beyond this policy declaration, the Subcommittee proposes the creation of a new organizational entity located in the immediate Office of the Librarian, where it will have continuing visibility and authority.

Several organizational alternatives were considered by the Subcommittee, two of which will be discussed below, but all proposals were designed to achieve the goal of increasing the Library's awareness of priority service for Congress and improving its overall quality.

The proposed new office would work closely with CRS but would focus primarily on the services provided by other departments of the Library. An inquiry control unit like CRS's might be established to receive some inquiries directly, but it would be used primarily to receive and reassign all referrals from one department to another (mostly from CRS). Such a control unit would help achieve the standardization of the Library's reporting of statistics on services to Congress and might utilize the automated Inquiry Status System currently being developed by CRS. The Subcommittee in no way wishes to delay response time by introducing another bureaucratic layer. Hence, it recommends that calls should be received directly when the caller already knows the appropriate unit to phone. All directly received requests, however, should be reported back to the proposed office for control purposes. Such centralized control would facilitate follow-up on Congressional requests to assure a timely response.

This office might also have responsibility for selective review of information going out of all departments of the Library to the Congress to assure a high quality product and to assure that responses conform to stated Library policies. This would not apply, in substantive matters, to CRS, which was given "complete research independence" by the 1970 Legislative Reorganization Act, nor to the Copyright Office, which has the statutory authority for administering copyright law, and, by necessity, offering interpretation of its provisions. It would also provide the impetus and administrative support for a more ambitious Congressional education program, which the Subcommittee thinks is essential to improve service to Congress (see earlier recommendations in this report). . . .

This office would provide a coordinating mechanism for Library services to Congress and would assist in the development of innovative and improved services for Congress. It would work closely with all the LC departments, serving as a focal point for liaison officers in each department. It would also provide a communication center when there is disagreement over the allocation of limited internal resources (computer time, personnel support, and other administrative services) when they relate to Congressional service. In addition, such an office would provide an appropriate locus in the Librarian's office for the receipt of Congressional recommendations and complaints.

One proposal the Subcommittee considered was to create an Assistant Librarian for Congressional Services to carry out the functions enumerated above. Such an office might include two subunits: an Office for External Liaison (encompassing the functions of the present Legislative Liaison Officer) and an Office for Internal Liaison. The latter would be composed of liaison officers in each department, whose principal responsibility would be coordinating and monitoring Congressional requests in his or her department. In those departments which do not have extensive dealings with Congress, these officers would doubtless have other responsibilities as well.

Elevating the Congressional services function to this level would accomplish most of the objectives the Subcommittee thought were important if the Library is to upgrade and improve its service to Congress. There are, however, several problems with the Assistant Librarian proposal.

First, an Assistant Librarian would likely have no actual line authority over the departments, and might not be any better able to effect change than a lower-level staff person. Second, there might be confusion over the relationship between an Assistant Librarian and the Director of CRS. While some felt this was minor and could be worked out, others felt that there may be some conflict with the statutory independence of CRS. Third, there was a consensus in the Subcommittee that it would be easier to upgrade a lower-level office than to do the reverse.

An alternative proposal the Subcommittee considered was the creation of a Coordinator of Congressional Services in the Office of the Librarian to coordinate and focus Congressional services Library-wide. The Subcommittee felt that such a Coordinator could carry out all of the duties envisioned for this kind of position without some of the attendant problems of the Assistant Librarian proposal.

The Coordinator would head up a committee of departmental liaison officers which would coordinate and monitor departmental services to Congress. This committee would provide an arena for communication and coordination, for resolution of departmental conflicts, and it would recommend improvements to the departments and/or to the Librarian. The Coordinator would be expected to achieve the following objectives: to exercise control over requests going to non-CRS departments, to standardize statistical reporting, to propose innovative services, to raise the level of interdepartmental communication, to educate the Library staff on the importance of serving the Congress, and to provide the impetus for the public relations project noted above.

The Subcommittee did not resolve the question of whether this position would include the functions of the present Legislative Liaison Officer or whether this would be a separate office.

> **Recommendation:** That there be created in the Office of the Librarian an Office of Congressional Liaison and Referral, headed by a Coordinator of Congressional Services.
>
> That there be designated in each department of the Library a liaison officer for Congressional services, who, with the Coordinator, would constitute a Library-wide committee to provide a mechanism for coordinating services to the Congress.

Legal Services for the Congress

Under the present organization of the Library, service to Congress involving general legal reference and research is divided between the American Law Division of CRS and the five divisions comprising the Law Library. The American Law Division provides reference and research services strictly in American law. The Law Library handles Congressional research and reference involving foreign law as well as providing "quick" reference answers in American law. It sends materials on loan from its facilities in the Main Building and from the Law Library in the Capitol, and it is the back-up legal resources center for CRS.

The responsibilities of the American Law Division are limited strictly to Congress. The responsibilities of the Law Library are first to Congress, secondly to the other governmental agencies, and then to the legal profession and the general public.

The question in this area considered by the Subcommittee was whether Congress is best served under the present system or whether some organizational change could improve that service.

The four major alternatives presented for the Subcommittee's consideration were:

1. No organizational change should be made. The system is operating well and any changes made should be internal improvements within CRS and the Law Library.

2. Keep the status quo as far as organizational structure is concerned but attempt to improve service to Congress through a closer coordination between the American Law Division and the Law Library. This would be accomplished mainly through liaison officers and a committee that would not only seek cooperation with respect to legal services but for services throughout the Library of Congress.

3. A new legal structure should be created, i.e., a National Law Center within the Library of Congress that would centralize all legal research and reference personnel and collections, providing service to Congress and all the other patrons currently served by the Law Library. Under this concept, the legal research leadership for the entire legal community as well as for the Congress would be centralized in the Library of Congress.

4. The Law Library, as presently organized, should be discontinued. The foreign law divisions should be more closely aligned with CRS (or with the Research Department). The American aspects of the American-British Law Division would be transferred as a Law Division to the Department of Reader Services.

The first and second alternatives would involve working within the present organizational structure. The third and fourth alternatives would probably require Congressional action before either could be implemented. Regardless of which alternative might be considered most appropriate, there was a general consensus of opinion by the Subcommittee that a strengthened Law Library would result in improved service to Congress as well as to its other constituents. The manner in which this might be accomplished was presented in various direct recommendations to the Task Force. The Law Library survey also pointed out some shortcomings that could be remedied. There are problems of bibliographic control of the foreign legal materials, of greater visibility for the services of the Law Library, of more autonomy in the areas of acquisitions and processing, and of more cooperation between the attorneys in the Law Library and in the American Law Division. Many of the programs pointed out in the recommendations, including an expanded publications program and the preparation of foreign legal information data bases, would involve increased space and staff.

The Subcommittee felt that the first alternative was not the most satisfactory. There is definitely a need for improved service and to achieve it some specific action should be taken, particularly in the area of cooperation between the attorneys in the American Law Division and the Law Library. This would involve some type of interdepartmental structure.

The Subcommittee felt that the second alternative could be accomplished in the short run with a minimum of disruption of the present structure. This would mean a strengthening of the cooperation between the various law divisions through the institution of a library-wide Coordinator for Congressional Services and departmental representatives for the Law Library and CRS who would work together within the organization to improve that service.*

A strong case was presented for the formation of a National Law Center, and several of the members of the Subcommittee were favorably disposed to this concept. The merits of the increased legal research capabilities inherent in such a plan would undoubtedly redound to the benefit of Congress in the long run. However, it was felt to be beyond the mission of the Subcommittee to recommend this procedure due to its many ramifications and the need for further study in this area.

The fourth alternative had no advocates on the Subcommittee and was not seriously considered. Being a divisive rather than a cohesive plan, it would tend to diminish services.

> **Recommendation:** That the Task Force consider the creation of some formal mechanism under the general authority of the Coordinator of Congressional Services to assure that the Law Library and the American Law Division of CRS work more closely together. This would be especially valuable at the attorney/researcher level. A more thorough understanding on the part of the two departments of their respective capabilities, as well as a greater exchange of ideas between them, would undoubtedly work to the benefit of Congress.
>
> In the longer run, the Task Force may wish to suggest that an upgrading of the Law Library to make it foremost in the country would be worth a major study of its own.

Congressional Loan Policy

There is now duplication of activity in the loaning of materials to Congress. Loan Division, of course, is responsible for charging and keeping records of all materials loaned from the Library's collections—to Congress as well as to other authorized borrowers—and for maintaining the official loan lists authorizing borrowing privileges for Congressional staff members. Loan Division also undertakes special searches at the request of Congressional users.

The Congressional Reference Division of CRS also does a substantial amount of searching for Library materials for Congress's use. Confusion is apt to result when the original requester tries to track down the status of

*In this connection it is interesting to note that some progress has been made in improving CRS–Law Library communications just through the vehicle of this Task Force process. Law Library staff are now able to receive annotated bibliographic citations (SDI) from CRS; Law Library services are now mentioned in the briefings which CRS regularly gives to interested Congressional staff; and the Law Librarian met with the CRS division chiefs to explain the kinds of services his staff provides to the Congress and to its other clientele.

his request and can't find it; usually because he originally called Loan Division to request the book and is now trying to determine its status through CRS. Complete automation of Loan Division's charge records files and of the CRS Inquiry Status System would alleviate this problem somewhat, but this is not likely to come to fruition in either department for a year or two.

More important than the record-keeping aspects of the loan of materials to Congress is the necessity for understanding the particular needs and demands of the Congress. This is necessarily part of the training of employees in CRS; it is not so likely to be emphasized in the Loan Division, whose principal function is as custodian of the general collections.

> **Recommendation:** That the Task Force explore the feasibility of rationalizing the loan and searching of materials for Congress and of maintaining the lists of authorized Congressional borrowers. (These lists are currently used by CRS to try to determine which Congressional staff members are "authorized users" of LC/CRS services.)
>
> At least two alternatives should be studied: (1) to transfer this activity totally to CRS, with provision being made for the retention of centralized record keeping in Loan Division; or (2) transferring as much as possible of this kind of activity from CRS to Loan Division, with an accompanying change in training emphasis for employees providing this service, in order that they may be more cognizant of Congress's special needs and demands.

LC Reference Centers and Book Rooms

The Book Rooms and Reference Centers of the Library now come under the jurisdiction of three different departments: CRS, Law Library, and Reader Services. In recent years, the functions of most of the rooms have gradually shifted from centers for collecting books being returned to the Library to centers providing reference services for Congressional offices located in the various office buildings.

CRS now oversees three of the Reference Centers, offering reference services and the use of specialized automated equipment in three locations: Russell, Rayburn, and Longworth Office Buildings. They will shortly open a fourth center in House Office Building Annex #2 (the old FBI Building on Third Street, S.W.).

The "Congressional Section" of the Loan Division runs the Cannon Book Room and the Library Station in the Capitol (which is the outlet for the Capitol Carrier or "tube" from the Main Building of the Library). The Cannon Book Room is basically a book collection and distribution center. Capitol Station, on the other hand, provides reference services to Member and committee offices located in the Capitol which are very similar to those offered by the CRS Reference Centers, as well as providing Congressional documents to the Office of the Librarian.

The Law Library in the Capitol also provides some of the kinds of services to Congress which are offered by the CRS Reference Centers, but its emphasis is solely on legal information and research. Its only linkage is to the Law Library in the Library's Main Building.

Another quirk which this mixed administrative structure introduces concerns deliveries to Congressional offices. The CRS messengers are responsible for delivering books and CRS materials to each office, but they must ride to the various office buildings on the Central Services Division truck. Once the truck arrives at the appropriate building, the CRS messengers unload their materials, sort them in the Reference Center, and then deliver them to each office. A Loan Division employee stationed in each Book Room or Reference Center is responsible for logging books in and out of the centers. In the Cannon Building, the Loan Division employee delivers books; the CRS messenger assigned to Longworth delivers CRS materials. Deliveries to the Capitol are handled by the Loan Division, using either the Capitol carrier or a messenger. The role of the Law Library in the Capitol is limited to the loaning and delivery of its own materials to Congress.

The differing departmental philosophies of CRS and Reader Services have caused a number of strains in the delivery system over the years and have made cooperation in delivery of Congressional materials difficult from time to time.

> **Recommendation:** That the Task Force consider placing all of the Library of Congress "outposts" under the general supervision of CRS, so that their functions can be more closely aligned and their purposes—to serve Congress in an outreach capacity—can be more strongly emphasized. A unified administrative structure would also simplify the problem of getting materials delivered to Congressional offices in a timely and efficient manner.
>
> That the Task Force give special consideration to the functions of the Law Library in the Capitol, and whether its role, as specified by law, can be strengthened to better serve the Congress. This kind of a study was beyond the resources of this Subcommittee.

The Reference Machine

The Subcommittee gave serious consideration to a proposal submitted to the Task Force concerning a new LC current issues reference service of "reference machine." The basic idea of the reference machine proposal is to utilize the significant resources that have been gathered in CRS in order to respond to reference queries from Congress and to answer questions from other sources as well. The rationale is that cooperation in the use of these resources would greatly enhance the overall reference capabilities of the Library of Congress.

The Subcommittee felt that the reference machine would indeed substantially augment the reference services now rendered by the Library—especially by the Reader Services Department—to the media, the American library community, and the general public. However, a number of negative factors presenting potentially serious ramifications were identified; among them was the impact on the CRS bibliographers.

At present, these bibliographers not only index and classify all the materials which they review and select for inclusion in the various CRS files and data bases, but they also serve as librarians to the CRS research divisions. Under the proposal, the Library Services Division, of which these bibliographers are a part, would be removed from CRS along with the Congressional

Reference Division and placed in a new reference department. This would obviously mean that the CRS bibliographers would not be available to serve as librarians to the CRS research divisions. Another problem raised was that it would compound the existing problems of assigning reference inquiries involving both the Congressional Reference Division and the CRS research divisions. At the present time, though the bulk of the reference inquiries are handled by the Congressional Reference Division, a considerable number are answered by the research divisions, and some concern was expressed about the effectiveness of coordinating Member and committee reference requests. There was also concern about maintaining preeminent service to the Congress in the face of the heavy demand that would undoubtedly be generated from the public and the media—increasingly so as the service became well known. In any event, it was the consensus of the group that the whole idea goes beyond the scope of what this Subcommittee could explore in depth.

> **Recommendation:** That the proposal for a reference machine be given further consideration by the Task Force and appropriate Library officials, including an in-depth study of its pros and cons and its ramifications for CRS and for the Library as a whole. It was thought, as an alternative, that it would perhaps be sufficient to stay within the constraints of the first step outlined in the development of the reference machine on the first pages of the proposal, keeping the basic files intact in the Congressional Research Service, but, through administrative procedures, making these files available for use by certain designated staff in other departments of the Library.

Reference Consultants for Congressional Offices

On the assumption that a new Member's office is inundated with printed information, the Subcommittee proposes that the Library do more to advertise its services to Congress than to mail packets of information to all offices. To supplement the printed word, the Library could offer the services of an LC librarian or other professional who could explain the LC/CRS services available, the value of an office reference collection, assist in organizing such a collection (and distribute the CRS multilith "Working Tools for Congressional Offices"–74/221 CR), and instruct offices in various areas (i.e., staff functions, the use of Congressional Reference Centers, etc.). This position (or positions) of reference consultant could possibly be filled from the staffs of the Reference Centers which would help to increase the visibility of the centers and their value as front-line representatives of the Library. This kind of instruction is currently available from CRS upon request and is occasionally provided.

> **Recommendation:** That the Task Force consider the feasibility and desirability of making available to Members' offices on a regular basis a librarian or other professional staffer to help organize an office reference collection, to explain LC/CRS services to Congress, and possibly to help in organizing the office staff.

One caveat should be added here: the Joint Committee on Congressional Operations publishes handbooks for the House and Senate to help Members manage their offices. Advising Members and their staffs on how their offices could most efficiently be organized and managed comes very close to the jurisdiction of the Joint Committee. If any steps—other than those that could be described as purely "librarian" in nature—are seriously considered, they should be discussed with the Joint Committee before going ahead.

Projection Equipment

The Prints and Photographs Division currently provides through its Motion Picture Section screening equipment for Congressional offices and projectionists for the equipment. However, the service is not well known to the Congress, and it is a low-priority activity in the view of the Prints and Photographs Division. There is a demonstrated need for the service; indeed, a special appropriation was sought from and granted by the Congress to purchase this equipment with the proviso that it be available for Congressional use.

Recommendation: That the Task Force consider transferring this audiovisual equipment to the Congressional Research Service and that it be located in the CRS Reference Centers. Staff in the Centers could be trained to use the equipment. Careful loan records should be kept in order that the equipment can be used to the optimum.

Specialized Braille Services

A suggestion was made to the Subcommittee that the Division for the Blind and Physically Handicapped [DBPH] might offer to transcribe into braille newsletters for Members of Congress. Since these newsletters are primarily of a partisan nature, the Subcommittee does not concur with this recommendation. The Subcommittee does see merit in the Division providing transcribing services for Members of Congress in writing and receiving mail from blind constituents.

Recommendation: That the Task Force explore with the DBPH the feasibility and desirability of transcribing letters written by Members of Congress to their blind constituents.

Study Facilities for Congressional Use

At the present time, because of pressing space needs, there are very few study rooms available in the Library for Congressional use. Over the years, Congressional offices have found these facilities to be very useful.

Recommendation: When the Madison Building is occupied, consideration should be given for one tier of study rooms in the Thomas Jefferson Building being reserved for Congressional use with a reference librarian on duty. Special messenger service for the delivery of books should be provided.

Congressional Center in the Madison Building

An oral history project for former members of Congress, already under way, offers the Library an opportunity to facilitate the collection, preservation, and servicing of unique primary source material for a study of the U.S. Congress and its members. This project, begun in 1970 by an organization known as Former Members of Congress, proposes to tape-record all former Members. Twenty-five oral histories a year are projected. In the fall of 1975, the Library agreed to be the repository for the tape casettes and transcripts; and in May 1976, the Librarian was presented with the first installment.

> **Recommendation:** That the Task Force consider the ways in which this important program of collecting and maintaining the tapes from the Former Members oral history project can best be developed and publicized. A Congressional Center in the Madison Building to house not only the oral histories but also other kinds of material which may be anticipated in the future (e.g., televised debates of the House and Senate), is one alternative.
>
> In lieu of creating a whole new office to run the Center, the Task Force may prefer to recommend that existing Divisions (Music, Manuscript, Motion Picture Section of Prints and Photographs) be utilized to perform the custodial functions that this project entails. In any case, its full development will require sophisticated treatment of the material in the form of catalogs, guides, subject indexes, etc., as well as adequate personnel and facilities for its servicing.

Congressional Papers

Another innovative service which could be offered to Members of Congress is advice and assistance concerning the arrangement and disposition of their papers. On an *ad hoc* and informal basis such a service already exists. For example, staff members of the Manuscript Division are occasionally asked to visit the office of a Member and are queried about the kinds of material which should be preserved for researchers and the most appropriate arrangement of the papers to facilitate research. Other questions concern access restrictions, literary rights in the papers, guides, indexes, and the like.

> **Recommendation:** That the Task Force consider regularizing and publicizing LC assistance on arrangement and disposition of Congressional papers. This could be done by including it in the multilith on "Working Tools for Congressional Offices," as is now done for the service provided by the [Library's] Central Services Division for the setting up of office files.

Maps for Congress

Additional potential services to Congress and its committees were suggested in interviews with officials of the Geography and Map Division. For example, the Division would like to provide computer-produced thematic maps and various kinds of maps in microform. There is a great need also for detailed street maps of Congressional districts. This type of map is especially important for the large urban districts. Although the actual number of these kinds of requests received by CRS at present is relatively small (10–20 per year), there would undoubtedly be a greater call for them if acceptable maps could be provided. It is very difficult for Members in urban districts (especially if their boundaries have recently been changed) to know exactly which streets fall within their district. A large wall map of their district, including streets, would be a great help to them.

> **Recommendation:** That the Task Force give consideration to exploring with the Geography and Map Division the feasibility of providing specialized Congressional district maps for Members of Congress as well as other kinds of particularized maps that they would find useful.

Bibliographic Services

Specialized bibliographies on a wide range of topics are requested and utilized by many Members of Congress. At the present time, most of these are prepared by CRS: some by computer, some by specialist librarians, some by analysts in particular fields. However, there is a great deal of bibliographic expertise in the Library that is generally not being tapped in responding to these kinds of requests, especially in the General Reference and Bibliography (GR&B) Division of the Reader Services Department. In terms of duplication of effort, instances were cited before the Subcommittee of long, comprehensive bibliographies on the same topic appearing at virtually the same time from CRS and other departments of the Library (such as Science and Technology Division).

> **Recommendation:** That the Task Force consider at the very least some mechanism for coordinating improved bibliographic efforts for the Congress.
>
> Another alternative would be to have all noncomputerized bibliographies prepared by GR&B. However, the present focus of GR&B on perfect bibliographic form would undoubtedly have to be altered so that they could meet pressing Congressional deadlines.

Automated Services

The Library of Congress offers a wide variety of automated services to the Congress. This Subcommittee did not go into the whole area of automated services for the Congress in any great depth because so much had already been written on the subject and because other Task Force Subcommittees were considering it.

However, it is evident that the Congress will rely more and more on the Library's services in the field of information retrieval, and the Library's resources should be adequate to the ever-increasing demand. One problem area which was specifically brought to the Subcommittee's attention is that of training Congressional staff to use the computer terminals and the various information files that are available.

At the present time there are some 122 terminals in the Senate and 93 in the House of Representatives for the purpose of direct access to the information files operated in the SCORPIO information retrieval system. All Senate and House staff members using these terminals have been given their initial training by the CRS Information Systems Group (ISG). Retraining, follow-up training, and training on changes in the files in the House has been a continuing responsibility of ISG. Follow-up training in the Senate has been the primary responsibility of the Senate Computer Center. Recently, however, CRS has been advised that during the 95th Congress the Information Systems Group will be asked to take over the greater share of training and orientation activity for SCORPIO users in the Senate.

Until now, most of the training activities carried out by CRS for system users in the Senate and the House have taken place in respective House and Senate offices. During the past year, however, the number of information files in SCORPIO has almost trebled, and at least four more files will be added during FY 1977. This will result in doubling the amount of time required for initial training of new staff, and an increase in the time required for follow-up training sessions. Experience in working with the House Commission on Facilities and Information as well as with the Senate Computer Center has clearly shown that training efficiency is significantly enhanced if the training can be conducted in a classroom environment free from the many interruptions inevitable in a busy Congressional office. In addition, personnel from several offices at a time may be trained in a classroom without any loss of effectiveness from the one-on-one situation. At the same time, the limited CRS training staff is much more effectively utilized.

> **Recommendation:** That the Task Force consider the feasibility and desirability of establishing a small, centralized training facility in the Library for use in training new SCORPIO users and for follow-up training of persons already familiar with the system and its files. This kind of facility could be used not only for training Senate and House staff, but also staff of all LC departments as well. The CRS Information Systems Group could form a nucleus of experienced trainers that could be supplemented by the part-time assignment of personnel from each of the other Library departments concerned with utilization of the on-line files within SCORPIO.

Concluding Thoughts

Serving the Congress is not an easy task. The needs of individual Members, of committees, of professional staff in the Congress vary widely. Their perceptions of how those needs can best be met differ considerably.

This Subcommittee feels that the Library of Congress can help to fulfill the needs of Congress by: first, setting the pace for priority service to Congress at the highest management levels of the Library; second, undertaking to educate the Congress about the kinds of expertise the Library has and the services it can provide; third, promoting greater internal coordination with respect to services to Congress between Library departments; fourth, continually evaluating the quality and level of the Library's service to Congress; and fifth, proposing new and innovative services that would be both useful to the Congress and appropriate to the Library's role.

The Task Force is undoubtedly aware that the functions and services of the Library of Congress, as well as of the other legislative support agencies, are currently under very close scrutiny by the Congress. Some of these studies have been alluded to in earlier sections of this report; many of them have not yet been published at this writing. But once they become available, they will form a very useful body of material with respect to the needs of the Congress and their perceptions of how well the Library is meeting those needs.

A final thought: although it was made clear to this Subcommittee right from the outset that the separation of Congressional services from the Library's other functions was not to be considered, the members felt that it should at least be mentioned. The Subcommittee did not give it any real consideration. However, other groups in the Library (notably, at the moment, the Congressional Research Employees Association) have thought about it and will continue to propose it. In that light, it should be kept in mind that some people do consider it as a viable organizational alternative for providing reference and research services to the Congress.

Report of the Subcommittee on Services to Libraries

Summary

The Subcommittee recommends that the Library continue expansion of its activities as a de facto national library in the following areas: (1) cooperative building and use of data bases, (2) interlibrary loan, (3) national periodical center, (4) national reference service, (5) national referral center for multiple disciplines, (6) increased coverage of specialized subject areas and forms of material, (7) establishment of standards, (8) research in preservation, and (9) acquisition of foreign materials.

The Library should establish a systematic outreach program through workshops, internships, and consultant services. It should publicize its services more widely through a directory, a referral center, and regular columns or contributions to scholarly and research journals, brochures, and newspapers. The Library should seek ways of making its products available at a price within the financial reach of all libraries. Finally, three special projects are recommended: (1) retrospective conversion of the *National Union Catalog* into machine-readable form, (2) development of a national on-line ready-reference data bank, and (3) establishment of an Office of Library Research.

I. National Library Service

There are five general areas in which the Library of Congress as a national library should exercise leadership and guidance.

A. The Library should assume a leading role in the development of a national library network. The following activities are among those which the Library should investigate with a view to developing independently or promoting under other auspices.

1. Cooperative building and use of data bases. The Library of Congress should take the lead in establishing or promoting programs for the cooperative building and use of bibliographic data bases. Experience to date in the CONSER Project for serials and planning for the implementation of an ongoing CONSER System to be managed and operated by the Library of Congress show that such cooperative or contributed data bases require both the adoption by participants of a set of agreed-upon practices or conventions with respect to retrospective as well as currently cataloged materials, and the authentication of contributed records by a central agency. More experience is needed before determining whether decentralized input is an effective technique. Further investigation is needed to determine the feasibility of decentralized input of holdings information for the production of union lists or catalogs. Projects under way will also provide experience in the cooperative use of data bases for serials and monographs. If technically feasible and cost-effective methods are achieved, such bibliographic and holdings files should be continued or developed for monographs, serials, microform masters, federal, state and local documents, and perhaps other forms or special groups of materials. The uses of commercial data bases and cooperation with them should also be investigated.

2. An interlibrary loan system based on the bibliographic and holdings information recommended. The system should include the following capabilities:
   a. Automatic switching of requests from one source to another, according to a programmed pattern, until all known sources have been queried.
   b. Automatic feedback to the requesting library on the progress of the search.
   c. Automatic fee charging and accounting *where applicable.*
   d. Automatic collection of statistical information as a basis for regular reevaluation of the system.
   Further research and design, taking into account work already done, is urgently needed.

3. A national periodical center. The National Commission on Libraries and Information Science is investigating the establishment of a national periodical center. The Library of Congress should participate in this investigation and consider instituting or promoting a program to make photocopies or microform copies of journals and journal articles available throughout the United States. A suggested model for investigation is the British Lending Library, which produces and distributes on demand photocopies of journal articles available in the United States in a speedy and economically attractive way.

4. A national reference service operating through local, state, and regional networks. The service should be designed to answer the query at the lowest level of the hierarchy without, however, undue delay in relaying it upwards, in order to supply a response within a reasonable time. As with interlibrary loan, the system should provide interim feedback, statistical reports, and a mechanism for charging for long searches *when appropriately authorized.* The National Telephone

Reference Service pilot project at the Library should provide valuable experience as the basis for the design of an ongoing service.

5. A national referral center for multiple disciplines. Services provided by the Library through the National Referral Center for Science and Technology should be expanded, as appropriate, for other disciplines. Research is needed to determine the disciplines in which this service is most needed, and the priorities for implementation.

B. The Library should assume leadership in the provision of specialized reference services and tools for various subject areas or forms of material. Given the strength of the LC collection and reference service in specialized areas, e.g., material for the blind and physically handicapped, legislative information, foreign law, audiovisual materials, maps, music, and exotic languages, the Library should make a special effort to expand or undertake cooperative acquisition programs, cooperative cataloging programs, publication of catalogs and bibliographies, and reference services operating either directly or through regional networks to the Library of Congress. These services should be extended through the automated system when feasible, but reference and other services could be developed on a manual basis.

C. The Library should provide leadership in the establishment of standards and guidelines in cooperation with the national and international library community. Technological developments in the electronic communication of bibliographic information have brought the Library of Congress and other libraries throughout the nation and the world to the point where cooperative data-base building and sharing are economically feasible. Such transfers of bibliographic data are possible only if identical or compatible bibliographic and technical standards are used. For retrospective materials produced before the advent of standards, conventions or agreed-upon practices will be needed. Progress has been made internationally through the development of standards for bibliographic description (i.e., the various ISBDs—International Standard Bibliographic Descriptions). Much work remains to be done in choice and form of entry, subject headings, classification schedules, and holdings statements. The problem of adopting an international agreement in the area of romanization and transliteration is crucial. The Library must continue and in some cases increase its participation in the development of such standards. Progress has also been made in the development of national and international machine-readable formats and of character sets for Roman-alphabet languages. More work is needed in the development of character sets for non-Roman languages, in protocols for computer-to-computer transmission, in the standardization of bar code equipment, and in many other areas.

The Library produces position descriptions, form letters, procedural guidelines, and other administrative documents that are frequently requested by other libraries. A program should be developed to make these available on a regular basis.

D. The Library of Congress has the trained staff, the expertise, and the national recognition to provide leadership in the development of a nationwide preservation program. A concerted effort, centralized and coordinated at the national level, is needed to solve the diverse problems of individual libraries. Through leadership in the development of a national preservation program, the Library could help to ensure the existence of this country's collections for future scholars.

E. The Library should pursue systematic acquisition of foreign materials. The Library has greatly expanded its foreign acquisitions in the last fifteen years through its PL-480 and NPAC programs. These programs vastly increased our acquisitions from some areas, but they have not covered all areas equally. A review of our programs with the aim of promoting acquisitions from areas requiring better coverage should be carried out.

A study should be made on the feasibility of expanding the Library's *acquisitions* efforts to cooperate in acquiring foreign materials for research libraries. Such cooperation might include the use of LC acquisitions officers overseas to identify or purchase such materials for research libraries. The desirability and legality of such a program should be investigated.

II. Outreach

In addition to performing the functions of a national library, the Library should establish a systematic outreach program to share its services and experience with other libraries and librarians.

A. Advanced institutes and workshops in librarianship/information science. Since many of the Library's staff members are skilled in the various aspects of library science, workshops could be held periodically at convenient locations throughout the country for outside librarians and library educators. The workshops, staffed by LC personnel, could be a forum for the exchange of ideas between both groups. General areas of interest for discussion at workshops could be LC automation and its influence on other libraries; career planning and placement, focusing on advancement and future employment; studies on modifications to classification systems and cataloging rules; and thorough explanation of the copyright revision bill and its impact on all libraries, stressing the use of photocopying, etc.

B. The Library could sponsor short-term internships in special disciplines and subject areas. Scheduling librarians (school, public, academic) for short-term internship programs on a regular and ongoing basis would serve to keep both the librarians and the Library of Congress staff abreast of innovations in the library field. Internships in special subject areas would also give outside librarians an opportunity to observe the Library's system and perhaps adopt its methods wherever feasible in their own libraries. This could be accomplished through apprenticeships in which an outside librarian works closely with a Library staff member in a special area. Parallel exchange programs could be designed by the Library of Congress and other large libraries to give participants greater experience and knowledge in various techniques.

C. Through consultant services, the Library could make its knowledge and expert skills available to others in foreign languages, copyright, services to the blind and visually handicapped, government documents, automation, multimedia cataloging, and storage and management skills. In response to expressed demand, Library staff could be available to analyze and evaluate existing programs, and to make recommendations as appropriate; the staff might also assist in writing program plans or proposals upon request. The costs for such services, who would pay for them, etc. should be investigated. Explanatory brochures on the Library's consulting services, including lists of subject areas covered and procedures for requesting consultants, should be made widely available. This would be especially helpful for libraries interested in subject areas unique to the Library of Congress.

D. The Library of Congress, within the framework of its outreach programs, should develop a procedure for regular and systematic planning and review of all services that it provides to libraries, professional organizations and societies, research, academic, and similar institutions. Responsibility for review should rest with the various divisions and departments providing the particular service. However, a central coordinating agent or office would need to direct the operations to ensure consistency and compliance.

In conjunction with the recommended overall review and planning, the Library should establish or devise a procedure for soliciting and obtaining from the clientele an appraisal of the nature, utility, and efficacy of the services the Library provides. Service evaluation feedback would be in the form of suggestions, criticisms, observations, etc., and would be expedited by the central agent or office mentioned earlier.

E. Further, in keeping with the program of open, responsive dialogue on the Library's services, a means for sharing experiences and ideas with other interested institutions should be established. For instance, the Library of Congress could disseminate information about ongoing research in the Library and publish technical papers and advisory reports on preservation, reference services, and library equipment. In short, the Library of Congress ought to move aggressively into participatory librarianship by widening the channels of communication between itself and its clientele and encouraging suggestions and criticism.

III. Publicity

A. The Library should publicize its services to libraries through a directory, updated regularly. The format should be looseleaf to allow for selective updating, additions, and changes. It should include a description of services, contacts for further information, printed sources, prices, etc. Indexes should provide access to the services by subjects, forms of materials, and activities, in addition to the office or division furnishing the service. The office assigned to maintain and publish the directory should regularly solicit up-to-date information from each division and office to ensure timely publication of update sheets or new editions, and the directory should be made available to the Library staff and the community at large by direct purchase, subscription, etc., since it should serve the information needs of Library staff, visitor users, and libraries and organizations outside the Library both in this country and abroad.

B. A referral service should be developed to provide Library staff and outside users access to offices and divisions responsible for developing or maintaining specific services or products. The referral service could be querying by telephone or online to determine the latest information on services already in existence or under development. Referral service staff could update the directory between editions or updates and ensure that outside and inside suggestions for services not yet devised reach the responsible office or division directly on a timely basis. The referral service would enhance the Library's role as a clearinghouse for library and research information by systematically channeling and capturing questions and ideas. The office assigned to handle the referral service should disseminate it among libraries and institutions in a formal and systematic manner to ensure the best and most appropriate use, and the office assigned to Library planning could systematically utilize the referral service input.

C. The Library should take a more active role in publicizing its services in the library and research community by working with editors of library and research journals to establish regular columns or contributions. These should serve both to establish and to broaden an awareness of the Library's resources and services. For example, the *American Libraries* feature "The Source" has columns on such things as ALA General News, Reference, Young People, Education, and Special Services. The Library might submit articles regularly to "The Source."

D. The Library should systematically develop and update brochures to provide an effective means of alerting potential users to specific Library of Congress services, both existing and newly created. Up-to-date, informative, and attractive brochures are timely, cost-effective responses to telephone, letter, and personal requests for information; they have high impact as handouts at conventions, meetings, and workshop displays. Each brochure proposal should be accompanied by a plan or program that provides for effective design, coordinates the individual brochure design with other related brochures in terms of text and illustrations, and identifies the audiences to which the brochure is directed and the schedule for updating and reissuing the brochure.

Brochure design should highlight both the unique characteristics of a service *and* the relationship of the service to a larger or related system or program; design should allow use of brochures separately or in groups, depending on communication goals. Offices or divisions responsible for services or products should play a key role in the development and updating of brochures, and the office assigned responsibility for the directory file and publication of the directory should participate in, if not coordinate, the development and updating of brochures. Use of techniques developed by commercial advertising agencies should be studied and implemented, as appropriate, and libraries and users should be selectively used to test the effectiveness of brochures and provide sources of new ideas and techniques for their improvement.

E. The Library should develop a special publication aimed at Library of Congress patrons and the library community. *Library of Congress Information Bulletin* (*LCIB*) serves both as the Library of Congress house organ and as a communications device to the library community. Because it is aimed at two different audiences with different needs and interests, it may be that *LCIB* serves neither audience well. Consideration should be given either to reformatting *LCIB* to include articles and bibliographies aimed at informing the library community about the Library's resources and services or to creating a separate LC publication for the library community. For example, one section (or separate publication) could be a staff newsletter including news of awards, personnel changes, in-house changes, more staff action photographs, events, etc. Another section (or separate publication) might contain items contributing to a "national library profile," e.g., meeting reports, service developments, bibliographies, improved and expanded information on new publications, etc.

F. The Library should establish a speakers' bureau. The Library of Congress has a wealth of subject specialists and experts in areas of concern to the library community. Staff members have formal and informal contacts and they frequently speak at seminars, workshops, consortia, and professional meetings. The library community, however, needs more widespread and better organized information about the human resources of the Library. A list of available staff specialists and their areas of expertise should be compiled, and its availability publicized widely in the library and research communities.

IV. Reducing Charges for Services

In order to make its services more widely available, the Library should issue the *National Union Catalog* on a more current basis and at a much lower price, possibly in microform, so as to place the *NUC* and the information it contains within the financial reach of all libraries. The Monographic Series card catalog now located in Building 159, Navy Yard Annex, Catalog Distribution Service (CDS), should be issued in an inexpensive printed or microform version financially accessible to *all* libraries.

Further, the Library should investigate the possibility and desirability of changing the 1902 federal statute governing the sales of the Library's cataloging to outside libraries, agencies, and individuals. The prices of all cataloging cards, proofsheets, book catalogs, technical publications, MARC tapes, computer printouts, online searches, etc., are set by this statute, which requires a return on such services of cost plus 10 percent. The investigation would determine if there are some desirable and practical alternatives for selling and distributing the Library's cataloging and classification for the benefit of the American library community. In view of rising postage and printing costs, the basis for determining the charges made to American libraries and librarians should be reviewed in depth. It may well be that the future of the American library system is determined by the price for such bibliographic services provided by the Library of Congress.

V. Other Projects

A. After the members of the Humanities Advisory Group had seen a demonstration of the capabilities of our computerized catalog, they turned to the Deputy Librarian to ask when the world's literature published before 1968 would be put in the system. Later discussions underscored their strength of feeling. A group of LC study facility holders reacted in precisely the same way. The user survey revealed that those doing historical research make up our largest category of users. Probably the same is true of other research and academic libraries. It is thus understandable that these users should aspire to the same powerful bibliographic machinery available to researchers using current materials. The Processing Department has established a list of computer-cataloging priorities suitable to the Library as a maker and distributor of current cataloging information to libraries. It is not adequate for the Library as the nation's supplier of bibliographic information to libraries serving the humanistic and historical researcher.

We therefore recommend that the Library undertake a cooperative project, similar to CONSER or COMARC, to put the entire *National Union Catalog* in machine-readable form. Perhaps several hundred research libraries would be required to assist and a generation needed to accomplish the job. The Library of Congress should provide the leadership to begin this task as soon as possible.

B. Reference librarians notoriously rediscover the wheel—or at least the name of George Washington's horse or the provenance of Lincoln's ten points—many times a year. Steps have been taken to minimize duplication— e.g., a column in *RQ*, shared form letters—but nothing could be quite so effective toward this end as a national online, ready-reference data bank. Ephemeral quotes, persistent myths, and topical trivia could all be entered and key words indexed with sources identified. Just as catalogers have for generations shared each other's work, so now an effective technique exists for sharing the work of reference librarians! The Library could "validate" the OCLC-like input of reference librarians throughout the nation and make available the findings to all.

C. Research in library technique and technology has in the past received paltry and sporadic support, e.g., occasional grants from CLR and peripheral research by manufacturers. It is surely appropriate for the Library of Congress as a national library to establish a well-financed permanent office to further knowledge in these two fields. Precedents for both can be found. The Library has undertaken research in preservation, automation, and technical processing. What remains is to expand and rationalize that which is already begun. Among many other topics, book retrieval, library security systems, teaching machines in library orientation, and the techniques of reference work all deserve detailed scientific investigation. We recommend that toward this end the Library establish an Office of Library Research, with one arm responsible for library technology (including auto- mation and preservation) and the other for library techniques. Each would support a research unit and a national clearinghouse. The clearinghouse could collect and distribute the reports of research done or to be done, anywhere. Thus the Library's research and that of other libraries could be fully utilized.

Appendix C: Advisory Group Reports

The generosity of several private foundations enabled the Library to enlist the help of eight outside advisory groups, chosen to represent the Library's various constituencies. The groups and their chairmen were: Arts, Patrick Hayes, Managing Director, Washington Performing Arts Society; Humanities, Jaroslav Pelikan, Dean, Graduate School, Yale University; Law, Phil Neal, Professor, University of Chicago Law School; Libraries, Robert Wedgeworth, Executive Director, American Library Association; Media, David Schoumacher, WMAL-TV, Washington, D.C.; Publishers, Dan Lacy, Senior Vice-President, McGraw-Hill, Inc.; Science and Technology, Gerard Piel, Publisher, *Scientific American*; and Social Sciences, W. Allen Wallis, Chancellor, University of Rochester. A total of 75 distinguished individuals from the United States, plus four from abroad, served as advisors. A complete list is in Appendix D.

All eight advisory group reports are included in this appendix. Each addresses questions pertinent to the Library's legislative and national roles, and several are also concerned with the institution's international role. The reports are unedited. As might be expected under the circumstances, two or three of the reports contain minor errors or misunderstandings regarding the Library's various functions. None however is serious. What is remarkable is that the members of the advisory groups, most of whom had never before visited the Library, gained such a thorough understanding of the institution within the confines of the one-year deadline and their own busy schedules.

The advisory groups were completely independent. Each met formally at the Library at least twice, and several three times. In addition, informal meetings were held in several cities. At the request of the advisory group chairmen, the Task Force chairman attended all formal meetings, keeping the groups informed of the activities of the Task Force and its subcommittees. Formal advisory group meetings were described, along with Task Force and subcommittee meetings, in various issues of the *Library of Congress Information Bulletin* (see the opening text to Appendix B).

1. Report of the Arts Advisory Group

Chairman's Comments

The Library of Congress is both the Library of the Congress of the United States and a national library.

It is a source of information for the world and a repository of knowledge and recorded history.

It fulfills primary functions of reference with books, prints, maps, musical scores, films, recordings, manuscripts—in the millions and millions of items.

In two fields the Library of Congress plays an activist role. The Music Division presents chamber music concerts for general audiences. The Research Department presents evenings of poetry readings, also for a general audience. These events are broadcast.

Now, in 1977, under a new Librarian of Congress, the Library is asking itself and many interested citizens for an analysis of where it is and in what possible new directions it should be going.

Arts Advisory Group members have written their thoughts and recommendations and criticisms. In the report now submitted, the panel comments fall readily into the categories of "Immediate," "Soon," "Eventually," or "For Further Search and Study."

This report, like the Boorstin era at the Library of Congress, is a beginning.

The Arts Advisory Panel met with the Librarian of Congress and his Task Force staff on two occasions in late 1976, early September and early November. The findings of many of the panel's members are set forth in the following pages.

The discussions of the panel on the two dates of meeting were lively, often provocative, and, on a major point or two, inconclusive. Our search was one for definition, definition of purpose, goals, projects, methods. Our questions dealt with what is primary, what is secondary, what is merely desirable. What if anything new should be undertaken? How can the old be enlivened as well as preserved?

The Library of Congress finds itself in the same city as the Folger Shakespeare Library, the National Archives, and the Smithsonian Institution. Clear definition and separation of materials and objectives are subjects which this panel is grateful not to have to deal with over the long run, and we wish the Librarian and his entire staff well in handling.

Those of us new to the world of libraries searched for the fine line between the repository role of the Library of Congress and its producing role. Its repository role is clear in all of its divisions. Its producing role is evident in the public concerts of the Music Division and the poetry readings of the Research Department. Consideration of possible future projects in theater and dance was discussed by the panel with the public stance of the Music Division in mind.

Some members of the panel, not all, see no conflict between the repository role and the producing role of the Library of Congress in the fields of theater and dance.

Noting that many suggestions of new paths to follow and objectives to pursue may prove well nigh irresistible, nevertheless the danger of proliferation should be heeded. There is just so much space, so much staff, so many staff hours and so many staff brains. And always there is just so much money.

The Arts Advisory Group saw its work as a beginning, in the spirit of the Librarian's own philosophy for his era at the Library of Congress. The members of the panel clearly enjoyed their role. Anyone with a mind enjoys being asked for his opinion. As the panel's suggestions are considered and perhaps framed for action, caution is urged that all present multiple services and activities of the Library of Congress be maintained at full strength and built up where necessary, as in the need of proper space for precious prints and for a good and commodious move of the Music Division into the Madison Library.

A current phrase on the Washington scene is "If it ain't broke, don't fix it." Clearly, from even a cursory observation, there are some things about the Library of Congress today that, if not broke, are not completely fixed and are in need of fixing. It is hoped that the comments and ideas and recommendations in the following report will be helpful.

Introduction

As a repository of knowledge, the Library of Congress is one of the greatest institutions in the world. It is rather exciting to consider its responsibilities and the dedication to its ideals of those who are involved in it. The Library has set up advisory groups in connection with the Librarian's Task Force on Goals, Organization, and Planning in order to sample the opinion of its various constituencies with the hope that they will suggest bold new ideas for the operation of the institution. Some users of the Library feel that the main concern of the Library should be to do the old things better. There may even be apprehension lest newly formulated goals deflect energy and money from traditional basic tasks.

As it now stands, the Library is already a creative force in American society. Any attempt to make it assume the role of stimulating creativity more consciously or more explicitly runs the danger of leading to the encouragement of academic art. What the Library needs is to make more widely known what it does, what it has, and what services it offers.

Despite problems of scale, the Library of Congress has provided the nation with remarkable guidance along with access to an impressive array of cultural resources. How can it more effectively encourage research and creativity in the interest of Congress and the nation? The role of the Library of Congress as cultural leader is presently unclear.

The Arts Advisory Group has identified a number of areas where the Library should move forward in this role. We have organized our thoughts and comments within these areas of concern.

Dance and Theater Material

In its role as the national library, the Library of Congress must assume the responsibility for preserving and documenting the cultural history of our nation. At present, the Library is doing a splendid job in the areas of music, prints and photographs, and motion pictures but, sadly, has neglected the areas of dance and theater. Within the "tradition of tradition," it seems self-evident that LC should establish dance and theater collections by analogy with the Music and Prints and Photographs Divisions of long standing. Hopefully, they will be as innovative in developing ways of preserving essential data as the older arts divisions were in pioneering the collection of sound recordings and films.

Organization

In developing an organizational and functional structure for establishing new arts units in the Library, one could hardly find a more apposite model than the LC Music Division. Theater and dance units should be planned for location as near as possible to the Music Division, as proximity would increase opportunities among the divisions for taking advantage of their natural, mutual affinities in an easily cooperative manner. If the Library decides to investigate the feasibility of subject units in these fields, it is reasonable to project a study period of three or more years to reach a pragmatic conclusion. It might be practical to seek funds for such a feasibility study from the National Endowments and from private funding sources.

In the music, theater, and dance collections of a large research library, the activities and techniques involved with each subject are significantly similar and interrelated. Characteristics of the three performing arts may be sufficiently similar to warrant grouping them together within the Library to form a performing arts division. This should be considered, however, only after theater and dance units have been formed and are functioning.

It is essential that professional theater and dance administrators be engaged by the Library to plan and direct the activities of these organizational units. We do not presume to recommend a list of candidates at this time, but do strongly recommend that the principle be considered.

LC should consider establishing an office to survey and document arts activities in the United States. Staff members should be sent to document activities (performances) and resulting material deposited in the Library.

Collection Development

A top priority in launching these units is the necessity to identify all dance and theater material in the Library's collections and to index (if not catalog) these materials. A survey of the main stacks should be conducted in classes GV1580–1789 to identify dance material and in classes PN1600–3299 and PQ for theater and drama. Subject guides should be created which include cross-indexing of related material in special collections throughout the Library.

Catalogs of copyright registrations in classes B, C, D, and G should be examined for the last 10 years and, if possible, the deposits in these classes should be examined and culled if they have not been destroyed or placed in special collections. A carefully formed policy should be established for selecting from continuing copyright deposits, unless a decision is made automatically to accept for the Library all pertinent deposits. The possibilities for collecting unique materials in these fields should be assessed with great care.

A comparison should be made with similar collections in other large research libraries. Identification of important gaps in dance and theater collections in other institutions by this comparison would permit formulation of an acquisition plan. A clear conception of availability, especially of unique materials, would be a prerequisite for determining what might be obtained through deposit or gift. Failing these approaches, requests for purchase funds from Congress, foundations, or individuals would need to be estimated on the basis of materials still available. In seeking special funds one could profitably study approaches that have been employed in obtaining the several endowed funds for the Music Division of the Library.

Commissioning New Works

Commissioning new dance and theater works using special funds, with the proviso that drafts, manuscripts, designs, etc., be deposited in the Library, could become a significant means of acquiring unique items. Commissions should go to young but worthy playwrights, choreographers, performers, and designers as well as to artists already established in their fields.

Master List of Dance Collections

Discrete collections of significant dance material exist in various locations around the country, but there is no master listing of these locations nor contents of these collections. LC should take the initiative in compiling such a listing for distribution to libraries or other interested parties. Great care should be given to developing a good working relationship with all extant owners of collections of theater and dance material.

Performances

We urge that performances in both theater and dance be considered a part of the Library's outreach program, but emphasize that these performances must reflect the goals and objectives of the Library and have direct and appropriate connection to the LC collections.

Revivals of plays of importance in the history of theater, but not necessarily "good box office," could figure in the Library's program. If based on important or otherwise valuable editions owned by the Library, scholarly publications of these plays could be financed by special funds.

Recommendation: In order to make better use of the Library's holdings in theater and dance, we recommend that the Library investigate the establishment of dance and theater custodial units either as separate divisions or sections within the Music Division as it now exists. The latter arrangement may eventually lead to the creation of a performing arts division.

We also recommend the immediate identification of all dance and theater material in the Library's collections, and the indexing (if not cataloging) of this material.

Certainly any broad program to make better use of the LC collections will include a much expanded relationship with museums as well as libraries and institutions of the performing arts.

Visual Arts

By virtue of the size and richness of its collections, the Library of Congress is a major national resource for the visual arts. Its collections invite research in art using extraordinary primary and secondary source materials, and appreciation and understanding of art through the display and publication of original works of art. This wealth of resources is to be found in non-book materials—manuscripts, drawings, fine prints, historical prints and posters, photographs, and motion pictures—as well as in the more traditional library formats—books, journals, and catalogs.

The separation of material by format which exists in the Library gives LC's art collections too low a profile. The visiting artist, art historian, or architecture student who is not already familiar with the compartmentalization of LC will surely be daunted by the seeming absence of an "art division," and may overlook important resources here in his search for material in several formats.

> **Recommendation:** It is recommended that the Library of Congress provide greater visibility of, and access to, its outstanding fine arts collections by identifying the "art division" that is implicit in parts of the present Prints and Photographs Division. The N class stack should remain near the division reading room, as it has been, and art books and journals should be placed in the custody of the Prints and Photographs Division, allowing the books to be serviced primarily through the division reading room. If at all feasible, the TR collections of books on photographs should also be shelved near, and serviced through, the division. The division should be renamed accordingly to become, e.g., "Art, Prints, and Photographs Division" or "Art and Visual Materials Division."

This is not a recommendation to break apart the present P&P Division, but rather a proposal to restructure it with a clearer articulation of the "art" elements in it.

The following comments are predicated upon the development of a re-structured "Art, Prints and Photographs Division" in the new Madison Building of the Library of Congress:

Staffing for this ideal division is one of the most important factors, and should include subject specialists in art, architecture, and photography, as well as American history specialists. The duties of the specialists would include: providing reference assistance to library users; reviewing and recommending art publications for acquisition; cataloging the visual materials that are regularly processed in the division; and conferring on occasion with the staff of the Processing Department on matters of art cataloging and classification for the book collection.

Hours of service in the division reading room would need to be extended to include evenings and weekends, with a subject specialist reference librarian on duty during those times. The reading room should be equipped with a fuller collection of reference books on art and architecture than P&P now has, and a complete catalog of the reference collection located nearby. CRT terminals complete the list of necessary reference tools.

Cataloging of the art book collections at LC seems to be under relatively satisfactory control. By contrast the collections of the prints and photographs need fuller cataloging if the researcher is to be able to find all that is available in his area of concern. Recent improvements in color processes for the production of microfiche, and increasing acceptance of fiche as a vehicle for fine arts publication, make this a potentially useful medium. Might not the visual collections housed in P&P be cataloged and then recorded on microfiche for study and dissemination?

The Library is taking a lead in the American library community in matters of preservation technology for paper, books, and film. The knowhow is there, or is being developed in LC's laboratories, but the actual treatment of thousands of items needing attention cannot keep up with present demands. The Library must secure additional staff and funding for preservation of all these media if countless national treasures are not to be lost.

All comments made here are made with the assumption that the Library of Congress intends to maintain (and improve) its strong art collections, for the benefit of the research community not only in Washington, D.C., but all across the nation. This is one of our basic recommendations. Washington, D.C., however, has a number of specialized art libraries, and there may well be some specific areas in which LC and these libraries will not want to compete or to duplicate holdings. The Library's role as the "national art library" should take these institutions into account, and coordination of collections and services must be considered.

In this regard, the Library of Congress should draft in some detail a written collecting policy statement for art, architecture, and related visual resources. The statement should be made available to the entire library community, with an understanding that such a policy must always be subject to change or reinterpretation.

Two visual media which have so far escaped comprehensive inclusion in the Library of Congress are videotape and 35mm color slides of works of art. The feasibility of their inclusion now ought to be investigated, with provision for both preservation and full cataloging.

Motion Picture Collection

We feel very strongly that the Motion Picture Section in the Library of Congress should be changed to the Division of Motion Pictures and Television. The importance of these two media in the cultural life of our country and the necessity for giving them individual concern and attention justify this change in the organizational structure of the Library.

Acquisition of Nonfilm Material

We would hope that the motion picture and television activities in the Library will be broadened to include the acquisition of more nonfilm material such as scripts (in various drafts), clippings, censorship records, stills, set designs, corporate records, film outtakes, and other materials that have not been copyrighted or otherwise deposited in the Library. This would also include records of programs and exhibitions at film centers around the country and other materials which would be valuable to researchers using the motion picture and television collection. The Library should also consider actively acquiring and displaying technical apparatus illustrating the history of motion pictures and television.

Motion Picture Preservation Program

As commendable as the motion picture preservation program is at the Library, there is an important area in which it has fallen behind dramatically. The Library does not have adequate storage facilities for its color films or videotape. Some extraordinary effort must be made to build these facilities as soon as possible since both of these kinds of material will disappear if not adequately preserved and stored.

Proposed Film Series

A number of thoughts have been given to ways in which the Library might present film series either at the building or via the Public Broadcasting System. As much as we are in favor of extending the availability of the Library's collections to the public, it must be kept in mind that these collections have been greatly enhanced by copyright deposits. If agreement of deposit which restricts public showing of motion pictures is not guaranteed, the Library's ability to acquire this material may be endangered.

There are, however, special film series and film lectures which could be offered when closely related to the LC collections and especially to those materials which are esoteric. In this way, the lectures and the screenings will not be in competition with the commercial interest of the motion picture industry, its producers, exhibitors, or distributors and, therefore, would not endanger the acquisition program.

Motion Picture Consultant

We recommend that the Library consider the possibility of appointing a consultant in motion pictures and television. The day-to-day operations and immediate problems of the Motion Picture Section require the full attention of the staff. A consultant would have the time to plan, develop policy, devote attention to acquisitions and to the promotion of bibliographic projects and research. The same person might coordinate the lecture/film series.

Motion Picture Space in Madison Building

We are dismayed with the plans for the Motion Picture Section as outlined in the Madison Building blueprint. There simply has not been adequate provision for space for the section in what is hopefully a building that will serve the Library's needs for the next 50 years. We urge that every effort be made to increase the space allotted or to move the motion picture reference collection to another floor. As outlined, there is inadequate office, reading, film study, and storage space, and no provision has been made for space for viewing and cataloging the various formats of television material.

Motion Picture Cataloging

The present system for cataloging motion pictures in the Library of Congress is inadequate. As commendable as it is for the Motion Picture Section to have a complete listing of its collection by title—something that almost no other film archive can claim—the real need is for an indexing system with multiple access. Most film research of any substantive nature requires that the researcher be able to enter the collection through other means, such as director, genre, production company, year, country, etc. As we understand, work has been done to make material in the Kleine and Roosevelt collections more readily accessible by cross-indexing, but great attention should be given to gearing up to include the entire motion picture collection. Serious scholarship can occur in motion pictures and television only when this multiple access provides the key to unlocking the collections.

Intern Program

We should like to see the Library consider an intern program which would place students/researchers in the Motion Picture Section for several months and then in the Museum of Modern Art for another five or six months. These individuals, having served in two of the most important archives in the country, would acquire experience in film study as well as in programming, study center activities, and in public education programs. They would be well qualified for positions in the various film archives in the United States.

Outreach

The Library should explore the possibility of sending to regional centers via cable prints of the motion pictures and television works in its collections. Just as it is desirable to create regional centers with video terminals that allow direct access to print materials in the Library, the possibility of making LC motion picture and television holdings available is very attractive. However, this is a very sensitive area and must be explored with great care and attention.

> **Recommendation:** We recommend that the Library establish a division of motion pictures and television to put the motion picture archive on a level with the other arts division in the Library. Holdings in this area should be expanded by the acquisition of related nonfilm material. The motion picture preservation program must be expanded to include adequate storage facilities for color films and videotape.
>
> We urge the Library to consider new ventures in the field of motion pictures and television, including the appointment of a motion picture consultant and the creation of a film series for public showing, an intern program, and a cable link to regional film centers. Indexes to the Library's motion picture collection must be improved to foster substantive film research and the inadequate space allotted for motion pictures in the Madison Building must be reviewed.

Music Division

Collection Development

A massive drive should be made to get a better and more complete representation of recordings made before the 1950s in the music collections of the Library. After that date, the collection is more than adequate, but the historical importance of recordings made before 1950 cannot be overrated. Priority perhaps should be given to recordings made in the United

States, but a representative collection of foreign recordings is equally important. This is a weakness that can be overcome only if funds are set aside in the very near future while material is still available for acquisition.

Manuscript Holdings

The manuscript holdings of the Music Division are not adequately cataloged. It is understandable that the Library of Congress should give priority to the cataloging which serves all U.S. libraries, but it is defeatist to rest with that. The unique holdings of the Library's special collections are a part of the national heritage as well. Their use is restricted until they are adequately described and indexed. Cataloging of the music manuscript collections should be undertaken energetically, and these collections should be publicized with the hope of attracting scholars to admire and use them.

Collection Maintenance

On our tour of the Music Division, we observed a large number of bindings in a poor state of repair. One would hope that each division of the Library would have an expert in restoration and repair attached to that division. (The division, which often knows best what kind of repair is needed, loses control over the repair process when material is removed from its custody.) It is tragic when very beautiful manuscripts have bindings that are beginning to crumble. In many cases, the state of deterioration is beyond repair, but with immediate attention to the matter there is hope for saving many treasures.

Performances

The role of serving some of the cultural needs of the Washington, D.C. community has, over the years, gradually devolved upon the Library. We do not think this responsibility should be altered or shirked. The concerts sponsored by the various foundations administered through the Library are an example.

The prestige of chamber music (and we refer here to the programs sponsored by the Coolidge Foundation) depends upon its being heard live. If the concerts are to reach out to the rest of the country, it should be by some means other than the makeshift of broadcasting. With the rising production costs of concerts, any attempt to go outside the Washington, D.C., area will mean finding additional funds. The effect of the Library putting its weight behind such a move would have an incalculably powerful effect on other centers of the country which both need and want music, but do not have the means to subsidize it.

Programming

The Library's concerts have, as we have pointed out, great prestige, but they have come to seem staid and unadventurous. This situation can be remedied by (1) adventurous programming of unusual or rarely performed works, and (2) more massive programming of series. (On the whole, unusual programs work best in a series.)

Collaboration with the Smithsonian Institution would seem an obvious move. They have the collection of old instruments, LC the music and recordings. Symposia, lectures, and programs would all be appropriate for cooperative effort.

> **Recommendation:** In order to strengthen its music collection, the Library must identify weaknesses which exist and focus acquisitions efforts accordingly. Cataloging of music material must be improved with special attention directed to bibliographic control of music manuscripts.
>
> The Library must strive to present more lively and challenging concerts through adventurous programming in its chamber music series. In addition to the established concert series, the Library should investigate cooperating with other institutions and organizations to sponsor and present symposia, lectures, and programs relating to the LC music collections.

Information Retrieval

The computerization of the Library has fascinating possibilities, though the project is still embryonic. We urge the Library to continue and expand its automation activities and to consider the retrospective computer cataloging of pre-1968 material.

As technology and finance permit, the Library should introduce computer stations to other libraries and information centers outside the Washington, D.C., area or, at the least, to offer access to its data bases and other computer services. Ideally, every American community of 100,000 or more should have an information retrieval outlet with a direct link to the Library of Congress.

We hope that the Library's computers will someday be able to tell us not only what is to be found in other U.S. libraries, but in foreign libraries as well.

> **Recommendation:** We urge the Library to continue and expand its automation activities and to study the feasibility of making its computer services available to libraries throughout the United States.

Arts Center

The concept of an "arts center" in the Library was introduced during the first meeting of the Arts Advisory Group. The question of the appropriateness of an arts center in a library was raised at that time. Even apart from the philosophical question of whether the best way to foster the arts is centralizing them in Washington, D.C., it seems a mistake for the Library to divide its energies by the increased assumption of "arts center" activities. These activities are essentially local in orientation and other organizations can do and perhaps are doing them better.

It is one thing to nurture new programs in themselves, and yet another to view them as pilots for the extended "arts center" concept. It seems quite important for LC to set up a businesslike, expert committee to review new LC programs specifically with a view to seeing which elements of them should or should not be taken as precedents for future programs. LC should not get further into arts programming for programming's sake. The only legitimate rationale for everything LC plans in the area of public programming should be to increase interest in and foster greater utilization of its own vast resources.

Projected LC "arts center" activities have been referred to as local in orientation, although there have been efforts in the past to provide for "outreach." Even with more successful outreach than we believe possible, the main thrust of an LC "arts center" would be to the Washington, D.C., area. From outlying areas, it is hard to drum up enthusiasm for draining off the energies of what is thought of as a *national* library in this way. Perhaps we must accept the fact that performing activities in Washington, D.C., will never radiate out to the country at large to any great extent. One can make available sound and video recordings of musical and staged events, but this is a pale simulacrum of the real thing and the people in the provinces know it.

We have difficulty with the notion of a great *library* as the natural force for a great center for the arts, at least in their contemporary manifestation. Other types of institutions—or perhaps no type of institution at all—would seem to be more appropriate. It is uncertain that the arts ought to be centered at all. The arts have proved to be increasingly unpredictable in form and context in this century so that the maximum imagination and the maximum flexibility are required to deal with them sensibly. A library with 84 million items and a staff of 4,600 cannot be all that light on its feet.

> **Recommendation:** We recommend that the final report of the Task Force affirm strongly the priority of "library" functions at LC in the broad areas of the arts, over "arts center" activities. The Library should consider its role as the national library, and, therefore, the repository of the cultural life of our country. Emphasis should be on obtaining and documenting our culture and not on creating a center for the performing arts.

New Programs and Services

The recurrent question of how far the Library should move in new directions is bothersome. Some group members share misgivings that major new programs will absorb staff energy which should be expended on current projects, or that they will conflict with or duplicate programs and materials elsewhere.

There is an awesome proliferation of programs at the cultural institutions of Washington, D.C., which should be considered by the Library in expanding its own horizon of activity. While not necessarily the controlling factor in a decision to go ahead with new projects in the arts, the possibility of duplication and undue division of the public's attention is a reality. Certainly film programming will take into account the nature and number of films and their devotees at the National Archives and the American Film Institute. New music recitals will be viewed in their local as well as national context, and somebody will have to decide to what extent new LC print reproductions will compete with those offered by the National Gallery. In a situation where the Folger Library has advanced from rare volumes and memorabilia to drama, concerts, and art and most other institutions reach beyond their traditional interest, the day has passed when any one institution can expand its activities unilaterally with some promise of profit and constructive mission.

The Arts Group feels that the preamble to every plan involving a new activity should resolve the question of whether the proposal fits comfortably within the LC mission as now perceived. Whatever the special circumstance of each new proposal, the best guideline may well be to restrict new LC activities to those clearly related to the collections on hand.

The advisory group discussed the Library's venturing into the following new areas.

Reconstruct Theatrical Performances

The essence of a great library is that it is a depository, a record of the past and of the present soon to become past. There is one subcategory of the performing arts which could focus most appropriately at such an institution, and that is the reconstruction of performances of the past. The new theater and dance division might well take leadership in guiding this new activity.

Use of Area Specialists

At present, the Library is not making full use of its erudite area specialists. The average doctoral candidate is not told in the Library's two orientation booklets nor in an initial Stack and Reader interview that through each special reading room specialists are available with language skills and a knowledge of the history and bibliography of their areas. Also, no mention is made of translating aid available.

Cross-indexing

Some effort should be made to provide extensive cross-indexing services for the reader who wishes to use the arts resources of the Library. The scholar, student, and user of the Library should be made aware of the fact that records in the Patent Office, for example, are of value to the motion picture research he may be conducting. He should be told that materials in the manuscript or music collections may supplement material from the general collections, etc.

Out-of-Print Periodicals

The Library should take a more active part in microfilming or otherwise acquiring certain out-of-print periodicals. Existing copies of important periodicals could be microfilmed by the Library for its collections and the negative held for microfilm orders from other institutions. Microfilm holdings should be widely publicized and orders encouraged.

Publications Program

There is an urgent need for the Library to initiate an active program of publishing bibliographies, indices, and checklists of its holdings. It would be of invaluable assistance to scholars to use guides to the LC collections when undertaking research.

A comment on current LC publications. Some design and improvement in the print quality of the Library's publications is in order. It is ironic that an institution so dedicated to the glory of the printed word issues publications in which so little importance seems to be attached to design and print quality. It is recommended that more be done in the way of commissioning outstanding designers, illustrators, typographers, and calligraphers to design LC publications, posters, and related materials. Color in the body of LC publications would be a welcome addition.

Archive of American Culture

As the national library and repository of the cultural life of our country, the Library of Congress should take an active part in obtaining and documenting American culture. There are so many materials that will never find their way into the Library through copyright deposits or through regular acquisitions channels.

The Library should consider establishing an office whose duty and responsibility it would be to survey activities happening around the country, send people to document these activities, and deposit these records in the Library. LC should also attempt to obtain as many other kinds of materials as possible which help to document and promote an understanding of such fields as motion pictures and television.

Exhibition Checklists

The Library might consider coordinating or preparing checklists of art exhibitions at various museums around the country. Researchers are not always aware that a particular museum has at one time had an exhibition or retrospective of an artist, genre, etc., or that it has on file a catalog, illustrative or descriptive material, or other items relating to the subject of a show.

Taped Interviews

The Library could consider an active program of videotaping interviews with living artists in order to obtain not only poets reading their works, but interviews with filmmakers, painters, sculptors, etc., who could talk about their life and their work. Videotaped interviews with artists and art gallery personnel should be encouraged, supported, and collected by LC. Similar projects should be undertaken elsewhere in the country with the assistance of LC. LC might consider having on standby the necessary filming and taping equipment to capture a record of events related to visiting artists.

Visitor Orientation

The Library should improve its orientation procedures for visitors by installing an orientation center near the main entrance of the LC Building. In simple, imaginative, and dramatic ways, an orientation presentation would tell visitors what the Library is all about.

Ideally, visitors would come away from the presentation with some idea of the physical distribution of the Library facilities, some understanding of library science, an appreciation of the Library's great collections, and guidance on how to use the Library.

A series of TV programs about the Library's activities might be broadcast over educational stations across the country. We do not have in mind simply explanatory documentaries, but rather dramatic stories related to the extraordinary collections and facilities of the Library.

Volunteer Program

Museums have had wide experience in working with volunteers, some good and some unhappy, because of the urgent need for motivation and the matching of skills with particular jobs. There is no question that volunteer work requires tight supervision. If each LC division needing help would maintain a list of assignments sorted by level of skill, there would seem to be the basis for a far-reaching volunteer program not excluding ushers, messengers, and docents.

If the Library were to issue more stack passes to scholars and research professionals, readers could in turn repay the Library by identifying misshelved books, tagging brittle material, or pulling rare material which is found in the general collections, etc.

Internships/Fellowships

LC's rich holdings attract the art researcher. At the same time LC might gain much by having one or more art scholars in residence for six months or a year. It is recommended that the concept of special consultants/fellows/interns be enlarged to include historians in art, architecture, and photography. Eventually the practicing artist or visiting art librarian might be brought into this fold. The talents of these specialists could be invaluable to the Library in assessing the importance of various collections in LC, in pointing out weaknesses, and generally by bringing into the Library fresh viewpoints. The library experience and the chance of turning up material for their own research while working would attract many individuals to the Library.

Exhibits

Exhibitions have long been an important activity of the Library, and must continue to be so. In addition to a refurbished Great Hall, there should be a permanent gallery space which is large, well-lighted, architecturally neutral, and completely flexible, permitting the installation of three or four major exhibitions a year. There should also be small exhibit areas in all of the buildings, in or near various division reading rooms, to accommodate a variety of topical exhibitions on a more modest scale.

Checklists of the small exhibitions should be made available whenever possible. For each major exhibition there should be a substantial catalog, well-designed, illustrated, and fully documented. Color should be used when suitable.

The Library has a long history of exhibits based exclusively on book, print, or music material. Exhibits have seemed simple, dignified, informative, and not without bookish charm, but against the imaginative displays developed over the past 10 years, they now appear pedestrian. We call for discreet changes which will make them more lively without losing their intrinsic dignity.

One solution is to introduce nonbook material which extends a theme or establishes a context. The Library might even borrow related material from other institutions when appropriate to the theme of an exhibit. Exhibit catalogs should accompany all LC shows.

Cooperative Efforts

With regard to the relationship of the Library of Congress to other institutions throughout the United States, we believe it would be a legitimate function of the Library to identify important materials and assist smaller libraries to properly catalog and preserve them and make them accessible to scholars. This function might even involve grants to such libraries if it is in the national interest that their materials be preserved and utilized.

The Library could play an extremely significant role in improving the quality of other libraries by sending out "distinguished guest librarians" to other libraries to foster LC-developed techniques and perspectives while at the same time bringing back to LC good ideas that originate in the affiliates. The regional libraries could also serve as something of a "farm system," sending up to the "big leagues" the best young librarians for periods of time. From this group might be drawn the future heads of the regional libraries. Possibly such a system of loose affiliation could be sponsored and coordinated through the professional associations.

Planning Unit

The size and complexity of changes contemplated for the Library of Congress suggest the need for a full-time planning office when the Task Force ends in January 1977. Many proposed changes will introduce skills new to LC, novel techniques and procedures, and a high visibility. Most will require budgeting, coordination in the efforts of LC divisions, and decisions on timing of execution. This overall planning function should be centrally located in a permanent office directly under the Librarian of Congress.

2. Report of the Humanities Advisory Group

The Library of Congress is a resource of inestimable value for humanistic scholarship. We propose that it become an active partner as well.

The charge to the Humanities Advisory Group was to address the needs of scholars and teachers in the humanities and allied fields who are concerned with contributing to knowledge and disseminating it. Our group consisted of the following: Morton Bloomfield, Victor Brombert, J. William Fulbright, J. Glenn Gray, Neil Harris, Bernard Knox, Jaroslav Pelikan (Chairman), and Donald W. Treadgold.

Our group has become aware that many agencies and organizations outside the Library of Congress have a stake in the services of the Library of Congress and are actively engaged in trying to solve the problems of the Library. Our group hopes that consultation with such groups will precede any steps to carry out the recommendations presented in this report. We hope, too, that a continuing advisory group will be created that will go on doing for the Library what we have begun.

As directed by the Librarian of Congress, the Humanities Advisory Group has attempted to view the Library in its totality and then to focus on those functions and services that directly affect the Library's humanistic constituency. Our discussions concentrated on four chief areas.

Facilities for Scholars

Given the enormous growth and proliferation of books, periodicals, and other kinds of publications and the expansion and continuing reorganization of the Library of Congress to deal with such phenomena, the scholar and teacher face formidable problems. Our inquiries have led us to believe that even the humanist who resides in the vicinity of the Library of Congress may experience substantial difficulties in using its services efficiently. Even more severe problems may beset the scholar or teacher from a distance who wishes to use Library material or would use it if it were possible and practical to do so. The following recommendations are intended to mitigate the difficulties faced by these users.

Recommendations:
1. A central reference desk for visiting scholars should be established, where basic orientation could be given or referrals made to reference librarians, bibliographers, or subject specialists with particular knowledge of the topic in question.
2. Research assistants should be available to look up call numbers, fill out slips, retrieve books directly from the stacks, or ascertain the location of material not in the main Library. These assistants might be recruited on a work-study basis from graduate students at local institutions.
3. The existing number of study desks and shelves should be substantially increased, and locked facilities for continuing use over a period of weeks or months should be provided for scholars who can qualify for the privilege.
4. Coordinated or combined with the reference desk for visiting scholars should be a housing desk for them. If combined, the desks would serve as a center for visiting scholars. Information regarding inexpensive housing for a period of several days, weeks, or months could be collected and distributed at the desk.

The following topics were also discussed and should be given consideration:

1. Preparing printed guides to each division of the Library, indicating the types of holdings, related services, and assistance available. They might be mailed to prospective applicants as well as distributed by the reference desk for visiting scholars.

2. The official designation "scholar in residence at the Library of Congress" might be made available to scholars on leave from their institutions to use the facilities of the Library of Congress.

3. The chief of the reference desk for visiting scholars might be charged with the responsibility of organizing discussions, seminars, or conferences including scholars in residence, representatives of relevant local institutions, and interested scholars on the Library staff.

If some or all of the above recommendations are accepted and carried out, suitable dissemination of information about these innovations should be undertaken through the publications of outside organizations as well as through those of the Library of Congress.

We considered, but we do not recommend, additional fellowship programs for scholars in residence at the Library. The Woodrow Wilson International Center, the Kennan Institute, and other such programs in the Washington, D.C., area already have governmental and private means for such purposes, and P.L. 90-637 (1968), establishing the Woodrow Wilson Center, might be an obstacle to the creation of programs appearing to serve the same purpose. We suspect, moreover, that many of the scholars and teachers who would benefit from our recommendations would probably not be likely to be chosen as the Woodrow Wilson Center Fellows. Any bona fide scholar or teacher from outside the United States should be eligible to receive any of the forms of assistance mentioned above as readily as U.S. citizens.

National Translation Center

There is a need for a national effort to promote the translation into English of creative and original works in foreign languages. At present no agency exists to identify such works or to help make them available to readers of English. Hard-pressed publishers find it difficult to meet the cost of such translated works, which recover their expense only over years, if at all. Consequently, they are forced to choose those publications of foreign presses that are prominent, not necessarily those that are important. Even so, our publishers are rarely in a position to seek out and compensate adequately the relatively few excellent translators who could guarantee adequate work. By contrast with those in certain other countries, translators in the United States enjoy little prestige or recognition in the practice of their exacting art. (In what follows, we have heeded Dr. Boorstin's injunction not to be concerned with problems of finance.)

We propose the establishment of a national translation center at the Library of Congress with the following principal goals.

1. To undertake a survey of outstanding books in the humanities published in foreign languages that should be translated (or retranslated) into English.

2. To assemble an up-to-date record of such books currently under translation or already commissioned for translation by American, Canadian, or British publishers.

3. To compile and distribute a roster of translators who have already published acceptable translations, in an effort to improve the low estate of the translating art in the United States.

4. To form a permanent national commission on translation, each of whose members would be delegated to select a subcommittee of senior scholars, native and foreign, specializing in the relevant language and culture. The subcommittee would be responsible for advising scholars in choosing appropriate works and translators.

5. To seek out those relatively few publishers in English-speaking lands who already bring out a significant number of translations, with

intent to aid them in finding subsidies for translations from governments, foundations, cultural associations, and private philanthropy. The center should likewise aid such publishers in appropriate ways to increase the sale of translations.

6. To publish a newsletter and later a quarterly journal that would inform the educated public of the work of the translation center and plans for future publications. The journal should also provide space for publication of articles on the theory of translation by English-speaking and foreign authors.

The establishment of a national translation center should proceed in carefully prepared stages, launched perhaps by a national conference of persons having experience in translation problems and publishing difficulties. Such a conference, in which other agencies like the American Academy of Arts and Sciences could be asked to participate, could also serve to call attention to needs and possibilities in this area.

Priority should be given to the selection of members for the permanent commission and a general secretary. The composition of the commission should include a few editors and publishers as well as scholars, perhaps distinguished free-lance authors and government officials as well. If necessary, a small steering committee could be formed from the commission to make urgent decisions. Commission members should be chosen not only for individual competence, but also for ability to work together without partiality to a particular culture or to particular translators known to members.

In drawing up the list of books whose translation is needed most, the general secretary should first canvass existing translation centers and committees, such as the Columbia University center and the PEN Translation Committee, as well as others here and abroad. Former members of the abortive national translation center at Texas are ready and willing to contribute accounts of their mistakes and suggestions of how to avoid them in the future. Once the work of assembling already existing material and earlier recommendations of works requiring translation is completed, the commission could proceed with some authority to gain agreement about priorities and reliable translators.

The commission should in due course endeavor to discover and encourage new translators by forming an editorial board whose function it would be to examine and criticize samples by prospective translators and to review completed works before publication. In some cases graduate students at major universities could be allowed to submit translations with critical introductions in lieu of dissertations now standard for the Ph.D. With the promise of publication, this would be a greater contribution to scholarship than many of the dissertations now accepted.

If and when the translation center and its commission have earned status and authority in the world of letters, it should not be impossible to attract the financial support needed to subsidize translations and translators to provide them the status and prestige presently enjoyed by traditional disciplines. Only when this goal has been attained will the educated American public have an opportunity to learn of the best artistic, religious, and philosophic thought beyond its language boundaries. We are convinced that this project has great promise for the future if realistically organized and pursued in single-minded devotion to making available classical foreign works in English at reasonable cost.

Recommendation: That the Library of Congress actively support the creation of a national translation center.

Bibliographic Access

Most American humanists are unable to get to Washington, D.C., often or for long stays. They employ the Library of Congress as a reference resource of last resort. Book catalogs, subject entries, and bibliographical publications of the Library are resources in themselves, guiding the researcher and suggesting materials that may be obtainable through interlibrary loan.

Because the Library of Congress has many orienting aids that are not widely known, it is difficult for many users to take full advantage of the national collections. Moreover, the printed material is simplicity itself when compared with the task of utilizing indices and clipping files of various kinds.

In the past few years there have been enormous advances in the development of data banks for the physical, biological, and social sciences. Computerized bibliographic data bases, frequently with digests or summaries of books and papers, are now available to paying subscribers. A large bibliography, frequently updated, and annual reports guide the novice through the maze of data bases.

Computerized Data Bases

Although most computerized data bases concern the sciences, there are several that relate to history, psychology, language and communication, social policy, law and jurisprudence, and other areas of great interest to humanists. If the New York Times service becomes retrospective, integrating its various years, it will obviously be of greater importance than it is now.

Several comments on these data bases seem appropriate: (1) most humanists are totally unaware of the existence of the data banks and therefore see little use for them; (2) librarians seem a little overwhelmed by the number of data banks; (3) such services are expensive, both in rental of terminals and in rates for individual queries; (4) there is a certain amount of duplication and a lack of coordination in running the various services; and (5) humanists are uninformed about data bases because there is no constituency within the university to press for subscriptions to certain data bases.

We would like to propose the following recommendations for consideration.

Recommendations:

1. That professional and academic organizations of humanists form committees on the library use of data bases.
2. That the Library of Congress (or some other institution) coordinate these committees and aid their communication.
3. That the Library of Congress consider ways of helping to stimulate or organize library education programs to acquaint

potential users with various data banks and to outline related services available from LC.

4. That the Library of Congress sponsor a conference of humanists to consider ways of utilizing data banks. (To consider ways of using existing systems is only half of the problem. The other part is to examine possibilities for creating new data bases and indices. Presumably a Library of Congress conference might place just such a question on its agenda.)

Newspaper Indices

In 1946 a survey of the existence of newspaper indices in the United States, concentrating on the second half of the nineteenth century, indicated that newspapers were underutilized despite the wealth of information they contain: "The task of searching through issue after issue presents problems which the average researcher has found insoluble with the limited time, facilities, and resources available to him." Such limitations restricted the scope of historical investigations, and frequently induced unproved hypotheses and dubious generalizations.

The situation has not improved significantly in 30 years. Documented in this early survey was a series of newspaper subject indices, usually covering five years or less, that were arbitrarily directed and undertaken, and are located in historical societies, special archives, newspaper offices, and public libraries. A few were projects directed by the Works Progress Administration. With respect to printed indices, there is only one of major significance that covers an extended period of time, that of the New York Times which, with a gap of several years in the first decade of the twentieth century, is practically complete from 1863 to the present. Other cities and other newspapers are less fortunate.

The value of systematic subject indices to newspapers would be immense. Even if the card indices now in existence were reproduced, a substantial contribution to the history of American culture and politics could be made.

It seems reasonable to propose that the Library of Congress establish a committee to survey existing indices of newspapers and periodicals, to make recommendations about selecting some for reproduction, and to make further recommendations about future indices constructed under professional standards for a selected set of American newspapers. In addition to the substantive issues that must be discussed, the Library should consider whether it will act simply as a searcher for funds among foundations and public agencies or whether it will serve as a continuing center for coordinating the indexing of American journals. Likewise, it is not clear which is preferable, to continue to rely on printed indices or to move directly into more efficient modes of retrieval. A committee of experts would have to consider this among other issues.

Recommendations:

1. That the Library of Congress establish a committee on indexing American newspapers or invite nominations from selected institutions for members of such a committee.
2. That the committee survey existing indices and make recommendations about their duplication and distribution.

3. That the committee determine whether the permanent administration of these projects be centralized or decentralized, within or without the Library of Congress.
4. That the committee make recommendations concerning the standards and formats of new indices, and the means of reproducing existing indices.
5. That the committee consider the ways these indices could be financed, and act to coordinate grant applications to foundations and public agencies.

International Relations

If the world is moving into a period of stress, intellectual institutions will inevitably suffer. In that case, an attempt to keep library services going throughout the world becomes more important than ever, and international field offices like those established by the Library of Congress will be indispensable.

An attempt should be made to set up an active international library agency that would improve conditions of international interlibrary loan and would move toward greater uniformity in library procedures. It would probably be better in the long run if the Library field offices could become the field offices of this international agency. However, all this is dependent on some kind of international cooperation and stability. It must be admitted that at present prospects for this look dim. Steps could be taken, however, to establish such an agency even if circumstances make its effective operation difficult for the present.

If such an agency could be created, there are many possibilities open for scholarly and technical exchange. Subject specialists could be supported for visits to the field offices to assist and cooperate with local experts. Computers could link the various offices, with data storage centers at major research libraries. There are many possibilities for learning and science in the broadest sense of the word to enlighten and help mankind.

The Library of Congress at present has a small number of offices throughout the world that serve as bibliographical centers for some of the more difficult areas of the world—difficult in the sense of bibliographical coverage and access. The following comments are based on a visit to the Library's Nairobi office made by one of our members, Morton Bloomfield, in July 1976. They should be recognized for what they are, speculations from a limited perspective.

The chief function of the Library of Congress field offices at present is to prepare lists of publications produced in an area and to acquire books and pamphlets for the Library of Congress and other American libraries. The latter function seems to be the one most prized by the Washington, D.C., office of the Library of Congress, for a complaint of the Nairobi staff is that their cataloging has been ignored and the work is duplicated in Washington. (It was admitted, however, that the Library is beginning to make use of the cataloging activities of the field office.)

The Nairobi center admires the freedom it is given and feels that this enables it to do a good job. The staff emphasized that the work of the field office was also useful to East Africa itself. There is no other bibliographical guide to the area that is as complete or as reliable as the one prepared by the

Library office. The model set by the Nairobi office opens possibilities for the greater use of the international office.

It may be said without contradiction that the Library of Congress is the greatest library in the world and that, perhaps even more important, it is recognized as such and is highly respected throughout the world by those who are in a position to know. The value of the Library's services and bibliographical knowledge is highly prized.

> **Recommendation:** That the Library of Congress join with other organizations and institutions to study the feasibility of creating an international library agency.

3. Report of the Law Advisory Group

Introduction

We have been urged by the Librarian to view the Library of Congress as an entity and to consider the field of law as a part of the Library's overall mission, rather than to limit our perspective to the Law Library itself. Consistent with that charge, our report does not emphasize issues of internal organization, management, or procedures within the Library. Rather, we have sought to help formulate a conception of the broad responsibilities of the Library of Congress as they relate to the field of law and then to emphasize certain functions that we believe require special priority at this point in the Library's history. Inevitably, however, our report takes as a point of departure the existing structure of the Library and reflects views and impressions about the functioning of the Law Library. As will be seen, we perceive a need for a more comprehensive and systematic outside study of the operations of the Law Library itself.

We conceive that there are three distinct roles our national library should be expected to fill if it is fully to discharge its responsibilities in the field of law.

> 1. It is the law library of the Congress and, in varying degrees, of other branches of the Federal Government as well. In this role it must be prepared to function as an efficient working law library, with such services and such special resources as are needed to meet the particular legal needs of government. Since these needs will almost certainly make themselves felt in the day-to-day functioning of the Library and will assert their own priority in the allocation of resources, we have not tried to assess the extent to which this role is being effectively served or might be improved. We do, however, call attention to what seems to us to be some ambiguity and overlap in the functions of the Congressional Research Service and reference operations within the Law Library as they have evolved over time.
>
> 2. The Library performs a critical service function for the law libraries of the country. The future strength of all law libraries depends heavily, and increasingly, on how effectively this service function is carried out, and on the extent of leadership the Library of Congress provides in solving technological problems, organizing cooperative efforts among law libraries, and supplementing the resources of other

law libraries. Most of the specific recommendations of our report are addressed to this aspect of the Library's role.

3. The Library is the principal national resource for building and preserving a record of the Nation's legal culture and for collecting the knowledge that is relevant to an understanding of law in the broadest sense. In this third role the Library of Congress has a special responsibility for continuing self-examination. This is true in part because the resources and potential resources of the Library of Congress are unmatched by any other libraries in the Nation. But it is true in part also because law libraries in general are mainly committed to special purposes, heavily oriented to professional services or professional training, and thus are far less suited than the Library of Congress to take so broad a view of their role in relation to knowledge and culture.

In thus describing the Library's major responsibilities, we have not overlooked the Librarian's admirable concern that the Library of Congress should be regarded as a resource for the people of the Nation and not merely for certain special constituencies such as the government, the legal profession, or law libraries. We believe this concern is properly reflected in the third role we have identified above. The ideal that the Library of Congress should be a resource directly available to the individual citizen is an important one, and opportunities to enrich the lives of citizens through publications, reference services, and direct access to its resources rightly occupy a high place in the attention of the Library. We believe, however, that those opportunities may be more limited in law than in some other fields, largely because of the technical and specialized nature of the use of legal materials, and that here even more than in most fields the Library must view its service to readers as taking place primarily through the support it can give to the Nation's library system as a whole. In providing that support, however, the Library must be alert to avoid having its own organization, acquisitions policies, and bibliographic efforts limited by the needs and perceptions of the habitual main users of legal materials or the horizons of existing law libraries. It is this caution and this responsibility that we mean to suggest in describing the third of the Library's main roles.

It follows from what has been said that the appropriate goal for the Library of Congress in relation to law is not adequately captured by saying that it should be the best law library in the country. Although there are important senses in which that ought to be the objective, to state the goal in such a fashion risks obscuring the unique functions the Library should perform and the distinctive perception of its role that it should hold. In relation to other law libraries, it should be an innovator and an organizer of cooperative undertakings. In relation to the Nation's legal institutions and culture, it should view itself as what can perhaps best be described as a great university library. The importance of this latter perception lies in the fact that the suggested role is one that is probably not consciously embraced by any of our existing university libraries, since responsibility for the field of law is almost everywhere delegated to a law library serving primarily the educational needs of a specialized clientele.

No doubt the broad purposes of the Library in relation to the field of law could be stated in other equally and perhaps more appropriate ways. We offer the foregoing propositions not because of confidence that they represent a final or model statement of objectives but to emphasize the importance we attach to an institution's self-view. In an institution as complex as the Library of Congress, and with as heavy pressures on its human and financial resources to perform the mundane day-to-day tasks, there is a danger that routine functions will overwhelm the awareness of more ambitious opportunities. Our necessarily superficial exposure to the workings of the Law Library leave us with the impression that it is functioning effectively, with dedicated and competent personnel, as a conventional law library of high caliber, although with considerable handicaps imposed by its physical space. Whether it is able, with its present financial resources and staff, to perform the tasks we emphasize in the remainder of this report is a question we have not seriously addressed, although we have little doubt that substantial additional resources will be required.

Our main concern is a question whether there is present a sufficiently clear and ambitious view of the place of the Law Library in relation to the other law libraries of the country, or a full awareness of its potential leadership in solving the problems about which law librarians are deeply concerned. To encourage the development of such a view is perhaps the most important service that we hope this report may provide.

With these general observations as background, we turn to the more specific recommendations of the Advisory Group.

Support for the Law Library System as a Whole

We believe the most urgent priority for the Library of Congress in relation to the needs of the legal community is the strengthening of the aspects of its work that involve cooperation with and assistance to other libraries. In this respect our report echoes much that is found in the report of the Task Force Subcommittee on Services to Libraries. Virtually every recommendation of that report is applicable to the library needs of the legal community. We believe there may be special urgency, however, in meeting immediate needs of law libraries. The needs for legal information are almost always instant needs. Accuracy and completeness of information, as well as rapid access, are at a premium. The inexorable tide of publication of legal materials, together with steeply rising costs, makes it ever more difficult for individual law libraries to keep up, and to meet the demands that are made upon the system. We understand, for example, that in some law libraries there are growing backlogs of uncataloged major current legal works due to the dependence on Library of Congress cataloging that has grown up in recent years and the slow rate of cataloging from the Library of Congress.

The support functions through which the contribution of the Library of Congress can be made significantly greater fall into three broad and somewhat overlapping categories: (1) leadership in creating a national bibliographic data base in law and a service network for users; (2) coordination with other law libraries in acquisitions, cataloging, preservation, and miniaturization, and the production of bibliographies and indexes; (3) improvement of existing processing and reference services.

1. A National Bibliographic Data Base and Service Network

Efforts are now being undertaken by law librarians to create a computerized data base covering publications in law and related fields. Such a facility will, of course, use MARC records generated at the Library of Congress, but it will also contain catalog records from other research law libraries. It is hoped that this service will eventually be expanded to include the indexing of periodicals, collections of essays, conference proceedings, and contents of monographs; indexing of primary legal sources, particularly in foreign law; and many other references required for legal research.

Such a data base will assist the acquisitions and cataloging functions in all law libraries and will support a wide range of readers' services. No other law library has the collection, staff, and resources to support the many bibliographic activities required in this undertaking.

We therefore consider it of the first importance that the Library of Congress take the initiatives that will enable it to exercise a strong leadership role in this effort. Without attempting to recommend how such an effort can best be organized within the Library, we believe that the specific commitment of funding and additional staff for this purpose should be provided. We are aware that there has been discussion of the desirability of having the Law Library formally designated as the National Law Library or of creating a National Law Center at the Library of Congress. One of the benefits of some such step might well be the reinforcement it would give to the kind of responsibilities and leadership we envisage the Library of Congress as assuming in connection with a national bibliographic data base in law, as well as in other activities mentioned in our report. We do not believe, however, that such a step is essential or that the desired effort should await the emergence of a concept such as a National Law Library. Rather, it appears to us to be well within the existing potential of the Library of Congress, and the Law Library, to exert the required leadership and influence over the direction that this important national effort will take.

2. Coordination of Programs with Other Law Libraries

The opportunity for strengthening the Nation's resources in relation to legal materials is not limited to the problem of a computerized bibliographic data base. It extends, as well, to other aspects of the Library's functions. We urge that a major objective should be to develop ongoing programs of coordination in as many activities as offer promise of fruitful joint effort, so that maximum efficient use may be made of the total available resources.

The collections themselves are an important case in point. The Library of Congress can no longer hope, if it ever could, to acquire and maintain all the needed and desirable legal materials. Along with other major law libraries, even now it does not adequately cover a number of important areas. This condition will become more serious with the passage of time.

Accordingly there is need for a national acquisitions program in law, in which efforts are made to allocate prime responsibility for collecting certain types of materials among different libraries in the country. The Library of Congress is the logical entity to bring about such a program.

By way of example, three fields which seem likely candidates for a coordinated effort may be mentioned. One is foreign materials. Recent sharp increases in the cost of foreign materials (along with but even exceeding such increases in the cost of domestic publications) have significantly reduced the ability of university law libraries to maintain strong foreign-law collections. This situation makes it of paramount importance that the Library of Congress should devote major emphasis to preserving and strengthening its splendid foreign collections, which constitute a unique resource. But the emergence of many new nations and the steady proliferation of legal materials generally will severely limit the comprehensiveness of even the Library of Congress' holdings in the future. If there is to be available within the United States adequate coverage of the vast spectrum of foreign legal materials, some allocation of emphasis and responsibility among libraries seems essential. Such coordination is needed not only because of the costs of acquisition and holding of the materials but also to insure that acquisition efforts are aggressively pursued in all appropriate areas.

A second area in which planning and coordination seems especially needed is the identification and collection of legal materials of historical importance, such as local court and governmental records. There is growing interest in American legal history among historians and legal scholars. This development provides both a reason and the means for a fresh stock-taking of the Nation's practices with respect to the preservation and accessibility of official records in which the evolution of our legal culture may be traced. The Library of Congress might well consider the convening of a group of legal historians for the purpose of reviewing its policies, and those of other concerned agencies, and to formulate a long-range program of cooperation among local and other libraries to bring archival materials of this type within a national legal bibliographic system, regardless of where the materials happen to be stored.

A third area relates to current materials pertaining to state and local government. A familiar inadequacy of even the strongest law libraries is the fragmentary character of holdings in these areas. A nationally coordinated system for collecting state and local legislative and administrative materials, combined with some comprehensive system of indexing and methods for making the materials accessible to users in all parts of the country would represent an important advance.

Related to the problem of acquisitions, but deserving of separate emphasis as a field for collaborative effort, is the reduction of legal materials to microform. The Library of Congress is now coordinating its filming of foreign official gazettes with the New York Public Library. Many other law publications, on deteriorating paper and requiring expensive storage space, can similarly be filmed on a cooperative basis. These include foreign legislative and statutory materials, particularly from provincial jurisdictions; nineteenth century American legal treatises; discontinued foreign and American legal periodicals; and many others. An important category is the records and briefs of the United States Courts of Appeals. We encourage the proposed plan to microfilm such documents at source for central deposit in the Library of Congress. This project can advance only with Congressional support, but once authorized, it should be expedited. It should have strong direction from the Library of Congress, with coordination through the Administrative Office of the United States Courts.

The development of a national program for microfilming legal materials, under the leadership of the Library of Congress, can accomplish far more than the Library can do alone or than can be done through individual efforts of separate libraries.

There are other processing and research activities in which cooperation with other law libraries can effectively advance bibliographic work. An expansion of the present shared cataloging program to include the authentication and acceptance in MARC of original cataloging from designated law libraries meeting applicable standards would aid the Library of Congress, other libraries, and library users everywhere. The accelerated application of K classification to retrospective holdings, and the much-needed revision of Library of Congress law subject headings are similarly desirable cooperative efforts. The preparation of new bibliographic guides to the law of various foreign countries and the development of a comprehensive computerized index to foreign law sources could also draw upon the resources and expertise available in other law libraries.

3. Improvement of Present Services to Other Libraries

The preceding discussion emphasizes two major paths of effort that we believe are important to the future development of the legal resources of the Nation. In addition to these major themes that in our view deserve new initiatives, there are numerous ways in which the existing services of the Library of Congress to other law libraries can be made more useful. We offer the following specific recommendations affecting these services.

1. Accelerated processing of legal materials by increased participation of the Law Library in processing activities; higher processing priorities for law materials; direct delivery of *all* continuations for immediate use in the Law Library, with the data necessary for processing to be forwarded by photocopy or other means to the Processing Department.

2. Completion and publication of the balance of the K classification schedules and development of an augmented program for their application to retrospective holdings.

3. Revision of Class JX (International Law) to reflect the many changes and new sources of law in that field.

4. Completion of the Law Library catalog to reflect all of its present holdings in all fields of law.

5. Revision of the subject headings for law, in cooperation with representatives of the law library profession, and publication of a revised list of subject headings.

6. Acceleration of the CONSER project and inclusion of the broadest range of legal serials. Commitment of resources at the Library for prompt editing and authentication of records to create a reliable national serials data base.

7. Full participation of the Library in the development of a national periodicals lending system as proposed by the National Commission on Libraries and Information Science, with the inclusion of the broadest range of domestic and foreign legal periodicals.

8. Provision of direct online access to MARC records at the Library of Congress for the use of law libraries.

9. Extension of the COMARC program to accept cataloging from selected law libraries according to Library of Congress standards, including not only updated entries, but original cataloging as well.

10. Improved processing of interlibrary loan, photocopying and microfilm orders, with simplified procedures and increased staffing to reduce present delays.

11. Distribution of major research reports and studies prepared in the Law Library and in CRS to law libraries generally.

12. Extension of the Library's recent experimental telephone reference service to selected law libraries, which could then function more effectively as regional reference centers for legal information throughout the country.

13. Development of educational and internship programs for training law library specialists at the Library, utilizing the expertise of the Law Library staff and its rich collections.

The Library and Legal Scholarship

Although much of this report is devoted to the service functions of the Library, we do not minimize the intellectual role the Library should aspire to occupy. We share with the Librarian the view that the Nation's library should be a center of intellectual activity and an active force in promoting the use of its rich resources. Ideally the Law Library (no less than other parts of the Library) should be an institution that attracts first-rate scholars to engage in research of a character that requires their being "in residence" for significant periods of time. The constant presence of even a small group of scholars working on substantial projects ought to have a variety of benefits for the Library. It would provide assurance that the exceptional resources of the Library were known to the community of scholars and were being drawn upon in important ways. It would strengthen the permanent staff's sense of connection with the world of scholarship and provide the stimulus of new perspectives. It should also be a valuable additional source of appraisal and ideas as to the goals of the Library and its effectiveness in meeting them.

We would therefore encourage the taking of all feasible steps, consistent with the other demands on the Library, to make the Law Library a leading research library for scholars. Such an emphasis implies cultivating particular fields in which the Library has or can develop comparative advantages over other libraries. The most obvious locus of such comparative advantage at present appears to be in the field of foreign and comparative law. Research in American legal history is another field in which the Library might well make a special effort to provide unrivaled resources. Other possibilities may suggest themselves to those who are most familiar with the special strengths of the present collection. One important element of an acquisitions policy should be to identify and give strong support to areas in which the Library can come to be regarded as the outstanding resource for research of a scholarly nature.

It is essential to such an objective that the Library provide working conditions as congenial as possible to the carrying on of scholarship, as distinguished from those which satisfy the needs of students, lawyers, and casual users of the Library. The present physical arrangements clearly fall far short of the ideal from this standpoint. Of greater concern to the Advisory Group, however, is that we are not satisfied that the plans for the Law Library in the new Madison Building give adequate attention to this problem. We have not studied those plans in detail and are not prepared to make specific suggestions, but it is our impression that significantly more space ought to be provided for well-designed study spaces that can be assigned to scholars for private use over some period of time. We urge a review of the projected new arrangements from the standpoint of emphasizing the function of the Library as a research library, as well as with an eye to the overall adequacy of the space provided for the law collection.

Finally, to foster the development of the Library as a center for legal research we strongly urge the consideration of a program of grants to enable selected scholars to spend a period of time in residence. Such grants might be for varying periods, ranging from several weeks to a year. As a supplement to sabbatical arrangements, foundation grants, and other sources of support, such a program might well be the means of assuring the existence of a nucleus of resident scholars. Such a program would, of course, take on added significance if it were part of a larger plan, involving the Library of Congress as a whole, to create a community of scholars within the Library. The existence of an informally organized group of scholars (perhaps designated as Fellows of the Library), with appropriate occasions for social and professional interchange, might enhance the attractiveness of a period of resident study and further reinforce the intellectual purposes of the Library.

Information and Publications

The Library's service to the general public, as well as to other law libraries, would be strengthened by a more active and systematic publishing program. In particular, the various foreign law guides produced by the Law Library over the years are now found in law libraries everywhere and have often materially assisted in the development of other foreign legal collections. But the appearance, supplementation, and revision of these guides is uneven. Given their unique character, a dependable schedule of publication should be determined and publicized. Another seminal work that should be revised and extended, possibly in book catalog format or even online as part of a larger computerized information-retrieval system, is McClenon and Gilbert's Subject Index to the Federal Statutes, long out of print.

Opportunities for developing new bibliographic guides and research tools should be the subject of continuing scrutiny by the law staff. There has been called to our attention, for example, the inadequacy of existing compilations and guides to the legislative law applicable to the District of Columbia. Although the Library of Congress cannot by itself carry out all or perhaps even a substantial number of the major projects of this sort that might be useful, it can well perform a valuable function in helping identify bibliographic needs and encouraging appropriate agencies to meet them. The function is one of sufficient importance that it might well be made a specific ongoing responsibility of designated staff personnel. For this as well as other purposes, we urge the development of regular means of liaison with the American Bar Association, the American Bar Foundation, the Federal Judicial Center, and similar entities concerned with improved service to the legal profession and the judiciary.

We believe there is also room for using the specialized resources of the Law Library to provide some publications of a more general sort, aimed both at the legal profession and at a wider public. One example that has been suggested to our committee is the need for better information about the legal systems of other countries, such as the Soviet Union and the Republic of China. Publications of a pamphlet type (such as the American Bar Foundation's widely distributed pamphlet on the legal profession in the United States) describing the legal systems of particular countries could make a significant contribution to public information.

We would also urge consideration of wider dissemination of the studies currently prepared by the Library's foreign law specialists in connection with reference requests. While some of these research reports may be of too narrow and specialized a focus to justify publication, we think there should be some regular means of publication of studies that may be of value to scholars and to the growing number of lawyers concerned with foreign legal problems.

There is need for improved communication of information about the resources and services of the Library in the field of law. The value of the Library to the legal profession, to other libraries, and to the public depends on wide awareness, especially among the particular constituencies of the Law Library, of the availability of its resources. A special pamphlet on the collections and functions of the Law Library would be a useful addition to the publications program. In addition, educational programs could be offered at the Law Library for general librarians to learn about the services and resources available there, as well as about the use and availability of legal materials generally.

Other Matters

It is apparent that there is now overlapping in the services rendered by the Congressional Research Service and the Law Library. Although a functional division of responsibility has been understood in the past, there has been an increasing tendency for CRS to provide reference services beyond Congress to the public generally. The growth of CRS and its own law division have involved some duplication of responsibility within the Law Library. Increased staff and new computerized information services have enhanced the effectiveness of CRS, while the role of the Law Library has been limited by constraints of space, staff, and funding. Fortunately, relations between the two units have been marked by cooperation rather than competition. However, a new clarification of their respective responsibilities would facilitate present operations and future planning.

Our committee received a suggestion that the Library of Congress might assume responsibility for the present District of Columbia Bar Association Library and maintain it as a working law library for lawyers in the District, law students, and out-of-town lawyers needing to do research in connection with their appearance before Federal agencies. Although the committee has no recommendation on the matter, the suggestion elicited sympathetic interest because of its relationship to another problem that concerned some members of the committee. That is the question to what extent the present functioning of the Law Library as a place of study for law students in the District may interfere with or divert resources from the primary objectives of the Library. As we have already indicated, we think the character of the Law Library should be that of a preeminent research library rather than an ordinary working library geared to the daily needs of law students and practitioners. The uses of available space and the services performed by staff are undoubtedly affected to some extent by the present emphasis on the latter functions. We urge further attention to the question of alternative means of meeting the needs of law students of the District, and in this connection the idea of establishing a satellite library, perhaps in cooperation with the local bar and local law schools, merits serious study.

Finally, our committee addressed itself to certain larger questions of the status and organization of what is presently the Law Library of Congress.

One such question is the status of the Library as a National Law Library, a concept that has received considerable support from the profession of law librarians. Implicit in much of what has been urged in this report is the notion that the Library should function increasingly in such a role, as distinguished from the historic concept of the Library as primarily an adjunct of the Congress. Whether the time has arrived to recognize, and perhaps enhance, that role by changes in the Library's de jure framework is a question that extends beyond the field of law and is related to larger issues concerning the whole Library of Congress. The concept of a National Law Library or a National Law Center is an important symbol of the purposes and opportunities of the Library. We urge that exploration and further refinement of the concept be kept high on the agenda of the Librarian and others concerned with future directions of the Library. In the meantime, however, we believe that much of the substance of the idea can properly be achieved within the present structure and status of the Library.

A second question is whether the historic separate identity of the Law Library should be retained, along with its semiautonomous position within the Library of Congress. A merging of law into the rest of the Library's collections and organization would serve to emphasize the place of law as an integral part of the universe of knowledge and might ultimately exert some influence on intellectual interests and attitudes concerning law. It might be urged that the present organization helps perpetuate a view of law as a special province of those whose vocational needs it serves. Whether in addition to such abstract justifications for a merger there are organizational efficiencies to be obtained we are not in a position to judge. Against any such advantages, however, must be weighed the importance to the legal profession, to the agencies of government and to the administration of justice, and to the law libraries of the country of a strong and vigorous Law Library supported in its own right. The Law Library is an ongoing institution with a long history, with a tradition of great distinction, and, we believe, with the potential to provide even more significant service than in the past to the important needs of the legal community. We would regret seeing that potential jeopardized by radical changes in the relationship of the Law Library to the rest of the Library of Congress, and we believe that the Law Library should be preserved as a distinct entity.

It follows from the view just stated that a systematic expert study of the internal organization and operations of the Law Library could be useful. Our committee has not attempted any detailed scrutiny of the present condition of the Law Library. We believe such a study would be desirable. Accordingly, our final recommendation is that a comprehensive survey of the Law Library be commissioned, to be carried out by a small group of outstanding persons expert in the field of law librarianship.

4. Report of the Libraries Advisory Group

Introduction

A periodic assessment of the activities of public institutions frequently results in a renewed commitment to basic institutional purposes, and can bring about revised objectives and new courses of action; it tends also to release hidden reservoirs of staff energy while reassuring the observing public. Therefore, it seemed appropriate and timely when the twelfth Librarian of Congress, Daniel J. Boorstin, in one of his first official actions, directed that a comprehensive review of the Library of Congress take place during 1976. It had been more than thirty-five years since the last review of the Library's activities was initiated by Archibald MacLeish.

In May of 1976 the Librarian appointed an Advisory Group on Libraries representative of the diversity of the North American library community, joined by the Director of the British Library, to assist in the Library's review process and make such recommendations as the group might deem appropriate. In his original memorandum of February 1976, the Librarian suggested several questions which might be addressed in the review of the Library of Congress.

During the six months allotted to its task, the twelve-member Advisory Group on Libraries toured the Library of Congress, interviewed members of the Library staff including the Librarian, consulted colleagues, and reviewed the printed record. The report which follows is not intended as a detailed examination of the enormous range of activities in which the Library is engaged. Rather, it is a selective review intended to suggest to the Librarian of Congress an agenda of paramount concern from the perspective of the library community.

Service is all too often an assumed objective in the rationale for technological and administrative innovations. The concept of the Library of Congress as the central element in a national network of libraries is not likely to excite the general public unless the public is aware of what the Library of Congress can and will do. The Library's support for the work of the research economist in San Francisco as well as the eighth-grade ecologist in North Carolina, its concern for the preservation of rare manuscripts as well as with the elimination of illiteracy, the Library's interest in folklore and music and in world technology, should in appropriate ways be made palpably evident through local public, academic, school, and special libraries in this country. For these and other reasons this report emphasizes the general educational and cultural role of the Library of Congress.

If it can be said that there is an element of genius in American librarianship it must be attributed primarily to the unparalleled development of bibliographic access to the many fine U.S. collections, thus overcoming the barriers of vast geographical distances and the inequitable distribution of resources. As the complexity of the task grows and costs increase, the creation of more sophisticated cooperative bibliographic arrangements becomes essential. The Library of Congress must continue to exercise its leadership in this area by pressing for the realization of a coherent national bibliographic system in a cooperative framework.

In its role as the research and information agency of the U.S. Congress, the Library of Congress has generated a number of specialized data bases which could form the basis for a generalized national information and retrieval service, provided that local libraries could gain access to them within a reasonable length of time and at a reasonable cost.

Internationally the Library of Congress must work to promote greater cooperation through the established mechanisms created by UNESCO, the International Federation of Library Associations (IFLA); the International Federation for Documentation (FID), the International Organization for Standardization (ISO), and other organizations concerned with library and information services.

Finally, libraries, like schools and hospitals, are too valuable to be influenced solely by professionals. Yet, the organized and informed opinions of the library community on basic questions affecting policy, function and organization, and specific advisory mechanisms must be established to improve continuity and utility.

In presenting this report to the Librarian of Congress the Advisory Group on Libraries wishes to express its appreciation for the opportunity to participate in this historic process. We also pledge our commitment to the many efforts to achieve a library and information service system worthy of the highest aspirations of the American people.

Cultural and Educational Role of the Library of Congress

The Library of Congress with the Smithsonian Institution, the National Archives, and the National Galleries shares an enormous responsibility for maintaining the record of culture past and present. As it acquires and preserves its collections in support of education and research it also reflects the complex and multifaceted heritage which defines our national identity. Yet the Library has another, perhaps unique, role to play. As the acknowledged leader of a network of similar institutions stretched across the nation, the Library of Congress is expected to provide extraordinary support for the program activities of other libraries. Although emphasis has traditionally been given to technical assistance, there exists an unlimited opportunity for the Library of Congress to enhance the image of all American libraries as cultural institutions by broadening its own cultural programs and by sharing its cultural programming capabilities with the rest of the nation's libraries.

The Library of Congress carries out a number of programs through which it is able to preserve and share materials unique to our heritage and to make a valuable contribution to America's cultural life. In 1975 the Library's traveling exhibits visited thirty-one separate locations in the United States. The concert series supported by special funds offers on a regular basis musical programs of distinction to library staff members and residents of the greater Washington, D.C., area. The symposia which are sponsored by the Library promote discussion, criticism, and the study of issues related to American life and letters. The Library's wide-ranging program of acquisitions supports this cultural role in that the Library is able to collect and preserve documents, records of original performances, and other materials which are special to the American past.

In developing its collections the Library must continue aggressively to seek and acquire those records which define the interest and achievements of the American people. Through its program of publications, exhibitions, and live and recorded concerts, the Library can share this record of the American heritage and offer a perspective on both the American tradition and other cultures. The Library of Congress must provide a setting which will encourage exploration into the Library's vast collections, and it must also work to sponsor and encourage research in those areas of its collection which are unique.

As the country moves toward a coherent national system of library and information services, the Library of Congress cannot supersede the research, public, and school libraries in this country, but should provide the leadership to enhance and supplement the capabilities of the many libraries which serve the American people.

Some specific programs for consideration are:

the expansion of the Library's traveling exhibits program to include a wide variety of topics and to reach a wider audience by means of a coordinated display schedule established by the Library in cooperation with local libraries across the country;

a program to offer the expertise of the Library of Congress to communities to assist them in creating local cultural programs. Other groups, such as the American Library Association and its chapters, the Special Libraries Association, the Association of Research Libraries, and the National Endowment for the Humanities, could be called on to join in the development and funding of such a program;

the sponsorship of cultural and educational programs that could be presented at locations outside of Washington, D.C., utilizing the resources of the scholars and artists in residence at the Library of Congress;

the support and development of high quality cultural programming; including but not limited to concerts, lectures, and readings, for television broadcasting;

expansion of the number of titles in the Library's publishing program, perhaps to include the issue of a journal of both high quality and popular interest reflecting a wide range of ideas and strengthening the perception of libraries as cultural institutions.

Bibliographic Services of the Library of Congress

There is no more fundamental problem facing the American library community than the effective organization of basic bibliographic services which provide access to our nation's wealth of research materials. The exponential growth in the quantity of materials produced and the increased cost of all materials have made it imperative that a method be found to reduce the unit cost of adding to and maintaining a library collection and to assure the identification and location of a growing body of materials for all users. The coordination of compatible or interrelated computer-based bibliographic systems appears to be the most promising current solution to this problem. However, such a system demands a high level of cooperation—it is not a task that can be assumed by any one institution, but must be undertaken cooperatively to facilitate the sharing of resources and to assure that equipment, standards, and scope are consistent.

The Library of Congress has pioneered in providing many essential services and tools to facilitate bibliographic control. The record shows that since 1902, when the Library of Congress first distributed standard cataloging data for titles received, it has offered the American library community an increasingly diverse variety of bibliographic services. The printed catalog card which is still made available through the Cataloging Distribution Service has been augmented by a variety of related services, including MARC tapes, Library of Congress proof sheets, technical publications, and book catalogs.

With the successful trial of the COMARC (COoperative MAchine-Readable Cataloging) there is the possibility that libraries will be able to contribute their own machine-readable bibliographic data to the MARC distribution service. Internationally, MARC has already been accepted as a standard for bibliographic exchange.

The Cataloging in Publication Program (CIP) provides libraries with cataloging data when the material is received; prospective publications are cataloged at the Library of Congress from galley proofs and the resulting cataloging information is printed on the verso of the title page. For the publication of the nearly one thousand publishing houses participating, CIP insures rapid and ready access to bibliographic information associated with their products. Further expansion, especially extension to foreign imprints, of the CIP is a welcome prospect.

The *National Union Catalog* provides both a full bibliographic description and information on location of the materials listed, thereby linking the collections of over 1,100 libraries.

The extent of the Library's holdings and its bibliographic records has been greatly increased by the National Program for Acquisitions and Cataloging (NPAC), by which "all library materials of value to scholarship currently published throughout the world are secured and cataloged." The main thrust of NPAC is foreign acquisitions; since the program began in 1966, more than 1.1 million reports have been searched and orders have been placed for 229,000 titles not previously acquired. Fifty-six libraries now receive depository sets of the resulting catalog cards.

The Library's participation in the CONSER (Conversion of Serials) project to build a national data base of serial publications and its direction of the National Serials Data Program (NSDP) are undertakings of great significance.

The Library's efforts at bibliographic description are not limited to the print media, however. With the collaboration of the National Information Center for Educational Media (NICEM) at the University of Southern California, the Library of Congress is able to catalog annually, using NICEM proof sheets, some 7,000 titles of new nonprint materials. These materials include motion pictures, filmstrips, slide sets, transparency sets, and video recordings. This effort is a good beginning but it should be noted that there are a number of nonprint materials that are not represented in the Library of Congress' system.

To provide a complete picture of the Library's bibliographic services the bibliographic functions of the Copyright Office must also be mentioned. The Copyright Office is the first source of transfer of materials to the Library. In the process of assigning a copyright registration number, the Copyright Office catalogs the materials for its own purposes and publishes a listing of copyrights in the *Catalog of Copyright Entries*. In 1975 the work of the Copyright Office Cataloging Division was expedited by the establishment of the first major online cataloging system in the Library. COPICS (Copyright Office Publication and Interactive Cataloging System) is aimed at the automation of all activities of the Cataloging Division; COPICS is able to supply regularly pre-sorted cards, a book form and a microform catalog, and a comprehensive machine-readable data base.

In addition to these specific services the Library has contributed its leadership and energy in cooperation with British, Canadian, and American library groups, to the preparation of a second edition of the *Anglo-American Cataloging Rules*.

Clearly the Library of Congress offers a number of highly valuable bibliographic services. However, there has been little evidence that the staff has taken a conceptual approach to the question of how to achieve a total national bibliographic system. On the contrary, the structure and internal organizational patterns of the Library often appear to have reinforced a fragmented and incomplete program of national bibliographic control. Nevertheless, the Library has, despite its organizational complexities, gradually introduced most of the basic components of a "United States national bibliography" (as understood within the context of the IFLA Universal Bibliographic Control program). It appears that with relatively little adjustment in terms of coverage, but with perhaps major reorganizational efforts within the Library, it would be possible to create an integrated U.S. national bibliographic system.

Since bibliographic control and access are two essential elements of library service in this country, the Advisory Group recommends that the Library of Congress give immediate attention to the following recommendations:

That the Library of Congress take the lead in developing a cooperative United States national bibliographic system encompassing initially a record of all works currently published in the United States, and that it grow to include bibliographic information for materials in all formats issued in the United States. That a group of cooperating libraries, including the Library of Congress, constitute the source for the bibliographic information comprising this system.

That the Library of Congress in mobilizing the efforts of other libraries in a cooperative national bibliographic system should recognize that the *National Union Catalog* and *Catalog of Copyright Entries* may need to be reconsidered. Consideration may be given to a cooperative dual structured system which would include an online computer-based bibliographic system with printed or micrographic products designed to meet the assessed needs of the national and international library community.

That the Library of Congress develop the capacity to offer both descriptive cataloging and subject analysis as well as to include both book and nonbook materials within the proposed U.S. national bibliographic system data base.

Reader Services

The reader services of the Library of Congress are seen to be varied and unique as the Library attempts to open its collection, interpret it, and make it accessible to all its users.

Basic reader services at the Library of Congress are handled by the Reference Department and the Law Library. In 1975 these two units accounted for the circulation of more than 2 million items within the Library and of over 200,000 off the premises. In addition, these units handled almost a million reference queries presented in person, by correspondence, or by telephone. In this role the Library has offered unparalleled assistance to other libraries in their support of education and scholarship.

Certainly the Library of Congress is unique among American libraries in terms of the extraordinary range and depth of the reference and research services it offers to its principal clientele—the U.S. Congress. Primarily through the Congressional Research Service (CRS) it will undertake almost any research activity, conduct a wide variety of literature searches, analyze contemporary issues, and provide access to a multitude of materials held in the Library's vast collections in support of the work of a member of Congress, the President, or other government officials.

In organizing itself to pursue these and other activities the Library has developed, in addition to the more traditional bibliographic aids, a number of specialized data bases which are accessible via computer terminals.

In 1975 the CRS answered over 244,000 inquiries from members of Congress; 709 major projects were undertaken and some 30,000 requests were answered by substantive reports, brief written responses, or consultation. This service has been enhanced by the development and implementation of the Legislative Information Display System (LIDS) which offers access to three legislative data files via computer terminals. This data base includes the bibliographical citation file of 75,000 references to CRS reports, official documents, and periodical literature, plus the major issues file of briefs on selected key issues.

To its general users, the Library offers an automated data base related primarily to the fields of science and technology. Named SCORPIO (Subject Content Oriented Retriever for Processing Information On-line), this system also includes access to three data bases developed by the Congressional Research Service: the Bill Digest File, its bibliographical citation file, and issue briefs. The system provides access by author, title, subject, LC classification number, or LC card number, to approximately 90,000 English-language monographs selected from the Library's MARC data base. In addition, the National Referral Center master file, consisting of descriptions of 10,000 information resources on virtually any topic of science and technology, is made available through SCORPIO. By means of the National Referral Center, the Library of Congress attempts to link persons having specific questions in science and technology with the appropriate organizations or individuals who can best answer their questions.

While the development of specialized data bases is the newest and most innovative reader service activity at the Library of Congress, certainly one of the Library's most successful undertakings has been its work in support of reader services to the blind and physically handicapped. Through a network of 54 regional agencies and 92 subregional outlets the Library offers braille, talking books, and cassettes to some 400,000 readers with diverse needs and interests.

This brief review of the Library's major reader services indicates that the Library of Congress has led the way in developing certain unique information services. The data bases and the related series of reports created by the Library's strong research arm are without equal. However, with the exception of the services to the blind and physically handicapped and the three-year plan to create a national bibliographic center for these activities, there seems to be little thought and no plan to share the data bases and appropriate special reports with other libraries in the country. Although it is recognized that certain of these services must maintain limited access provisions so not to hinder the work of the Congressional Research Service or indeed the Congress, SCORPIO was conceived as a public reference tool. By making available its various data bases and reports to the national library community, the Library of Congress would make a tremendous contribution to the revitalization of America's libraries' reference services, and, in turn, would directly offer all the American people a higher level of information services. At present, it is a frequently heard criticism that information requests received by the Library of Congress are not treated in a consistent manner depending on how the request is received. The development of local information services of high quality would enable the Library of Congress to refer information requests to the local level for response when appropriate and promote a compatible national level of information services.

A greater sharing of material resources is needed in other areas affecting direct services to readers. In recent years, serial publications have come to be of greater importance to scholars and researchers. The Library of Congress has an expansive collection of serials and periodicals, but even this great Library cannot hope to collect every periodical to meet the needs of its users and encourage access to its collection. Efforts are now under way to create a national periodicals system including a national lending system. Such a national pooling of periodicals resources would both expand the Library of Congress' collection of serials and make it more accessible to other libraries.

In light of these comments, the Advisory Group on Libraries recommends:

> That the Library of Congress in developing data bases for public reference use explore means of sharing access to these data bases with the American library community, perhaps in a similar manner by which the National Library of Medicine data bases are made accessible.

> That special reports by the Congressional Research Service on topics

of major interest be made more accessible to the public through some type of systematic distribution to libraries, possibly a depository arrangement.

That the Library of Congress encourage and participate in the creation of a national periodical system designed to insure timely access to serials resources throughout the United States.

International Role of the Library of Congress

All great research libraries must be involved in international activities, since scholars and scholarship, unable to survive without libraries, thrive best in conditions which permit the free flow of ideas from country to country and from culture to culture. No country's library and information system can be self-sufficient. Many countries have always had to rely to a great extent on information obtained from outside, and now, such is the volume and complexity of material generated, even the largest and most industrially developed countries are no longer able to collect all the information relevant to their needs.

Currently libraries and information services are seeking to discover how to optimize their services by drawing on the best available material whether at home or abroad. As a consequence, many international organizations are now showing interest in such questions as how to acquire, process, and disseminate information in the most effective and useful manner. Prominent among these are intergovernmental organizations such as UNESCO, Food and Agriculture Organization (FAO), World Health Organization (WHO), and other specialized agencies of the United Nations; regional intergovernmental organizations such as the Organization for Economic Cooperation and Development (OECD); and nongovernmental international organizations such as the International Federation of Library Associations (IFLA), the International Federation for Documentation (FID), and the International Council on Archives (ICA).

Because of the extraordinary range of its collections, encompassing unsurpassed stores of material dealing with American and other cultures, taken together with its wide-ranging and sophisticated service potential for meeting the needs of both national and international users, the Library of Congress is a natural focus point for United States involvement in international library and information service programs.

For the Library of Congress the most important international developments have been in the context of two groups of related program activities— NATIS and UNISIST—which are being developed under the aegis of UNESCO. UNISIST was initially concerned with science information, and NATIS was aimed initially at libraries and library services. However, the principles governing their basic program activities are essentially the same. Both are concerned with developing national and international resource sharing networks; both recognize the role of the national library in promoting these activities; and both identify program areas in which the national library has an important role to play.

Recently, UNESCO brought together most of its UNISIST and NATIS activities into a general information program under the supervision of an intergovernmental steering committee, the Information Systems and

Service Council, on which the United States is represented. The Library of Congress should play a major role in the affairs of the new Council and in the briefing procedures to be adopted by the State Department for guiding the United States representation on the Council.

Through the National Program for Acquisitions and Cataloging the Library of Congress collects a wide range of foreign material. In the case of some developing countries the Library may hold more comprehensive collections than the countries themselves, and the Library's foreign accessions lists may be even more timely and comprehensive than the national bibliographies where these exist. As a result, the Library is singularly well-placed to play an effective and valuable role in the international program for Universal Bibliographic Control (UBC) and related programs of UNESCO and IFLA.

The purpose of UBC is to insure that in each country some agency will record and describe all indigenous publications as well as produce and distribute appropriate bibliographic records according to international standards currently being developed under UBC sponsorship. The Library of Congress might encourage the development of national bibliographies where none exist by making the national libraries of these countries concerned the exclusive agents for publication of the contents of appropriate Library of Congress accessions lists within their national boundaries. Consideration might also be given to making available microform copies of out-of-print works to enable these libraries to fill gaps in their collections of indigenous materials.

Another vitally important area for international cooperation lies in improving world arrangements for increasing the availability of published materials of all kinds by means of rapid loan or photocopy services. The Library of Congress should initiate steps to establish appropriate international loan procedures for use by libraries within the United States.

Earlier reference was made to the traditional role of the Library in assisting international scholarship. More might be done to increase the extent to which the wealth of the Library's collections is mined by scholars from abroad by developing a visiting fellowship program.

In all of these activities the international credibility of the Library of Congress will be largely dependent on the degree of national support it receives. What may seem desirable internationally may create substantial problems nationally unless there is careful preparation. Moreover, recognition should be given to the substantial international programs of the other American national libraries and of the major library associations, so as to minimize conflict and duplication while enhancing opportunities for cooperation. It is therefore essential that appropriate consultative machinery be set up to insure that the leadership of the Library of Congress in international matters can be responsive to the library and information community it serves.

Specific recommendations are the following:

That the Library of Congress take steps to assure that appropriate representation of the U.S. library and information services interests will be made to the new Information Systems and Services Council of UNESCO. Further, that representatives of the Library should be inti-

mately involved in the briefing procedures adopted by the State Department in guiding the U.S. representation on the Council.

That maximum effort be exerted toward the implementation by UBC
by improving U.S. arrangements for the production and distribution
of bibliographic records; by extending national input to the International Serials Data System (ISDS); by developing the international
MARC system and MARC data-base exchange arrangements; and by
assisting in the design and implementation of appropriate international
standards for bibliographic description of all types of materials,
for transliteration, and for exchange of machine-readable records.

That consideration be given to the possibility of encouraging the
development of national bibliographies by making the national libraries
of the countries concerned exclusive agents for publication of the
contents of the appropriate Library of Congress accession lists within
their own boundaries.

That the Library establish active interagency communications with
other groups in the Federal network on matters of international concern and that appropriate consultative mechanisms be set up to insure
that the Library can be responsive to the needs of the American
library and information community.

That the Library of Congress assist in the organization of improved
arrangements for international interlibrary lending.

That consideration be given to the development of a visiting fellowship program aimed at making the wealth of the Library of Congress'
collections more accessible to foreign scholars.

The Library of Congress and the American Library Community

By appointing the present Advisory Group on Libraries, the Librarian
of Congress continues a tradition of involving the American library community in major discussions regarding the future of the Library of Congress.
In 1896, just prior to the move to the first new building, the Joint Library
Committee held hearings on the Library and its services. ALA sent witnesses to testify at the hearings. At the invitation of Archibald MacLeish,
the library community again participated in a review of the role, function,
and organization of the Library of Congress. While the record gives considerable evidence that the Library has consulted with the library community on basic questions affecting policy, function, and organization,
the relationship between the Library of Congress and American libraries
has suffered from a lack of continuity. Discussions have been all too in-
frequent and usually associated only with the formal review and planning
activities of the Library. An optimal advisory mechanism to the Library of
Congress from the library community might be appropriately constructed
within the following framework:

The relationship should be sustained over time.

The relationship should be multi-level, recognizing that the type of
advisory mechanisms required will vary in terms of the subjects being
studied.

The relationship should be pluralistic, recognizing that library and information services today are complex and that the interests of state, public, college, school, and special libraries need to be represented along with the concerns of the large research libraries.

The relationships should be both formal and informal, recognizing that both the Library of Congress and the American library community are far too complex and diverse for a single advisory mechanism to serve adequately.

Just as the American library community should stand ready to assist the Library of Congress in considering its mission, the Library of Congress should seek to serve American librarianship by acting as a focal point for activities which are in the national interest and have impact upon all libraries. For example, in the years ahead, greater attention must be given to the area of research and development to improve library methods and practices. Although the extent of the need exceeds the Library's present capabilities, there are some areas in which the Library could work cooperatively with other institutions. One especially critical area of concern is the preservation and conservation of library materials. The Library of Congress is currently engaged in advanced research to study the deterioration, preservation, and conservation of library materials. Expertise and knowledge of this type should be shared as widely as possible.

In the area of education and training the extent of the Library's activities and interests make it a valuable resource for the continuing professional development of librarians. A program of mid-career internships, supplemented by a series of training programs on specific topics, would allow librarians to advance their own skills, share their knowledge and imagination with the Library of Congress staff, and be exposed first-hand to the rich resources which the Library of Congress offers.

Some specific recommendations for consideration are:

That an advisory mechanism for the Library be created to represent various types of libraries, scholars, and other appropriate groups to assist the Library in articulating its national objectives and coordinating its activities in light of these goals. The Library should continue to select specialists to act as advisors to the various projects the Library undertakes.

That the Library develop appropriate means to share widely the Library's knowledge on the deterioration, preservation, and conservation of library materials.

That the Library establish a series of formal educational and training programs to provide continuing career development both for library professionals already on the staff of the Library of Congress and for librarians from outside the Library.

5. Report of the Media Advisory Group

As the world's largest library, the Library of Congress is involved in the collection of millions of items annually that add to its storehouse of information. But that information is worthless unless it is used. The true measure of whether the Library of Congress is a "great" library is its success in disseminating that information.

Any journalist given the opportunity to tour the Library, as we were, could not help but be impressed by the scope and quality of its material. It is the most remarkable institution of its kind in the world. We were left, however, with the impression that the Library's resources are not being used by the media, i.e., press, radio, television, as much as they could be. This is not entirely the fault of the Library.

The Library and the media have suffered from a kind of mutual benign neglect. In the case of the Library, the cause appears to be an unstated policy of not encouraging use of its facilities by the media. In the case of the media, the problem appears to be one of ignorance of the services available, caused at least in part by the Library's low-key approach to the media and public relations in general.

As surrogates for the public, the media are the principal information link between the public and its elected representatives. With its vast potential as a source of information, the Library of Congress is in a unique position to enhance that information flow and to improve both its quality and quantity.

We sense that one of the Librarian's priority goals is to make the Library better known to the public, so that the public can appreciate and make better use of it. We congratulate Dr. Boorstin for his initiative and leadership in seeking ways in which the Library can do more for the media and for all its patrons. In a democracy that depends on the education of its people for the formulation of policy, the Library is poised to perform a vital public service. It lacks only the mandate.

As a result of discussions and papers prepared by group members, the Media Advisory Group recommends changes in policy or service in the following areas of concern.

Publicizing LC Services to the Media

Ignorance on the part of the media about the Library of Congress and its services appears to be widespread. A check with a small sample of the approximately 1,500 members of the Washington, D.C., press corps, conducted informally by Richard Stewart, indicates that only a fraction of them are familiar with the resources and services available from the Library.

Any move to improve and expand the Library's services to the media requires abandonment of the Library's present low-key approach in favor of high-quality promotion and public relations, consistent with the dignity and integrity of the institution. Services and information should be the focus of any such program. Self-promotion, of course, is out of character with the Library's role and should be eschewed.

We urge that (1) services offered by the Library be outlined in a brochure distributed to all members of the House and Senate galleries and mailed to all local offices of major dailies, television and radio stations; (2) a mailing list for selected out-of-town mailing be drawn up to distribute brochures outside the Washington, D.C., area; and (3) announcements of LC services be placed with appropriate trade journals and professional organizations. (We must emphasize that brochures and announcements are meant to supplement the Library's attempt to personally speak to as many media personnel as possible. There is no substitute for telling the LC story on a one-to-one basis.)

> **Recommendation:** The Library must be more active in acquainting members of the Washington, D.C., press corps and the media outside Washington with the services it can provide. This can be accomplished by personal contact with local media representatives and by letter or telephone to the media outside the Washington, D.C. area. A brochure listing LC services to the media and listing LC liaison personnel should be widely distributed. Announcements of LC services to the media should be placed in appropriate publications.

Distribution of Products of LC Research

The Media Advisory Group was impressed by the scope and volume of research conducted by the Library of Congress. Clearly, products of LC research would be of great interest and assistance to media personnel working in related areas on both short and long-term assignments. Reports prepared by CRS are of particular interest to the group, as subjects are timely and well researched and data is current. The Library should publicize the availability of these reports in the galleries, over the wires, and by word of mouth.

> **Recommendation:** To the maximum extent possible, the Library should make available to the media CRS reports and other products of research conducted by LC specialists. We recommend that the Library draft guidelines which would permit CRS to release certain kinds of information about current topics in answer to inquiries from the press. Shopping lists of reports currently available from the Library should be widely distributed and frequently updated and instructions for obtaining copies of the reports clearly and concisely stated.

Provide Media Access to LC Computer Data Bases and Services

Unanimously, we believe that each of us and the organizations we represent could greatly benefit from access to LC computer data bases and services. Computers have a major potential for the future. (Many newspaper-television-radio offices already use them.) A national computer link that would allow the media to obtain printouts in their offices from the Library's growing computer banks would be a vital service and should be encouraged. Obviously, this would also serve thousands of libraries across the nation.

At this point, we are uncertain as to the technology involved in establishing such a media/LC computer link, but we do wish to register our interest and enthusiasm for the project. (Note: Some consideration might be given to user fees for this service and other services LC might offer the media, since the media, while performing public service, generally consists of profit-motivated business firms. The issue of fees should receive further study, possibly by a joint committee of media and Library personnel. It is possible, consistent with public law, that funds from such services could be specifically earmarked for use in improving media services.)

Recommendation: We urge the Library to consider the possibility of offering computer services and the use of its data bases to the media. Local media representatives in Washington, D.C., would particularly benefit from access to the Congressional Record and Legislative Index data bases, and the Library might consider a pilot project to place terminals which access these data bases in the House and Senate galleries.

Improve Media Access to Special Format Material in the Library's Collections

As we toured the special reading rooms on our first visit to the Library, we were impressed by the variety of material in the special collections.

Discussion of these collections turned attention primarily to the Prints and Photographs and Motion Picture material, because we frequently need appropriate material to illustrate print, film, or televised pieces. Unfortunately, discussion with the custodians of these collections revealed alarmingly numerous restrictions on the use of the material. Regrettably, copyright or donor restrictions and the time involved in obtaining required permission for use make this material inaccessible to all but a handful of media representatives.

Could the Library investigate the legalities of obtaining a blanket release for media use of various parts of these collections (as a public service or in-the-public-interest)? In the meantime, a system of coding materials in these collections, as to restricted or nonrestricted material, would greatly aid media researchers in identifying those items which are immediately available for reproduction.

Because time is of the essence in nearly all news assignments, researchers need to receive greater assistance from LC reference librarians who work with these special collections. These librarians hold the key to the collections and can reduce time spent on searching by discussing a project with a researcher and sharing their knowledge of the material.

A room for on-the-spot filming of items from these collections would save a great deal of time as well as wear-and-tear on the materials.

Recommendation: We strongly urge that the Library improve its reference service to the media in the areas of special format material. Direct access to reference librarians in these areas would save time spent on research and greatly facilitate selection of material. The Library should investigate means for removing some restrictions on use of special format material by the media and initiate a system for coding restricted and nonrestricted material so that researchers on a tight deadline can identify those items which are immediately available to them. We recommend that the Library provide a room for filming material from these special collections—a room equipped to handle special lighting requirements and stocked with easels, backdrops, and other equipment for filming. The Library should encourage media use of the Library's special collections for documentaries and other long-term assignments by publicizing these collections and outlining reference services provided.

Speech Writing by the Congressional Research Service (CRS)

In recent years there has been a tendency on the part of some Members of Congress to ask the Congressional Research Service to write speeches for them. In some instances the requests have been for partisan speeches. As Library officials realize, partisan speech writing is not an appropriate role for the CRS or for the Library of Congress. It is questionable if even nonpartisan speeches should be provided by CRS, since their drafting would seem to belong more properly to Congressional staffers.

CRS should confine its role to providing the data and information from which speeches are drawn. That is a logical function for CRS in serving the needs of Congress. We were told that speech drafting represents less than two percent of the CRS workload, but considering that workload, this is a considerable amount of work. It takes time from more vital services that CRS should be performing and contains within it the seeds for the politicizing of CRS, a circumstance that can only work toward the detriment of Congress and the Library.

Demands for partisan speeches are not dissimilar to demands made on CRS for partisan position papers. The dangers are inherently the same. Both could have a long-range effect on the integrity of the Library as a place of scholarly research. CRS currently provides background research to Congress on issues and includes various options on both sides of the issues. It is the role of each Member of Congress to weigh those options and decide for himself/herself which of them best serves the public interest.

> **Recommendation:** The Library should reinforce its credibility by declining to draft speeches of a partisan nature and avoiding any research that even has the appearance of partisanship. Such practices, when they occur, present a constant danger to the Library's hard-earned reputation for nonpartisanship, intellectual integrity, and independent scholarship. Ways must be found to isolate any such activity from the Library proper and to avoid the labeling of partisan research with the Library imprimatur.

Announcements of LC Events

LC events have not been publicized as widely as they could be. The Library and the media can and should work together to improve this situation. Care should be taken to alert all local papers, magazines, and broadcasting stations, including the wire services, well in advance of a special event at the Library. Exhibits, literary programs, concerts, and all special events should be announced to a wide circulation as early as possible.

> **Recommendation:** The Library should step up its campaign to publicize its special events, notify the media of events as far in advance as possible, and notify all potential sources of publicity.

Comments and Considerations

The following innovative services were discussed at our meetings or were addressed in working papers prepared by group members. They are presented here for consideration.

1. The Library of Congress could supply to the media on a regular basis briefing material on topics in or about to be in the news (background on nominees to political appointments, subjects/bills before Congress, holiday/seasonal notes, anniversaries of note, etc.).

2. The Library could provide interesting items to the press on a regular basis (historic, believe-it-or-nots, etc.) for use as filler.

3. Encourage greater media use of Library facilities by offering tours of LC, providing meeting space for media groups, scheduling periodic lectures/seminars on appropriate subjects, opening CRS topical briefings for Members of Congress to media personnel working in related areas, sponsoring debates on major public issues, etc.

4. Mail the LC *Information Bulletin* to media representatives on a regular basis.

5. Increase telephone information services, already available but underutilized, to assist reporters working against deadlines. However, this type of service should not be used by the media as a source of material requiring extensive research that could be done by the reporters themselves at the Library. Make it possible for a reporter to speak directly to the specialist who will work on the inquiry to avoid distorted transfer of information through middlemen and to allow a reporter to discuss a topic informally with knowledgeable sources. We cannot emphasize too much the value of this personal contact with Library specialists.

6. The use of telecopiers should be examined for transmission of documents of brief length to the offices of correspondents. This service might further be expanded to provide similar material to media offices outside the Washington, D.C., area. In such instances, however, the media can reasonably be expected to assume the transmission costs.

7. Consider changing the title of the Assistant Librarian for Public Education. "Education" has an institutional connotation and might better be changed to "public affairs" or "information."

Improving service to the media, and through it the public, would enhance rather than detract from the vital services being performed for Congress by the Library of Congress. In fact, expansion of such services could also, in the following ways, serve Congress:

a. The media, because of its ignorance about the Library, often resorts to subterfuge by using Congressional offices to secure information from LC. Direct use of the Library staff and resources would remove the burden from Congressional staffers and save considerable time.

b. Direct access to the Library would eliminate this media dependency on Congress, with its potential for undue influence on media reporting.

c. Access to LC expertise would improve the quality of reporting of national issues vital to both Congress and the public. The people, the Congress, and the media would all benefit.

d. The investment of funds for operation of the Library of Congress would return added value by introducing a new dimension—improved popular education on public issues through a better informed media.

6. Report of the Publishers Advisory Group

Chairman's Comments

All of us on the Advisory Committee I am sure enthusiastically support the general objectives for the publishing program envisioned in the first part of this report (The Publishing Program of the Library of Congress). We all believe that it would be very desirable for knowledge of the Library's collections to be much more widely known, for the fruits of their use to be more broadly published, and for otherwise unavailable materials in the collection to be brought into print.

I must confess, however, to some personal reservations about the practicality of some of the particular means of accomplishing these objectives suggested by the subcommittee that prepared the first part of this report. Since, because of time pressures, it has not been practical to clear the report with all the members of the committee, I do not know what their views would be on these particular reservations. My personal view is that it would not be possible for the Library to have an actual publishing house analogous to a university press without a number of changes in the law that would give it freedom to manufacture books where it chose, to copyright them, to market them independently from the Superintendent of Documents, and to retain and reinvest income from the sale of books. There would be considerable Congressional opposition to these amendments, and if approval could be obtained at all, it would only be at the cost of using up a considerable amount of the Library's good will in Congress. Even if these obstacles could be overcome, however, the experience of all but a very few university presses suggests that publishing programs of this sort can be carried on only with a very substantial subsidy, and such a subsidy might impose quite a considerable burden on the Library's budget.

If the Library is not to have a genuine publishing operation functioning similarly to a university press, I feel some personal discomfort about referring to its publishing operations as "the Library of Congress Press." Simply as a matter of accurate nomenclature, I think this use of the word "press" ought to be confined to institutions like the Yale University Press.

This is, of course, not to say that it would not be desirable to push ahead actively with publication of the sorts of books envisioned in the subcommittee report. But, I would think that this could be effectively done by arrangements with existing publishing houses, including both commercial houses and university presses, in which the Library stood in the role of author or sponsor of the publication, receiving royalties or perhaps granting subsidies, depending on the possible market for the book. There will be no lack of publishers willing to work with the Library in bringing out any viable book.

There should certainly be an active and vigorous office of the Library headed by the sort of person who might make a very successful university press director that would be charged with developing such projects, seeking out publishers, dealing with publishers who come up with project development of their own, and working out the necessary contracts.

I suspect that in this area we are talking about a difference primarily of name and that the subcommittee's recommendations and mine really do not differ basically.

On the magazine front, I certainly share the view that there should be a journal of the Library of Congress that would reach a broader audience and have a more comprehensive and perhaps livelier content than the present *Quarterly Journal*. I worry some, however, about the reference to such publications as the *Smithsonian* as a possible model. *Smithsonian* is highly commercial in its nature, dependent like commercially published magazines on advertising revenue for its support, and highly competitive with commercial magazines for both advertising and circulation revenue. It uses very expensive, hard-sell mail-order promotion to develop circulation revenue. It is a successful and very valuable publication because of the extraordinary ability of its editor, because the highly pictorial resources of the Smithsonian lend themselves to such a magazine much more readily than do those of the Library of Congress, and because the Smithsonian is technically a private corporation able to handle the manufacture, marketing, and the receipt of funds in ways that permit a commercial operation.

I don't think anyone has the thought of recommending that the Library of Congress undertake the publication of a similar commercial magazine, but if it should attempt to do so, controversial legislation would need to be enacted; and even if it were enacted, commercial success would be very doubtful. I wonder if what we need is not a better supported, vitalized, broader-ranging version of the existing *Journal*. This would cost some more money but not the sort of enormous investment that would be needed to launch something like *Smithsonian*. Its range would almost necessarily be confined to the scholarly and relatively intellectual community, but that in itself is a broad one. Articles of a popular sort about the Library or its collections could be initiated or stimulated by the publications office referred to and placed by it in more popular magazines.

Here, again, I think we are simply talking about slightly different approaches to a common goal.

Introduction

The members of the Publishers Advisory Group are enormously impressed with the incomparable resources of the Library of Congress and with its potentialities for service to the nation and, indeed, to the whole world of scholarship. Our two days' visit to the Library and our discussions with its executives and staff have reinforced the admiration of that institution we had all felt as individuals. We feel privileged to have been asked to make recommendations to the Librarian's Task Force. We do so in the memorandum that follows, but with diffidence, for we are keenly aware that it would take months, rather than the hours we have been able to spend, to achieve any comprehensive knowledge of the Library's activities and resources that are relevant to this memorandum.

The Publishing Program of the Library of Congress

It is, clearly, the obligation of a national library to publish—an obligation recognized for at least the past dozen years by the publications officer of the Library of Congress (see the 1967 report from the Library of Congress to the National Advisory Committee on Libraries) and now given new impetus and prospects by the new Librarian and the Assistant Librarian for Public Education. The Publishers Advisory Committee of the Library's Task Force wishes to support this obligation with the conviction and backing it plainly deserves.

To this end we urge the establishment of (1) a new and strengthened book publishing operation to be known as the Library of Congress Press, and (2) a new and imaginative periodical to represent the arts and humanities resources of the Library.

To clear the way for such moves, the Library needs (1) to secure from the Joint Committee on Printing of the Congress the necessary dispensations to insure freedom on the part of the Library to improve the printing and distribution of its books and periodicals, as well as to provide such copyright protection as may be necessary to make feasible negotiations with outside book publishers, whether university or commercial, for occasional publication under a joint imprint (the use on the title page of "Published for the Library of Congress Press" or "A Library of Congress Press Book") and (2) to seek additional funds, both from the federal budget and from additional outside sources of endowment.

The Committee was asked to consider other existing programs and resources under the Library's publications and it has done so, but its two major recommendations are given above. Additionally, we wish to make the following observations.

1. The *Quarterly Journal* (*QJ*) is an important and well-edited scholarly journal dealing with the Library's collections. It should be carried forward, with added resources for design, illustrations, and compensation for authors; with sufficient effort it can undoubtedly attract a larger audience. Begun during the MacLeish librarianship and budgeted as a supplement to the *Annual Report*, the *QJ* has, it has been observed, enlisted many staff contributors to examine and display, largely for in-house or least ingovernment purposes, material from the rich treasures that make up the Library of Congress today. Its circulation (3,500), its format (comparatively old-fashioned), and its low GPO price should all be reexamined. But more importantly, as the Library's Task Force has already pointed out in its January 28th, 1977 report, the *QJ* needs refocus—to establish its publishing purposes and to test its contents against this standard.

2. The Library's bibliographic publications and catalogs are indispensable tools for the American and indeed the world library and scholarly professions. Unquestionably their program should be enlarged and strengthened. It also seems apparent that these publications, with exceptions when warranted, should continue to be "published" by the Govern-

ment Printing Office in order to enter the public deposit and exchange programs.

But now we will return to perhaps the two most important considerations.

Library of Congress Press

Such an imprint, backed by a suitable staff and money, is long overdue and we suggest to the Librarian and his Task Force that its establishment could become a front-rank feature of his administration. To set up such a publishing arm, designed in the first and last instance to provide an outlet for the glorious and extensive materials already available in the nation's library storehouse, three moves need to be made at the outset: (a) the appointment of an experienced and qualified director selected from the ranks of university or commercial publishing executives—young enough to understand and develop the opportunity, old enough to grasp and make manageable the special problems of such a new publishing arm, (b) an advisory board composed in equal parts of Library brass, scholars, and outside publishing executives; and (c) a new financing program designed in realistic terms of both Congressional budgets and outside private gifts.

The first of these steps is a matter of recruitment; the third should result from a plan drawn up by the new director and his advisory board. Suffice it to say that the existence of Trust and name funds will provide both precedents and leads.

What to publish? Again the director and his advisory board should hammer out a program, again drawing upon the Library's previous experience to date and the rich resources already listed by the outgoing publications officer and from the fertile imagination of the Assistant Librarian. Many of their suggestions have already been cataloged in various reports and memos from these two professional individuals. Build from there. The problem will be one of selection, not search—at the outset at least. But it should be said that the Committee believes it of considerable importance for the new director of the Library of Congress Press and his inside and outside advisors to devise as early as possible a precise definition of its mission and the kind of books it will publish. The same applies to the "New Periodical" described below. Neither venture should be launched, we are saying, without the benefit of such thinking.

It should be added that we see the new Library of Congress Press bringing out some books on its own and others under a joint imprint with outside publishers, university or commercial, as the case may be.

The New Periodical

It would be handy and even helpful if we could suggest a title but we prefer to let that result from the sharpened thinking of those directly concerned inside the Library. We do cordially suggest three existing magazines which should be studied as models in the process of definition: the *Smithsonian*, the *Times Literary Supplement*, and *American Heritage*. From these it can be deduced that we favor a magazine for both the scholar and the lay intellectual—broadly conceived and produced with verve and skill. But, above all, a degree of innovation which will lead to a natural and thus an expanding audience. Obviously, the same ingredients are obligatory: (a) a talented editor; (b) a supporting advisory group; and (c) money. It is also plain that an editorial program for such a publication comes first. Here again the Assistant Librarian can offer a running start out of his own experience and forward thinking.

Summary

All it will take, in the last analysis, to inaugurate these two ventures is money and determination. Such money to develop each, including a mock-up for the periodical, can come to no less than $100,000 for each. To guarantee a secure beginning for each through a proving period of five years, from five to ten times that amount will be needed. The proving period ought to bring each project to at least 75 percent of self-sufficiency in realizable income.

The other need at the outset, we suggest with all due respect, is advice—competent as well as visionary, to assist the Library's officers with the best that the private sector can offer. However constructed, such advisory bodies ought also to provide buffer states between the Library and the Congress, on the one hand, and the Library and the private sector on the other; to engage the attention and the pride of the one and to neutralize and make constructive the support of the other.

Finally, as any useful component of any task force, we ask what can we do next, provided these recommendations enlist the attention of the Librarian and his associate, to assist in bringing off these enterprises?

Copyright

The Advisory Group has not undertaken to concern itself with the substantive provisions of copyright law. The question has been raised, however, whether the Copyright Office should continue to be a part of the Library of Congress. Certainly it has become a very large organization that consumes space and administrative support to a perhaps burdensome degree.

But as emphatically as we can state it, we believe the Copyright Office must remain in the Library. The copyright law provides by far the most important contribution of the Federal Government to the fostering of art, music, and literature. It is essential that its administration be in the hands of an agency dedicated to those ends. Responsibility for the Copyright Office indeed gives the Librarian one of his most important opportunities to exercise major cultural leadership.

Preservation of Library Materials

Through the Library of Congress Preservation Office, a good deal of attention is being focused on the question of preserving books. The problem is being examined from three perspectives: (1) preservation of the intellectual contents of materials so embrittled that they cannot be used without damage, but not of sufficient intrinsic value to justify preservation in the original format; (2) preservation of rare and intrinsically valuable materials in the nation's libraries which require the attention of expert paper conservators; and (3) preservation of present and future publications which are being printed on paper with a life expectancy of 50 years or less.

New Books. According to Frazer Poole, the Library's Preservation Officer, there are now about a half dozen mills that produce alkaline paper. The number is increasing at a very slow rate. Through various associations such as the Association of American Publishers (AAP), the Book Industry Study Group, BMI, etc., publicity and educational programs of all types should be conducted to make publishers and paper manufacturers aware of the need for considering preservation requirements when drawing up specifications for books. Publishers should always be represented on preservation task forces or committees that are being established under LC's program. The Library of Congress Preservation Office is proposing at least two alternatives to the problem in view of the difficulties of quickly getting all appropriate books produced on long-lasting paper. The first of these is to have a copy of all books or all appropriate books stored under controlled environmental conditions. The second is to have all books microfilmed and programs established to have the microform master stored under appropriate environmental conditions. Either of these alternatives could be facilitated by appropriate changes in the depository requirements of the copyright law. American publishers' support of these techniques could help obtain the necessary legislative action.

Old Books. The Library of Congress has prepared extensive proposals for seeking foundation and federal funding for a massive preservation and restoration program for previously published books. Although research continues on large-scale approaches like vapor phase deacidification, the outlook, at the moment, is not promising enough to provide clear-cut directions. Therefore, the Library is suggesting a large-scale microfilming program for old books. The Library of Congress realizes the enormity of this task, and that many commercial companies, including members of AAP, have extensive programs already under way. Any effort in this direction will require the full cooperation of library and publishing organizations. Publishers will want to stay in touch with this program because of the copyright implications and the opportunities for duplicating microform copies of books from materials filmed under the umbrella of a book preservation program.

In conclusion, American publishers can aid in the commendable effort to assure the preservation of our nation's publishing results by: (1) individually and collectively working to increase the availability and usage of long-lasting papers; and (2) individually and collectively cooperating in efforts designed to establish programs for assuring the availability of materials printed on short-lived papers.

Automated Bibliography and Cataloging

These are matters in which the library profession rather than the publishing industry has the primary concern, but the following suggestions deal with these aspects that particularly touch publishing:

1. *American National Standards Institute* (ANSI). Library of Congress membership on ANSI Z39 Subcommittees should be reviewed and strengthened. The Library should be well represented especially on ANSI Z39

Subcommittees engaged in developing standards for Standard Account Numbers (SC 30) since this numbering system will be assigned eventually to libraries and library systems. The Library should be encouraged to take a more aggressive role in educating librarians about their availability and in urging their application.

2. *International Standard Book Numbers.* ISBNs are now captured in the MARC system, input primarily, one assumes, through the Library of Congress Cataloging in Publication Program. The Library should apply the check digit validation in its computer handling systems and study the feasibility of notifying publishers about erroneous numbers. A study is currently in progress of the actual and potential uses of ISBNs in libraries (Helen Schmierer, University of Chicago, for the Committee for the Coordination of National Bibliographic Control). The ISBN system is now an integral part of Universal Bibliographic Control (UBC) programs, so positive steps should be taken, particularly in machine-based systems, to minimize the transfer of incorrect and invalidated numerical data.

3. *Cataloging in Publication.* As CIP becomes a reality internationally (it is happening) the Library should continue its leadership efforts, with extreme care to ensure that CIP in the United States remains beneficial to librarians and to publishers in this country. Information bulletins and CIP progress reports should be prepared and disseminated to publishers and to librarians to keep the program vital and responsive to real needs.

4. *Forms for collection of publisher data.* An effort should be made by the Library of Congress, in cooperation with the private sector (Bowker, Wilson, etc.) to make data-gathering forms as compatible as possible to reduce redundancy and minimize the labor employed in completing forms and keypunching by librarians and publishers alike.

5. *Data transmission, machine-readable codes, etc.* Experiments should begin on feasibility of machine transfer of selected data exchanged by publishers and the Library. Specific example: input and return of CIP data.

6. *Nonbook publishing.* The Library should increase its study of and involvement in bibliographically controlling audiovisual and other non-print media, working in cooperation with professional organizations (AECT, AMP, etc.) and with the private sector. The Library of Congress and private sector centralized bibliographic data-service organizations should schedule regular meetings to update each other, to point up unfilled needs for new services, and to encourage innovation. New technologies, are worthless in themselves; new applications must be sought that are both cost-effective and intellectually useful.

7. *Cataloging.* The Library should continue to move the library world here and abroad to rapid acceptance of standardized cataloging to make records prepared in one place more universally acceptable.

8. *Copyright Office.* The bibliographic and cataloging procedures and records of the Copyright Office should be made better known to potential users, including members of the private sector.

The Library, from its overall view of national activities in all these areas, has a responsibility to spot gaps and make these known so that other agencies and/or commercial enterprises can provide new services to help fill them. This appropriate sharing of the work load should benefit all concerned with improving bibliographic control. The Library of Congress is also in a position to discover needs of smaller publishers and attract them into the bibliographic mainstream, at the same time sharing this information with appropriate groups in the private sector.

Creation of an Archives of Publishing

An important service could be performed by the Library in providing leadership in the selection, preservation, and recording of archival material of the publishing industry that would document a major aspect of American cultural history. It would obviously not be practical for the Library itself to house in one central collection all the publishing archives that should be preserved. Indeed many important bodies of records have already been deposited in various university libraries. It is recommended, however, that the Library initiate a study which should involve not only the Association of American Publishers but probably also the Authors' Guild and leading literary and cultural historians to work out a broad plan for the preservation of important records of American authorship and publishing. Such a plan might include a definition of the types of materials that should be selected and preserved, articles or leaflets setting forth a plan, and the establishment in the Library of a central register of unpublished materials on publishing and authorship, in which could be based a guide to collections of these materials, revised and issued from time to time. If the Library wishes to exercise such leadership, the committee will be glad to urge the full cooperation of publishers.

International Activities

The Library has had an increasingly important, indeed, indispensable, responsibility in the acquisition and cataloging of foreign material not only for itself but for American research libraries generally. And the Copyright Office and the Register personally have been playing outstanding roles in international copyright. Perhaps in reaction to what some regarded as an earlier overcommitment, the Library's role in international matters over the last decade has otherwise been a relatively passive one. We believe that it is in the national interest for the Library to play an increasingly important part in international cultural affairs, one consonant with its preeminence in resources and professional stature. We are sensitive to the problem the Librarian and his senior colleagues must encounter in dealing with important competing demands for their time and attention, but we hope that it may be possible to develop and enlarge the international activities suggested below.

Executives of the Library and particularly the Librarian should, we believe, interest themselves in the affairs of UNESCO. For example, when in Paris, senior library personnel might call on the appropriate people in the Secretariat. The Library might well take an interest in the appointment of Americans to senior UNESCO posts (a number of posts to which Americans might now be appointed are vacant and will probably be filled by nationals of other countries in the absence of qualified American applicants). The Library should be informed with regard to appointments (by the White House) to delegations to UNESCO General Conferences and other major UNESCO-sponsored meetings. The International Book

Committee, which emerged from UNESCO's International Book Year, might command special interest as might the International Book Award and the UNESCO conferences convened from time to time on a regional basis to consider the supply of books and the fostering of publishing and library service in developing countries.

The Library, while staying meticulously within its division of labor in the federal establishment, could do much to revive and strengthen U.S. participation in UNESCO through appropriate liaison with the UNESCO office of the Department of State, and by maintaining contact with an active interest in the U.S. National Commission for UNESCO. The Library should exercise initiative in insuring that each newly appointed Chairman of the National Commission and other key members of the Commission feel that the Library is one of the bases most useful to touch in Washington; a major source of information, expertise, and moral support.

The foregoing is said with full cognizance of the political sensitivity that has inhibited U.S. participation in UNESCO in recent years. One may hope that this situation has improved, and that the efforts of American institutions and leaders concerned with international cultural relations can be usefully devoted to improving and strengthening UNESCO.

We also think it important that the Library strengthen its interest in the International Federation of Library Associations through personal participation of executives of the Library and through active involvement in the nascent organization of national libraries which is proceeding under IFLA auspices. Activity in IFLA may be particularly important because of the opportunity it affords for professional contact with major cultural institutions in eastern Europe and in the third world.

We would hope also that the Library might become substantively involved with the Government Advisory Committee (GAC) on International Book and Library Programs. This Committee provides senior publishers and librarians with an opportunity to discuss matters of mutual concern with those government agencies involved in book and library matters abroad. The primary government auspices of the Committee are the Department of State (Bureau of Education and Cultural Affairs), AID, and USIA, but other agencies (e.g., Commerce and USOE) have from time to time been actively involved. The Library frequently sends an observer (at one time the Deputy Librarian). The Register appears before the Committee for occasional reports and consultation. We believe reasonably high-level and consistent *participation* in the work of GAC by the Library would be mutually productive.

We recommend study of the possibility of giving more visibility in the publishing and library communities to the Library's Field Directors abroad. Publishers who have been in contact with those representatives have found them well informed about local publishing and library affairs and most helpful for general orientation. We see possible reciprocal advantages to increased contact between the Library's representatives and senior American publishers and librarians traveling in countries where such representatives are stationed.

The Library might suggest to the Chairman of the American Library Association's International Relations Committee willingness to have an observer attend the meetings of that Committee with a view to yet further strengthen collaboration between the Library and ALA with respect to international exchanges and other matters.

Possible Cooperation in Support of American Libraries Generally

During the latter 1950s and the 1960s the Federal Government followed a consistent policy of strengthening libraries. The Library Services Act (later revised as the Library Services and Construction Act), the National Defense Education Act, the Elementary and Secondary Education Act, and the Higher Education Act all contained provisions for Federal funding of library services. Among them they covered all levels: school, public, college, university, and research libraries. Although the principal support of libraries continued to come from state and local funding, the Federal appropriations made possible major extensions of service—to rural areas, in elementary schools previously without libraries, and through outreach programs to serve residents of depressed urban centers and other impoverished areas who had not been library users. This period of Federal support culminated in the work of the National Advisory Commission on Libraries, and the enactment by Congress of its recommendation of a formal statement of national policy that all Americans were entitled to library service adequate to their needs and that the Federal Government in coordination with programs of state and local governments and private institutions should move toward the accomplishment of that goal. A National Commission on Libraries and Information Services was created to make plans for the achievement of these policy goals.

But the policy was abandoned even before it was announced, and the Nixon Administration consistently recommended that all Federal programs for the aid of non-Federal libraries should be given zero funding and in effect be terminated. Though Congressional determination to continue library support partially frustrated this effort, Federal funding has not begun to meet inflationary costs. This partial withdrawal of Federal support has coincided with a critical funding problem of state and local governments, colleges and universities, and public school systems. As a result library support has been cut to critical levels all across the country.

The publishing industry had been very active in lobbying for library support in the 1950s and 1960s. It joined forces with the American Library Association in all its lobbying efforts, it provided the largest single component of the financial support for the Committee on Full Funding, it joined with the American Library Association in founding and supporting the National Book Committee to serve as a public voice for books and libraries, and it initiated, supported, and provided professional public relations and advertising support for National Library Week. We believe that these efforts may have had some part, perhaps some considerable part, in the extraordinary flow of library support in the late 1950s and 1960s. But for a variety of reasons, including perhaps controversies over copyright matters, publisher efforts also dwindled and substantially disappeared in the 1970s.

Now may be the time to revive joint efforts. A new administration is coming to power, with probably a greater concern for libraries and education. Copyright controversies have been amicably resolved. And the White House Conference on Libraries and Information Services has at least been called.

The role of the Library of Congress in catalyzing the sentiment for more generous national library support can perhaps be most effectively discharged by the Librarian personally through speeches, articles, Congressional testimony, cooperation with NCLIS, and similar actions. No doubt the Library will want to explore a variety of ways, perhaps through a continuing library advisory committee to maintain a close association with the library profession generally throughout the country. Perhaps one useful exercise of that leadership would be to convene a small group of publishers, authors, librarians, and distinguished public figures to explore the possibility of the creation of a new body to fill and greatly to enlarge the role of the former National Book Committee though acting with greater scope and independence than the earlier committee.

Possible Activities of the Library of Congress in Relation to the Role of the Book in American Culture

Obviously the entire function of the Library relates to the role of the book in American culture, but it may be appropriate to plan activities that can more vividly symbolize that role. This will be the more effective in view of the present Librarian's recognition as a distinguished scholar, author, and intellectual leader.

One thought that has occurred to the members of the committee is that the Library might be the sponsor of an annual event, a sort of Festival of the Book. There are various possibilities for such an occasion. It might occupy three or more days. Arrangements might be worked out with the National Institute of Arts and Letters to have the National Medal for Literature presented during the festival. A distinguished actor or actress or a group might give readings from great literature. An outstanding literary figure might give a major lecture on some aspect of literature. An outstanding foreign author might be invited as another major speaker. Seminars or discussions on intellectual freedom, here and abroad, would be important. Panel discussions of the practical problems of librarians, authors, booksellers, and publishers could take place. Government officials concerned with books and education and interested members of Congress and of the diplomatic corps should be drawn into participation. A chamber music concert, a reception or dinner in the Great Hall, appropriate exhibits, and similar events might add flair and color. We believe a truly exciting, internationally notable event, growing in importance over the years, can be achieved.

Members of the committee will be glad to be helpful if they can in any plans the Library may have for such an event.

But the Library's role, and that of the Librarian himself, should certainly not be confined to a single annual festival, important though that event may become. For most of its history, for example, the Library gave little attention to children's literature, yet its resources equip it to be a major center for the study of books and of reading motivation for children and young people. Public television affords a channel through which the Library may reach a broad audience with book-related programs. As the Library begins to develop programs of this sort, many other possibilities will suggest themselves. If, as suggested in the previous section, a successor to the National Book Committee is created, it could share responsibility for what can be a very exciting program.

7. Report of the Science and Technology Advisory Group

Introduction

In order to render the service to Congress for which it was created, the Library of Congress has to be the national library as well. Congress can accept no limit on its power of inquiry. Its Library must seek to place within the reach of Congressional inquiry, therefore, all of the resources of human knowledge and experience that can be encompassed by library technology. The National Commission on Libraries and Information Science, mandated by Public Law 91-345, has called for the organization of the "disparate and discrete collections of recorded information in the United States . . . [in] an integrated nationwide network"; the Commission recommended that the Library of Congress be designated for this purpose as the National Library.

The Library of Congress falls short of that designation—and of its Congressional designation equally—to the extent that it fails to bring the current literature of science and technology into its collections, its bibliographic services, and even into its Congressional Research Service. That literature has escaped comprehension by traditional library methods. It is expanding at a still-increasing rate. The unit of reference is not a book or the issue of a journal but a paper published in a journal. The most actively searched and consulted part of this literature is the most recent. What the librarian is called upon to manage here is not an archive but a forward-running shock-wave.

By and large, the access to this literature in the depth and precision required by its users has not been developed by libraries but by scientific societies, commercial enterprises, and a few government agencies in this country. These services have been pioneering the adaptation of computer technology to the uses of the library. They have demonstrated its considerable power to facilitate the fine-grained indexing of the highly structured literature of science and technology and for the rapid searching and retrieval of information from it. There is a rising demand among users of these services for improved common standards of indexing and for compatibility of machine access to them, as echoed in the call by the National Commission on Libraries and Information Science for "an integrated national network."

That demand will be met by the Library of Congress or by another agency. In the latter case, the nation would have to consult two (or more) national libraries, one for "culture" (excluding science and technology) and the other(s) for science and technology. This is a prospect to deplore at a time when questions posed by the advance of science so heavily condition the goal and value choices that confront the nation and the individual. Nor would the Library of Congress be able to carry on its Congressional mission, if command of the current literature of science were delegated to another library.

Even as the demand for new enterprise in the librarianship of science and technology has overtaken it, the Library of Congress is hard pressed to keep up with the work it has been doing so well. Science and technology are not the only fields of human activity characterized by exponential curves. The volume of publication in all fields runs ahead of other social indicators all around the world. At its present rate of accumulation, the printed record begins to overwhelm the storage capacity as well as the cataloging and retrieval procedures of the traditional library. A rising percentage of it originates in the 400 languages other than English represented in the Library's collections. The permanency of the printed record is threatened meanwhile by the "embrittlement" of the sulphite paper that came into wide use around the middle of the last century; measures thus far developed to rescue the most precious books could never be applied to the Library's entire collection. In addition, a still more rapidly growing electronic "literature" of sound and graphic image awaits collection, cataloging, and preservation.

For the challenges, tasks, and problems that now confront the Library of Congress the current rapid development of information science and technology promises a choice of new tools and strategies. The reduction in the cost of machine memories, for example, has bearing not only on the cataloging and storage of library collections but also on the problem of preservation, whether of graphic images, sound, or text. As will be discussed at greater length below, the digital encoding of information in such memories makes the record secure against decay even as the record is reproduced, generation after generation, to rescue it from the decay of its physical carrier. In sum, it can be said with confidence that the new science and technology of librarianship makes it possible for the Library of Congress to fulfill the role of National Library and thereby better serve its principal client, the Congress.

This report will present its findings and recommendations under two headings: (a) what the Library of Congress should be doing about the Librarianship of Science and Technology and (b) what the Science and Technology of Librarianship can do for the Library of Congress. The recommendations of this report are here briefly stated.

Recommendations:

1. The Library of Congress should take the leadership in designing and organizing the central switchboard of the national— and international—network that is needed to integrate the scattered and disparate libraries and information banks of science and technology. In this connection, the Library should secure—by negotiation with the proprietors of those libraries and information banks or by invocation or appropriate amendment of the new U.S. copyright law—the contents of those banks to its own fair usage in its service to Congress. The Li-

brary's leadership in the organization of the central switchboard can help to settle otherwise the many open questions that
surround the rights of the ultimate copyright holders and the
standardization of the technology required to keep book on and
exact payments for such rights.

2. The Library of Congress should promote and organize the collection and cataloging of certain bodies of "fugitive" literature
   in science and technology that have relevance to contemporary
   public policy and are central to the history of science and technology. This includes the studies and reports produced for
   public and private decision on major engineering undertakings
   that are otherwise lost to public access in the proprietary files
   of industry and the overlooked files of governmental agencies.
   It also includes computer programs, the "software," in the
   mainstream of the rapidly evolving information-communication technology.

3. The Library of Congress, as the central switchboard in the
   library network, should take measures to place itself in
   command of the rapidly expanding resources of information-
   communication technology. The projected Library planning
   office should be supported by a strong research office, charged
   with keeping abreast of the technology and pushing the theory
   and practice of librarianship forward as technology lifts logical
   and material constraints.

4. The Congressional Research Service should seek its own continued development as the model of librarianship required to
   bring the work of science and technology into rational connection with the social and political processes that make public
   opinion and policy. At its highest level that connection must be
   made, as it is now made through the Congressional Research
   Service, by dedicated and disinterested scholar-librarians. The
   policy analyses, position papers, and reviews of the literature
   prepared by the staff in response to inquiry from Congress
   should be regularly published in order to bring this important
   work into the mainstream of the literature of science policy.

5. The Library of Congress should sponsor the development of
   digital-encoding technology for the preservation and the restoration of the present and future record of sound and graphic
   images and, possibly, even of the text record that is threatened
   by "embrittlement."

6. The Library of Congress should soon address the development
   or urgently needed criteria for the sampling, preservation, and
   retrieving of the fugitive "literature" of the electronic media,
   in both sound and graphic image, radio and TV.

7. The Library of Congress should bring the wealth of computer-
   mediated imagery into the reach of its clients, including especially the new atlas of the world generated every day by
   earth satellites. The Library should give leadership to ensuring
   that the much more detailed and live atlas in the custody of
   the National Security Agency is not lost to the interests of more
   constructive human purpose.

8. The Library of Congress should sponsor the development of the software and hardware of information-communication technology for making the record of human knowledge and experience accessible to the electorate as well as the the informed searchers of the record it has hitherto served. The aim of this recommendation is the development of the "transparent library," accessible not only in Washington but at every site in the country where demand will sustain the allocation of the necessary physical resources.

9. The Library of Congress Division for the Blind and the Physically Handicapped should be supported in its good work by all of the developments in information-communication technology sponsored by the Library in connection with its total mission.

The Librarianship of Science and Technology

The traditional technology of librarianship turns upon service to searchers of the printed word. The unit of search is the book or the "volume" of a periodical. The Library of Congress has long had the leading role in the standardization of the broad subject headings and subheadings in the library catalog. The Library's MARC system is now displacing the card catalog in the country's major libraries.

In cataloging scientific books, the Library has pushed established procedures to provide more detailed categorization of their contents. Because the structure of the work of science is so much more highly ramified than that of more humanistic writings, a scientist searching the Library catalog finds its descriptors and the depth of indexing upon which they rest to be inadequately small compared to the systems that now provide access to the periodical literature.

The Information Bank Switchboard

In the indexing of the periodical literature, in common with other libraries, the Library has not undertaken to reach below the title of the journal. The unit of search in science and technology is not, however, the journal or a volume of it but a paper published in a given issue. Such papers carry the primary record of the work of science. They are the unit of search until their substance has moved into the textbook knowledge from which the next generation of scientists begin their search of the literature. This literature is not, therefore, a settled record for consultation in an archive. The very transience of the need to consult it is a measure of the urgency of the demand to have its contents accessible.

That demand has been met not by the familiar library but by highly specialized agencies set up to track the literature of this and that field of science and technology. Such services have been developed by scientific societies (e.g., American Institute of Physics), by commercial firms (e.g., Data Courier, Inc.), and by government agencies (e.g., National Agricultural Library). Supported largely by fee-for-service payments, they have been able to develop novel techniques for abstracting (e.g., Chemical Abstracts Service of the American Chemical Society), for key-word indexing (e.g., Excerpta Medica), and for citation indexing (e.g., Institute for

Scientific Information). The last provides a powerful method for detection of trends in research as well as for the illumination of hindsight.

Needless to add, these enterprises have drawn heavily upon and have also contributed to the development of the software of information and communication technology. Responding to the *ad hoc* emergence of markets for their services, they have each perfected their own idiosyncratic adaptation of the technology. They offer, as a result, great variation in standards of referencing and low compatibility in system design. A few major enterprises have undertaken to bring assortments of these systems together in comprehensive information banks, e.g., Lockheed Information Systems in the private sector and National Technical Information Service in the Department of Commerce for the output of U.S. government agencies.

None of the existing systems—super- or otherwise—satisfies the increasing demand for ready access to the total current literature of science and technology felt so urgently in every field. Nor do they provide reliable access to the literature originating outside of the United States (e.g., the numerous bibliographic files, data banks, and addresses in Europe listed in the current edition of the ASLIB-EUSDIC directory) that records a rapidly increasing percentage of the total world output of the enterprise of science and technology. The universality of science, transcending national and cultural boundaries, requires that the literature of other nations be as accessible to the searcher as that of his own.

As the National Library and one of the principal international libraries, the Library of Congress is ideally positioned to proceed with the organization and design of the central switchboard needed to make these immense resources accessible to their users. The task implied by Recommendation 1 of this report is entrepreneurial and administrative. It is not proposed that the Library engage in the collection of the ultimate physical documents or in the in-depth cataloging and indexing now conducted so well by others. Rather, it is the Library's function, according to this recomendation, to take the lead in bringing the many parties at interest together to secure agreement on the design of the central switchboard and see to its realization and perfection. That will require the promotion of standards for indexing and abstracting and the improvement of the compatibility of the many free-standing systems for linkage to the switchboard and to one another.

This report advances the recommendation that the Library of Congress bring the content of existing U.S. information banks into its own access without fee for the fulfillment of its Congressional function. In performing its Executive Branch function of administrating of the copyright law, the Library finds itself in possession of a copy of every printed work (and of much else besides!) put under copyright protection. Considering that the information banks will be operating under that protection after 1 January 1978, even though their contents are not on deposit, the Library should be entitled to free access to those banks. What is more, most of the demand for as well as the supply of the material referenced in those banks is generated by the expenditure of tax-levy funds; the Library should, therefore, be able to advance an eminent-domain argument to the same end.

In sum, the Library of Congress should have free use for its own purposes to all information accessible through the central switchboard. On behalf of the ultimate copyright holders, the Library can help to secure rights otherwise to compensation for use of proprietary information by taking initiative in settling the economic and legal questions surrounding such rights and in standardizing the technology for keeping book and exacting payment for use of such rights.

Many of the same public-interest considerations call for the cataloging and preservation of the neglected literature for studies and reports developed in connection with public and private decisions about large-scale engineering enterprises, as proposed by Recommendation 2 of this report. Despite its massive size, this is a fugitive literature. Its inaccessibility occasions frequent reinvention of the wheel; the last product of accumulative experience does not contribute to improvement of the next. This literature often bears more directly on public policy than does that of fundamental scientific research. Again, the Library need not itself undertake the collecting of the physical documents provided it makes appropriate arrangement for their preservation and for access to them through the central switchboard.

A subset of this category of unpublished and unprinted literature is the accumulating body of computer programs developed for research, engineering, and system-management purposes. These should be brought into access through the central switchboard by appropriate legal procedures.

Because the entire literature of science and technology is characterized by high specialization and yet also by an equal degree of interpenetrating relevance from one end of the spectrum to the other, the requirements of its users overrun the standards of indexing and cross-referencing that satisfy searchers in other fields of knowledge. The Library of Congress should encourage the continued development of key-word and citation indexing and of other pathways into the labyrinth of this literature. This should be a major preoccupation at the research office, the creation of which is urged in Recommendation 3 of this report.

The National Referral Service sends the searcher on to primary sources outside the Library. Especially pending the period of the development of the central switchboard, this service should be kept well tuned and operational. It will have a role even after the switchboard is perfected and operating, as providing a human interface between the searcher and the primary sources.

The Congressional Research Service

The Congressional Research Service transacts the Library's principal business with Congress. This remarkable organization, exhibiting at once the character of a newspaper city room and a think tank, is central to the concerns of this report. The Congressional Research Service conducts the librarianship of science and technology at the highest level. Going beyond the passive reference and annotated bibliography that are the standard output of library science, it produces critical syntheses and interpretations of the literature that relate its substance to the choices and decisions of the political process. The Congressional Research Service may be regarded, therefore, as a paradigm of librarianship as it may become, when its routine functions are delegated to machines. With the mechanization of the hierarchic logic of the index, the librarian will be freed to bring into action the uniquely human capacity for associative logic.

The quality of the data-gathering and analytical services supplied to Congress by the Congressional Research Service are of crucial immediate importance for two reasons. First, these services are at the heart of the statutory function of the Library; to maintain their excellence is a primary obligation *de jure*. Second, the Congress needs not merely adequate, but excellent reference services now as it never has before; the great technical complexity of much current legislation attests to the urgency of this need.

The Congressional Research Service is distinguished by the intellectual vigor and dedication of its professional staff. That is not belied by the further observation that its work product does not always display the same excellence.

The "city room" aspect of the Congressional Research Service ranges from instant response on specific points of inquiry, to the preparation of short background papers, to the anticipatory assembly of documentation on an evolving public issue or piece of legislation. Demands at these levels on the staff are rapidly increasing. Moreover, the Congress itself is taking a more active interest in technical matters, as evidenced by the presence of increasing numbers of technically sophisticated personnel on Congressional office and committee staffs and of Library-access terminals in Congressional offices. The increased traffic in inquiries and the availability of alternative routes of access for the members of Congress and their staffs suggest that there should be a critical review of procedures at these first levels of inquiry. Two areas that should be considered for possible reorganization are these:

1. Priority determination: Members of Congress invoke Library of Congress services for a variety of purposes. Unless the resource (in this case, Library of Congress staff time) can be provided in superabundance, allocating it properly requires some determination of priority. Consideration should be given to differentiating inquiries as to purpose; for example: the answering of constituents' questions as against the preparing of a piece of legislation.

2. Treatment of requests by complexity: The present "triage" system, which assigns Congressional inquiries to level of response, may not be the best for future needs. The availability of Library terminals to members of Congress suggests the organization of a primary data bank or service to provide first-level response almost without involvement of Library staff. Further study could reveal ways in which instruction of members of Congress and their staffs by Library personnel could produce substantial cost-savings.

An especially important problem, at all levels of service, is the quality of material available for response to inquiry. These reflect the deficiencies of the Library in the librarianship of science and technology. The overwhelming bulk of such material belongs to the secondary literature. For the most part, it comes from popular or semipopular magazines. Thus, although the Congressional Research Service "Magazine Manual" lists *Science* and *Nature*, it does not include *Proceedings of the National Academy of Sciences, U.S.* nor any one of a number of other extremely important comprehensive or review journals in the sciences which are themselves nearly secondary. This situation occasions considerable alarm because of its probable consequence for the legislative process. In the growing number of areas in which understanding of science and technology is critical to achieving good outcomes in public policy, it is hard to imagine anything worse than the reinforcement of "conventional wisdom" that is likely to result if the policymaker has access only to the least professional version of scientific opinion. Attention should be given to upgrading the depth and authoritativeness of the data banks available to answer Congressional inquiries.

At the top level of the triage come the major reviews, position papers, and policy analyses prepared in response to requests, often initiated by committees of Congress. These documents represent the professional peak of the Library's work. At their best they are extended, demanding, and highly influential works of scholarship. The group of scholar-librarians responsible for their production is extraordinarily well qualified; in terms of scholarly ability they equal or exceed equivalent professional staffs at the National Academy of Sciences, the Office of Technology Assessment, or other agencies responsible for Federal output in the area of science and public policy. They do their work, moreover, under time pressures normally greater than that experienced by, for example, personnel of the National Academy of Sciences.

The quality of the output from the top professional staff of the Congressional Research Service is generally high. Members of Congressional staffs and scholars who use them concede, however, that the quality is not as steady as might be wished and that some of the reports lack either the depth or the discrimination of important from unimportant matters required to make them maximally useful. Certain improvements in circumstances in which the work is done can be recommended to help a first-rate staff produce a more consistently excellent work product.

First, it has to be said again that the current periodical scientific literature is not adequately represented in the information banks available to Congressional Research Service staff for policy research. The sources that are available consist too much of secondary material, with the attendant dangers of reinforcement of secondary notions alluded to above. Thus, on a fairly typical subject of current political interest (nuclear fuel elements) the Library's own reference system yields only books, government publications and general-circulation magazine articles. To get beyond this level of discourse, the searcher must call in the Lockheed system which, on the question at hand, surfaces a good many significant entries in the technical literature (including important work in Canadian and Indian journals). The log of the access terminals shows, however, little use by the Library staff of these "outside" data banks. Against their use there stands, among other obstacles, the matter of a fee payment on which this report makes a recommendation above, in another connection.

The second circumstance has to do with the conditions under which the scholar-librarians of the Congressional Research Service must now work in relation to their peers. Most of the significant works of the group are published only in Committee prints or other Federal publications; they are poorly catalogued, even in the Library of Congress. As a consequence, they are, in most instances, lost to the literature of science and public policy. These circumstances isolate the Congressional Research Service staff from professional colleagues elsewhere. The absence of a more regular mechanism of publication deprives them of the beneficial effects of peer review and of critical dialogue in professional journals. As a result, there is a danger that the Congressional Research Service staff will, despite the best intentions, grow apart from the standards of their own professional peer group.

If this work product could be brought more into the mainstream of scholarly publications in science and public policy, that would improve the quality of work provided by the Congressional Research Service staff to the Congress. It would also make work at the Congressional Research Service more attractive to two categories of other scholars: first, those who might wish to join the senior professional staff at the Congressional Research Service but who may hesitate to do so because of fear of isolation; and second, those who might wish to join the Library of Congress for a shorter period of time as visiting scholars.

With respect to the latter possibility, the Library of Congress should take advantage of the Intergovernmental Personnel Act (P.L. 91-648) to bring in qualified personnel from other Federal agencies as visitors for a half or whole year at a time. In fact, the Library should seek to bring in, on a temporary "flow-through" basis, as many people as possible from other government agencies, state and local as well as Federal, and from academic and business circles. These visitors could amplify the not-too-large research community of the Library of Congress and reduce the present isolation of that community from the "real" world outside. Such interaction is essential to personnel engaged in the at once journalistic and scholarly task of making reliable information flow in response to the political process.

There is, finally, the matter of the relationship between the "think tank" function of the senior Congressional Research Service staff and the rest of the Library. A certain tension between the librarians of the Science and Technology Division and the members of the Congressional Research Service staff now prevails. This relationship needs to be improved for immediate reasons, having to do with the harmony and efficiency of the present staff. But there is a long-range reason, too. The Library is, plainly, evolving toward a set of services which will bring its great resources to users through an extended computerized library network. The highest level interface in such a system must be supplied by people; by scholars and scientists who comprehend a field of learning and can contribute to its application to human need in the midst of the social and political contests that attend technological change. In this function the senior Congressional Research Service staff must be joined by senior librarians in other divisions who have equivalent experience and scholarly ability, and by others brought more temporarily to residence at the Library of Congress. They will not only conduct the highest function of the Library by their mastery of the Library's resources; they will also contribute to those resources by their work.

The Science and Technology of Librarianship

The "state of the art" of librarianship, as practiced at its best by the Library of Congress, developed around the collecting, cataloging, and retrieving of books. It is now taxed to the limits of its command of those functions by the steeply rising tide of publication in all fields in all countries. More ominously, perhaps, it is entirely bypassed by the increasing proportion of the record of human experience that is not recorded by the printed word.

These circumstances are forcing a revolution in librarianship. Technologies developed under other auspices for other purposes are not only supplying solutions to needs and problems as recognized by traditional librarianship; these novel technologies are bound in the end also to change the nature of the library. Plans for the future of the Library of Congress must reckon with its transformation from an archive accessible to trained and determined searchers into the organizing center of a web of communications that will make its resources accessible to the electorate at large.

The Library Research Office

The Library of Congress must place itself in command of new developments in information-communication technology if it is to remain in charge of its own destiny. This does not mean that the Library research office, the creation of which is urged in Recommendation 3, should itself undertake research and development in these technologies. It should work neither on hardware nor software, but rather on the "front-end" questions of library science. The new research office can count, for example, on indefinite continuation of the annual 30 percent decline in the cost per bit of active computer memory. It must reckon with the possibilities for compression of storage space represented by the 10^{10} bit capacity of the N.V. Phillips-MCA videodisc that is about to enter the U.S. consumer-electronics market. For the Library's long-range planners, the research office should take note of the wiring of American cities by cable-TV networks—that can become, along with other high-capacity networks, channels for two-way communication, for consultation of a library. It can also figure that the future holds early prospect for retrieving the text along with the reference in many fields of knowledge. Thus, through its research office, the Library must acquire intimate current familiarity with all of the relevant technologies if it is, in the words of J. H. Shera, to ". . . rise above the computer, above the engineer, above the systems analyst" and seize the opportunities for more effective service to Congress and to the public made possible by the rapid progress in relevant technologies.

The Library's first ventures into use of the new kinds of hardware betray its lack of connection elsewhere to science and technology. For example, the quality of images in its microfilm and microfiche files is generally wretched; the Library should be setting the standards for these technologies. The Library's first venture into photocomposition has given it a system that has no diacriticals and so is useless for composing in at least one major realm of Library concern, linguistics. Competitive and equally available systems, such as the UNIX time-sharing system, could have supplied diacriticals and capacity to format mathematical equations as well. The Library's music department ought to know of the system developed by Leland Smith at Stanford University that can input a musical score from a standard keyboard and establish a computer file from which orchestral parts can be automatically extracted. With the sophistication in science and technology it ought to possess for larger reasons, the Library can maintain secure standards of flexibility and quality in its employment of new hardware.

In the development of the MARC system, the Library of Congress has made the kind of contribution to the science and technology of librarianship for which it is best qualified. The conversion of the library card catalog to machine-readable form constitutes a major contribution to the development of the central switchboard of the ultimate national and international library network. Again, proceeding from a solid grounding in the front-end questions of library usage, the development of the SCORPIO system sets new precedents for making computer files responsive to innocent inquiry. Experience with this system from the many terminals in use on Capitol Hill will show how its reach can be extended beyond the in-house files now accessible to it.

On the output side of the switchboard, much of the work required for the building of the network of user libraries in this country, at least, has already been accomplished by the Ohio College Library Center. That agency now has 930 libraries in 48 states tied into a computerized file of bibliographic information located at Columbus, Ohio, for online consultation on cathode-ray-tube terminals through dedicated telephone lines. Membership in the network permits a single library to share with all the others in the on-line union catalogue of 2.5 million records; in shared cataloging (in which an entry by one library serves for all, most entries made before the hard-pressed Library of Congress crew gets around to them); in serials control; in acquisitions; in interlibrary loan communications; in retrieval by subject. This network is designed for incorporation in a future national or international network without major investment in new software.

On the input as well as output side, the task of the Library of Congress is facilitated by the Research Library Group organized by the libraries of Harvard, Yale, and Columbia and the New York Public Library. These libraries share many of the burdens of collection and cataloging carried by the Library of Congress.

In sum, as the Library of Congress takes up the challenge of supplying leadership in the development of the national and international library network, it will find many elements already in being. To put the pieces together, however, will prove to be an objective challenging enough for the world's foremost library. It will require, in addition to statesmanship, the kind of command of information-communication technology that is urged on the Library in this report.

Preservation by Digital-encoding Technique

The relevance to library science of the information-processing power of the computer was easily recognized; it is now being put to work by systems such as MARC. The potential saving of shelf and storage space by the new technologies is celebrated by spectacular numbers: the N.V. Phillips-MCA videodisc could capture the entire printed record held in the Library of Congress on 30,000 discs. A less well-recognized and celebrated boon is the prospective cure of the problems of preservation that is to be had from the technique of digital-encoding of information.

The digital record alone is secure against the breakdown of the medium on which it is carried and against loss of integrity as the record is reproduced onto the next generation's carrier. The point can be best understood by contrasting the nature of the digital record with the more familiar analogue media. The most familiar analogue medium, a photograph, records on a continuous gray scale, or on the continuous scales of saturation of a set of dyes, a more or less satisfactory analogue representative of the original. However satisfactory, reproduction of the record onto the next generation of photographic film entails loss of faithfulness to the original, not only from decay of the image on the aging master but from unavoidable aberrations in the chemistry and physics of the darkroom. With respect to text, the contrast between black and white is too great, of course, to be lost in the aging of the master; most loss of contrast can be corrected by enhancement in reproduction to the next master. At present Library of Congress performance standards, however, illustrations are all but lost in the first generation microfilm and microfiche. The storage and reproduction of analogue signals on a magnetic tape is attended by analogous and equally unavoidable imperfection and deterioration, owing to the dependence of the record on the qualities of the medium.

Digital-encoding makes the record independent of the medium. The unit of recording is the black-or-white, on-or-off, yes-or-no presence or absence of the threshold signal. In whatever medium the record is made, the discrete digital signals may decay differentially as compared to one another, but the record remains unimpaired so long as the medium, for example a magnetic tape, holds the signals above the threshold. Should signals be lost, they may often be confidently reinstated upon logical analysis of the record. By the same kind of procedure a parent analogue record may be restored and enhanced upon encoding in a digital record.

This technology commends itself to the Library of Congress for preservation of its graphic arts and music collections. For the digital-recording of the Library's collection of motion picture film, existing television technology offers what amounts to nearly off-the-shelf equipment. Development of the gear for the digitalizing of the Library's music collection presents no deep questions. Color and pitch can be securely established to calibrate future performance and reproduction from such digital records by completely objective and reproducible instrument readings.

Combined with optical scanning, the digital-encoding technique might even be used to secure the preservation of text. A by-product gain would be the freeing-up of shelf space. Since analogue methods are adequate, the possibility turns on economic considerations and the further evolution of digital-encoding technology.

The Librarianship of the Electronic Media

The recently enacted copyright law requires the Library of Congress to set up the American Television and Radio Archives, to maintain and publish catalogs and indexes of the archives, and to make its holdings available for study and research. This requirement poses new problems and fundamental new questions to library science. Archiving the massive and continuous flow of the symbolic environment created by television and radio raises issues different from those of archiving printed and film media.

The consumer's "use" of broadcasts, especially television, is relatively nonselective. Viewers and listeners select not so much titles and programs as periods of time for viewing and listening to whatever is on the air. Sampling of material to be archived should reflect, therefore, the structure of programming and of program exposure, rather than only the selection of specific programs. Archiving should include contextual materials (news, commercials, etc.) as well as data on audience size and type, and indicators of trends over time.

The specification of the unit to be archived and indexed becomes, therefore, a complex problem of purpose and flexibility, to be determined empirically. Traditional program (or other genre) classifications have little meaning or validity in the archiving of broadcast material. An analytical scheme and typology suitable for indexing the time, space, thematic, demographic, and action structures of dramatic, documentary, news, and commercial (as well as perhaps musical) materials must be developed and tested. The investment is too great and the accumulation of materials too rapid to risk false starts or undue obsolescence.

A user-oriented search and retrieval system and a financially and technologically feasible retrieval and display system will have to be developed. The complexity and novelty of these and other tasks related to the adequate archiving of broadcast materials require a substantial period of development and pilot testing.

Computer-mediated Graphics and the New Atlas

The record of human experience and understanding is finding its way off the printed page through the development of another technology for generating and communicating graphic images. This is, for lack of a better generic term, computer-mediated graphics. With a mounting traffic of its own alongside that of television, this technology has an increasing role in getting the world's work done. It is the medium through which the computer interacts most responsively with its operators. An image on the cathode-ray tube or the plotting board may embody the analysis and synthesis of a room full of computer printout. Computer-mediated graphics is equally the medium through which earthbound man continues his exploration of the solar system by far-ranging robot spacecraft. From satellites closer to home—from the Landsat and the synchronous-orbit weather-monitoring satellites—the most spectacular images made by the new technology are imprinting the public consciousness with a new vision of the Earth and of man's place on it.

The Library of Congress should see to it that the software of this technology is collected and indexed along with the computer programs mentioned in Recommendation 2. Again, so long as the Library sees to it that these materials are collected and indexed by some responsible institution and are accessible through the Library-centered network, it is not necessary for the Library itself to be their physical custodian.

The maps that issue from the Landsat and weather and other satellites on similar missions stretch the terms of the traditional map collection. With great virtuosity the Landsat satellites are turned from day to day on surveys of the Alaskan biome, of Antarctic land forms, of the marine resources of the Gulf of California; to monitoring the moisture in Nebraska wheat fields; to classifying the timber resources in the Rockies; to assaying the mineral resources of Arabia; to the planning of land use in Israel; to making ethnographic and archeological maps of Central America. Bibliographic trails into this wealth and variety of material should be laid from all the disciplines it enriches. NASA is well qualified to maintain custody of the rapidly expanding collection; it is accessible and retrievable by wire. The Library of Congress should plan soon to equip itself with terminal facilities to put this resource of imagery readily at the disposal of its clients.

A still richer resource of the same kind remains, for the present, beyond public access. This is the enormous daily output of the military satellites in the custody of the National Security Agency. That runs not only an order or two of magnitude larger than that of the NASA satellite program; it also presents images resolved close to the detail of "ground truth." The resolution of these pictures, sufficient to measure the thickness of the wall of a missile silo, brings human cultural activity into the new atlas. Thus, the technology has immediate relevance to city and town planning, with power to monitor, in time as well as space, the live evolution of a community. The Library of Congress should press the progressive declassification of this vast wealth of imagery in all its unexplored relevance to human well-being. Through the appropriate committees of Congress it should make sure that its paramilitary custodians are sensitive to their obligations as trustees of this material in the interest of happier human concerns. The civilian satellites give us 1:100,000,000 and even 1:250,000 images of the entire Earth such as were hitherto drawn by centuries of ground-surveying for only the most prosperous countries. From the military satellites the new world atlas is ready to capture a graphic index to the life of our species.

The Transparent Library

As the National Library, prospectively if not actually, the Library of Congress owes a service to the electorate somewhere between that which it renders to Congress and what it offers to the tourist. While it is not committed to teaching, it is obliged to render its wealth of resources accessible to the citizen-at-large engaged in those pursuits—from electing a Congressman, to learning for the pleasure of it, to the browsing discovery of new "covetables"—which occasion a broadening need for information. The Library has recently experienced a vivid demonstration of the positive correlation of use to accessibility. Removal of its great map collection from the central complex has reduced its use over the past year by 30 percent. Conversely, increase in the accessibility of the Library as a whole can be expected to put the Library into correspondingly active contact with the electorate. In framing its contribution to the possibilities of "found education" for its ultimate constituency, the Library needs to make a new synthesis of what it holds and to take a demanding view of the problems of presentation.

The freeing-up of the Library's splendid monumental spaces by the removal of presently misplaced activities to the new Madison Building offers the ideal setting for the venture into accessibility. Whatever is undertaken here must not only respect the setting, however, but take from it the example of hospitable attention to detail and verve for communication.

A first task for this space is to make the Library and its workings more legible to those within it as well as to visitors. By models, video displays, interactive terminals, and other appropriate devices, this exhibition could demonstrate the Library's physical layout and use of space; the duties and the interaction of its people; the volume, sources, and destinations of the flow of information; its services to Congress, and, finally, its systems of classification and access—there and ready in a computer terminal to engage the visitor in a branching dialogue.

The meta-browsing of the Library as a whole that begins at this point should be continued in the series of exhibitions and demonstrations beyond. They should take the visitor in greater depth into the Library's holdings and services; for example:

Film flips through the Library's collections of visual material:
circus posters
stereo cards
architectural drawings
photographic "studies"
aerial photographs.

Some experiments with very fast data retrieval and other interactive demonstrations of the new technologies of the Library.

Displays from the foreign-language libraries within the Library; each display offering a choice of film introductions (India: present commerce, cultural history, literature, or the look of the land).

In a baffled room, a sample of the Library's corpus of folk-song recordings or a performance by the Budapest String Quartet on the Library's instruments.

In a small theater, a changing program of vignettes:
the pleasures and frailties of the printed book;
the history of printed illustrations;
the notion of copyright; its past and future;
the state-of-the-art of library science, including some prospects in automatic content retrieval;
the future of publishing; how recent technology has changed the relation between a text and its book.

One fairly spacious pavilion would describe in some detail the scope of the Congressional Research Service and display some of its recent projects for Congressional committees. A terminal in this area (similar to those in Congressmen's offices) could access a computer simulation of the U.S. economy.

A SCORPIO terminal, with a special introductory dialogue, could offer a limited but real contact with the resources of the Science Reading Room.

Plainly, whatever can be done to increase the accessibility of the Library of Congress in its main building in Washington, D.C., the same can be appropriately reproduced in "regional bibliographic centers" of the National Library—one in each major city. These regional centers could be developed as extensions of the MARC distribution service, alongside or in existing university and other libraries that subscribe. The hardware and software of information-communication technology are now fully equal to realizing the vision of the transparent library.

Library for the Handicapped

Much in the new technology has relevance to reducing the barriers between the contents of the Library and handicapped citizens. The Library of Congress may soon find that its hitherto standard services are being displaced by devices and services more easily used by its handicapped clients. In this period of high flux in the technology, it is important that the Library maintain its monitoring and standard-setting function on behalf of these clients.

8. Report of the Social Sciences Advisory Group

Chairman's Comments

I am pleased to submit the report of the committee appointed to consider the relations of the social sciences to the Library of Congress. The Committee met at the Library of Congress twice, on September 9–10 and on November 12, 1976. Since much of our time had to be used in learning something about the Library, we had little time to formulate the comments and suggestions which follow, so we are not in a position to offer them as formal recommendations.

Relations of the Library of Congress to the Social Science Community

Information about the holdings and services available at the Library should be disseminated more effectively. At present, the visibility of the Library among social scientists is low.

Orientation services for research workers at the Library would be valuable.

The Library might establish a number of Visiting Social Science Scholars. These might be people who not only would use the resources of the Library, but would in some way contribute to the resources.

The Library might establish a social science reading room, which could serve not only as a comprehensive bibliographic center for the social sciences but as the focus for social science work within the library, e.g., as an information center for users, a base for visiting scholars, and a center for acquisition and classification policy, as in the case of other subject specialties.

The Library should consider the extent to which it might become a depository for basic research data, as well as for research studies based on such data.

A standing Advisory or Visiting Committee of Social Scientists might prove useful to the Library, with regard to acquisition and classification policy, review of holdings, contact with the field, oversight of CRS, possible lecture series, etc.

The Library should send representatives to professional meetings in the social sciences, where they would present briefings such as those now given by the National Science Foundation, the National Institutes of Health, etc.

The new planning office at the Library should support continuing social science research on libraries, for example, operations research on the role of the Library in the total system of libraries.

In view of the Librarian's ambition to make the Library more of a center for scholarly activity in the Washington, D.C., area, the Library might consider sponsoring a series of lectures or seminars in the social sciences by visiting users of the Library's resources, authors of studies in the social sciences that were substantially based on the Library's resources, and others who could contribute to increasing the Library's role as a center for social science work and discussion. Similarly, reports on Library-based studies in the social sciences should be sought for the newly reformed *Quarterly Journal*. The Library could establish some form of affiliation with the Library, designated by a title such as "Associate of the Library of Congress." This affiliation could be available on application to the Library, and be actively offered to visiting scholars, members of local university faculties, institutes, research organizations, and professional association staffs, as well as to members of Congress, the federal judiciary, and executive agencies. Affiliation could entitle one to eat in the dining-room-to-be, to participate in various seminars and lectures, to attend occasional receptions for ceremonial events, and—most important—to special orientation to the Library's holdings and services, with easier access to stack or study facilities.

Congressional Research Service (CRS)

There needs to be a careful scholarly review of the operations and output of the CRS, probably by an *ad hoc* committee appointed for the purpose (which, if indicated, might be continued as an advisory board to the Service; or that function could be taken by the general advisory committee, if one is formed). The committee would appraise the CRS product and distribution, as well as its relation to the total legislative process as an important policy tool in the social sciences; consider the publication of CRS studies, which would not only be a useful service in itself but would lead to appropriate critiques of CRS studies by social scientists at large.

As a way of both upgrading CRS scholarly work (through peer review) and keeping it more closely in touch with the social science community, the Library might consider appointing visiting scholars and graduate students to the CRS staff for term periods.

SCORPIO Computer System

The Library should try to make this system available at other libraries.

Additional materials might be included in the computer system, for example CRS materials and holdings of other libraries.

Consideration should be given to modernization of social science classifications and subject headings. If a Social Science Advisory Committee is established, or if Visiting Social Science Scholars are brought to the Library, they might participate in this.

Appendix: The Library of Congress as a Depository for Basic Data of the Social Sciences

This appendix was prepared by Hugh F. Cline

During the past 15 years, the social science community has generated an increasing number of very large numerical data sets, which are proving extremely valuable for multiple research uses. Encouraged primarily by the enormous capacity of digital computers for analyzing such large-scale data sets, we have generated such files as the one in 1,000 sample of the decennial census, nationwide economic surveys of samples of families, from national opinion surveys. These files are now maintained in a wide variety of institutional settings, including university computing centers, research institutes, and social science data files. In addition, there seems to be some interest in developing a capacity within the libraries for assisting scholars in using computer programs for data reduction and statistical analyses of these files. It is not clear to me whether this is a desirable development for increasing the utility of such data files in social science research, but it is an interesting possibility and deserving of serious consideration.

Currently, these data files and the computer programs for analyses are maintained in a wide variety of formats. It is still exceedingly difficult to transfer either a data set or a program from one university computing center to another. There is need for some standardization in this field—a standardization which will increase the exportability of these computer fields, without imposing a premature closure. Unfortunately, no local university computing center or social science research institute has yet demonstrated the ability to address the problem with an adequately broad perspective. The task of collecting, cleaning, documenting, and disseminating such data files is, indeed, very similar to the activities of many libraries in maintaining their holdings. Because of the similarities in these processes, the question of libraries serving as depositories for these research data files should be thoroughly explored.

There is no question that this type of new service would offer an opportunity for expansion and challenge to libraries. The Library of Congress could take a leadership role in exploring this question, and would certainly increase its visibility in the social science community.

Appendix D: Task Force Members and Subcommittees, and the Advisory Groups

＊

1. The Librarian's Task Force on Goals, Organization, and Planning (January 16, 1976–January 28, 1977)

John Y. Cole, *Chairman*
Alan Fern, Research Department
Beverly Gray, Reader Services Department
Tao-Tai Hsia, Law Library
Edward Knight, Congressional Research Service
Lucia Rather, Processing Department
Lawrence S. Robinson, Administrative Department
Norman J. Shaffer, Administrative Department
Robert D. Stevens, Copyright Office

Elizabeth F. Stroup, Congressional Research Service
Glen A. Zimmerman, Administrative Department
Task Force Staff:
    Janet Chase, Office of the Librarian
    Nancy Mitchell, Office of the Librarian
    Christopher Wright, Office of the Librarian
    Robert Zich, Reader Services Department

2. Subcommittees

Area Studies

Beverly Gray, Reader Services Department, *Chairman*
Georgette Dorn, Research Department
John R. Hébert, Research Department
Paul L. Horecky, Research Department
Tao-Tai Hsia, Law Library

Louis A. Jacob, Research Department
Zuhair E. Jwaideh, Law Library
Mary Ellis Kahler, Research Department
David H. Kraus, Research Department
David Littlefield, Processing Department

Edward MacConomy, Reader Services Department
Marlene C. McGuirl, Law Library
Rubens Medina, Law Library
Renata Shaw, Research Department
Ivan Sipkov, Law Library
Robert D. Stevens, Copyright Office
Warren M. Tsuneishi, Research Department
Julian W. Witherell, Reader Services

Automation and Reference Services

John W. Kimball, Reader Services Department, *Chairman*
Jane Collins, Reader Services Department
Nancy Davenport, Congressional Research Service
James Godwin, Processing Department
John Kaldahl, Congressional Research Service
Hylda Kamisar, Reader Services Department
Mary S. Lewin, Administrative Department
Marlene C. McGuirl, Law Library
Myron W. Phillips, Reader Services Department
William H. Poole, Copyright Office
Barbara B. Walsh, Reader Services Department
John Wolter, Research Department

Bibliographic Access

Suzy Platt, Congressional Research Service, *Chairman*
Elisabeth Betz, Reader Services Department
Susan Biebel, Processing Department
Janet Hill, Research Department
Jeanne M. Jagelski, Law Library
David Littlefield, Processing Department
John Panko, Processing Department
Lynn Pedigo, Reader Services Department
James Roberts, Copyright Office

William J. Sittig, Research Department
Daisy Tagge, Processing Department
Melissa Trevvett, Congressional Research Service

The Bibliographic Role of the Library

Ronald Gephart, Reader Services Department, *Co-Chairman*
John R. Hébert, Research Department, *Co-Chairman*
Patrick Bernard, Processing Department
Constance Carter, Reader Services Department
David Eastridge, Copyright Office
Evelyn Eiwen, Office of the Librarian
Ruth Freitag, Reader Services Department
Edward MacConomy, Reader Services Department
Ann Hallstein, Processing Department
Armins Rusis, Law Library
Richard Stephenson, Research Department
Julian Witherell, Reader Services Department

Collection Development

Robert D. Stevens, Copyright Office, *Chairman*
Beverly Gray, Reader Services Department
Tao-Tai Hsia, Law Library
Lawrence S. Robinson, Administrative Department
Renata Shaw, Research Department
Michael H. Shelley, Copyright Office

The Cultural Role of the Library

Dorothy Pollet, Reader Services Department, *Chairman*
Susan Aramayo, Office of the Librarian
Lewis Flacks, Copyright Office
Marvin Kranz, Reader Services Department

Maria Lacqueur, Reader Services Department

Jerald Maddox, Research Department

Rubens Medina, Law Library

Frederick Mohr, Office of the Librarian

Gerald Parsons, Research Department

Donna Scheeder, Congressional Research Service

Carolyn Sung, Research Department

Sandra Tinkham, Office of the Librarian

Jean Tucker, Office of the Librarian

Michael Walsh, Processing Department

Documents

Beverly Gray, Reader Services Department, *Chairman*

George Caldwell, Reader Services Department

Nathan Einhorn, Processing Department

Agnes Ferruso, Processing Department

Alma Mather, Processing Department

Floris McReynolds, Congressional Research Service

Eugene Nabors, Law Library

Robert Nay, Law Library

Robert Schaaf, Reader Services Department

Maurvene Williams, Congressional Research Service

Donald Wisdom, Reader Services Department

Loan and Photoduplication Services

Norman J. Shaffer, Administrative Department, *Chairman*

Larry Boyer, Law Library

Beverly Brannan, Research Department

Everett Johnson, Reader Services Department

Thomas Nichols, Copyright Office

Robert Schaaf, Reader Services Department

Suanne Thamm, Reader Services Department

Melissa Trevvett, Congressional Research Service

Warren Tsuneishi, Research Department

Howard Walker, Reader Services Department

Margaret Whitlock, Congressional Research Services

Robert Zich, Reader Services Department

Serials Management

Joseph W. Price, Processing Department, *Chairman*

George Atiyeh, Research Department

Jane Collins, Reader Services Department

Ann Gardner, Reader Services Department

Rita Harrison, Law Library

Edward Kapusciarz, Copyright Office

Jennifer V. Magnus, Processing Department

Emma G. Montgomery, Research Department

Mary E. Sauer, Processing Department

Michael Shelley, Copyright Office

Donald Wisdom, Reader Services Department

Donald Woolery, Processing Department

Services to Congress

Helen W. Dalrymple, Congressional Research Service, *Chairman*

Peter Bridge, Processing Department

Susan Finsen, Congressional Research Service

Anthony P. Harrison, Copyright Office

Paul Heffron, Research Department

Jane Lindley, Congressional Research Service

Adoreen McCormick, Office of the Librarian
Nancy Mitchell, Office of the Librarian
Robert Nay, Law Library
Charlene Woody, Administrative Department

Services to Libraries

Lucia J. Rather, Processing Department, *Chairman*
David Carrington, Research Department
Paul Edlund, Processing Department
Prentiss Gillespie, Administrative Department
Ellen Zabel Hahn, Reader Services Department
Marlene C. McGuirl, Law Library
Josephine Pulsifer, Processing Department
David Remington, Processing Department
Jacquelyn Ricketts, Copyright Office
Christopher Wright, Office of the Librarian
Robert Zich, Reader Services Department

Services to Staff

Winston Tabb, Congressional Research Service, *Chairman*
Charles Brookes, Law Library
Milton Collins, Processing Department
Catherine M. Croy, Administrative Department
Kay Elsasser, Processing Department
Veronica M. Gillespie, Research Department
Katherine F. Gould, Reader Services Department
Beth Jenkins-Joffe, Reader Services Department
Margrit Krewson, Reader Services Department
Arthur J. Lieb, Office of the Librarian

Victor Marton, Copyright Office
James McClung, Office of the Librarian
Laverne Mullin, Law Library

Training and Staff Development

Kimberly W. Dobbs, Law Library, *Co-Chairman*
Louis R. Mortimer, Congressional Research Service, *Co-Chairman*
Susan Aramayo, Office of the Librarian
Keith Bebo, Administrative Department
Edith Belmear, Processing Department
Phillipa Butler, Administrative Department
Elizabeth Carl, Processing Department
Kathleen Christensen, Processing Department
Sylvia Cook, Congressional Research Service
Catherine Croy, Administrative Department
Robert David, Processing Department
Fay Diggs, Processing Department
Robert Ennis, Congressional Research Service
Maryann Ferrarese, Processing Department
Lynda Fox, Processing Department
Jacqueline Granville, Office of the Librarian
Gerald Greenwood, Administrative Department
Walter J. Hadlock, Congressional Research Service
Asa (Bud) Hardison, Administrative Department
Bruce Harris, Processing Department
Patricia Hines, Processing Department
Joyce Holmes, Congressional Research Service

Oxana Horodecka, Processing Department

Georgia Joyner, Congressional Research Service

Lucinda Leonard, Processing Department

Robyn Levine, Congressional Research Service

Arthur J. Lieb, Office of the Librarian

Peter Lu, Processing Department

Jack McDonald, Reader Services Department

Hugh McNeil, Processing Department

Thomas Miller, Congressional Research Service

Joe Nelson, Congressional Research Service

Rhoda Newman, Congressional Research Service

Ruthann Ovenshire, Congressional Research Service

David Remington, Processing Department

James Richardson, Congressional Research Service

Anne Ritchings, Congressional Research Service

Janet Schacter, Administrative Department

Judith Schmidt, Processing Department

Virginia Schoepf, Processing Department

Frank Seidlinger, Processing Department

Susan Tarr, Congressional Research Service

Jeanne Temple, Law Library

William Underdue, Administrative Department

Patricia van Ee, Office of the Librarian

Susan Vita, Processing Department

Eugene Walton, Administrative Department

Eugene Whetstone, Administrative Department

Clay Wilson, Reader Services Department

The User Survey

Robert Zich, Reader Services Department, *Chairman*

Roy Aguirre, Reader Services Department

Nancy Benco, Office of the Librarian

Dan Burney, Research Department

Jane Collins, Reader Services Department

Georgette Dorn, Research Department

Walter Gallagher, Administrative Department

Katherine Gould, Reader Services Department

Louis Jacob, Research Department

Beth Jenkins-Joffe, Reader Services Department

Everett Johnson, Reader Services Department

Hylda Kamisar, Reader Services Department

Jerry Kearns, Research Department

David Kraus, Research Department

Jane Lindley, Congressional Research Service

Judy McDermott, Processing Department

Marlene McGuirl, Law Library

Waldo Moore, Copyright Office

Jon Newsom, Research Department

William Sartain, Reader Services Department

Patrick Sheehan, Research Department

Ivan Sipkov, Law Library

Carolyn Sung, Research Department

Winston Tabb, Congressional Research Service

Melissa Trevvett, Congressional Research Service

Howard Walker, Reader Services Department

John Wolter, Research Department

3. Advisory Groups

Arts Advisory Group

Patrick Hayes—*Chairman*, Managing Director, Washington Performing Arts Society

June Arey, Consultant, The Rockefeller Foundation

Frank Campbell, Chief, Music Division, New York Public Library

Jack Delano, Rio Piedras, Puerto Rico

Joseph Kerman, Professor, Department of Music, University of California at Berkeley

Alan Kriegsman, Dance Critic, *Washington Post*

Fisher Nesmith, Consultant, Museum of African Art

Warren M. Robbins, Director, Museum of African Art

Charles Rosen, Department of Music, State University of New York at Stony Brook

William B. Walker, Librarian, National Collection of Fine Arts/National Portrait Gallery, Smithsonian Institution

Tom Willis, Music Critic, *Chicago Tribune*

Humanities Advisory Group

Jaroslav Pelikan—*Chairman*, Dean, Graduate School, Yale University

Morton W. Bloomfield, Professor, Department of English and American Literature and Language, Harvard University

Victor Brombert, Professor, Department of Comparative Literature, Princeton University

J. William Fulbright, Legal Counsel, Hogan and Hartson, Washington, D.C.

J. Glenn Gray, Professor, Department of Philosophy, The Colorado College

Neil Harris, Director, National Humanities Institute, The University of Chicago

Bernard M. W. Knox, Director, Center for Hellenic Studies

Sherman E. Lee, Director, The Cleveland Museum of Art

Donald W. Treadgold, Professor, Department of History, The University of Washington

Law Advisory Group

Phil Neal—*Chairman*, Professor, University of Chicago Law School

Morris L. Cohen, Librarian, Harvard Law School, Harvard University

J. S. Ellenberger, Law Librarian, Covington and Burling, Washington, D.C.

Lawrence M. Friedman, Professor, Stanford Law School, Stanford University

Marian G. Gallagher, Law Librarian and Professor of Law, University of Washington

William J. Kenney, Criminal Division, U.S. Department of Justice

Judge Harold Leventhal, U.S. Court of Appeals for the D.C. Circuit, Washington, D.C.

Sidney S. Sachs, Chairman, Standing Committee on Facilities of the Law Library of Congress, American Bar Association

Edwin M. Zimmerman, Covington and Burling, Washington, D.C.

Libraries Advisory Group

Robert Wedgeworth—*Chairman*, Executive Director, American Library Association

Dorothy Blake, Coordinator of Planning for Media Resources and Utilization, Atlanta Public Schools

Lillian M. Bradshaw, Director, Dallas Public Library

Ethel S. Crockett, State Librarian, California State Library

Louise Giles, Dean of Learning Resources, Macomb County Community College, Warren, Michigan

Warren J. Haas, Vice-President for Information Services and University Librarian, Columbia University

Doralyn J. Hickey, Dean, School of Library Science, University of Wisconsin at Milwaukee

Harry T. Hookway, Deputy Chairman and Chief Executive, The British Library Board, London, England

Frederick Kilgour, Executive Director, Ohio College Library Center

Richard Rademacher, Librarian, Wichita Public Library

F. William Summers, Dean, College of Librarianship, University of South Carolina

Miriam H. Tees, Librarian, The Royal Bank of Canada, Montreal, Canada

Media Advisory Group

David Schoumacher—*Chairman*, WMAL-TV, Washington, D.C.

Ed Guthman, National Editor, *Los Angeles Times-Mirror*

Edward P. Morgan, McLean, Virginia

James B. Reston, Washington Bureau, *New York Times*

Joan Richman, CBS News Department, New York, N.Y.

Richard Stewart, *Boston Globe*

Jerold TerHorst, Washington Bureau, *Detroit News*

Publishers Advisory Group

Dan Lacy—*Chairman*, Senior Vice President, McGraw-Hill, Inc.

Robert Asleson, President, R. R. Bowker Company

Simon Michael Bessie, Senior Vice President, Harper & Row Publishers, Inc.

Ed Booher, Director, National Enquiry into Scholarly Communication, Princeton, N.J.

Townsend Hoopes, President, Association of American Publishers

Chester Kerr, Director, Yale University Press

Kenneth McCormick, Senior Consulting Editor, Doubleday & Company

Carol Nemeyer, Staff Director for General Publishing, Association of American Publishers

Charles Scribner, Jr., President, Charles Scribner's Sons

Theodore Waller, President, Grolier Educational Corporation

W. Bradford Wiley, Chairman, John Wiley & Sons, Inc.

Science and Technology Advisory Group

Gerard Piel—*Chairman*, Publisher, *Scientific American*

Charles Eames, Venice, California

George Gerbner, Professor, The Annenberg School of Communications, University of Pennsylvania

Donald Kennedy, Professor, Department of Biology, Stanford University

John R. Pierce, Professor, California Institute of Technology

Derek de Solla Price, Avalon Professor of the History of Science, Department of History of Science and Medicine, Yale University

The Right Honorable Ritchie-Calder, Edinburgh, Scotland

Cornelius Smit, Infonet BV, Amsterdam, The Netherlands

Social Science Advisory Group

W. Allen Wallis—*Chairman*, Chancellor, The University of Rochester

Bernard Berelson, Consultant, Population Research Council

Hugh F. Cline, Consultant, Educational Testing Service

Stanley L. Engerman, Professor, Department of Economics, University of Rochester

David Goslin, Executive Director, Assembly of Behavioral and Social Sciences, National Academy of Sciences

George Lowy, Chief, Social Science Center, Columbia University Library

Dorothy Ross, Professor, Department of History, Princeton University

Eleanor B. Sheldon, President, Social Science Research Council

Index

THE LIBRARY OF CONGRESS IN RETROSPECTIVE

1800　The Library of Congress is established in the new capital city of Washington.

1802　Congress sets forth the rules for using the Library.

1814　The 3,000-volume Library is destroyed when the British burn the Capitol.

1815　Congress purchases Thomas Jefferson's comprehensive 6,000-volume personal library, considered "a most admirable substratum for a National Library."

1830　Congress extends the use of the Library to other government officials.

1864　Ainsworth Rand Spofford becomes Librarian of Congress.

1867　The purchase of Peter Force's notable collection of Americana makes the Library of Congress the largest library in the United States.

1870　A revised copyright law centralizes all U.S. copyright activities at the Library of Congress and the Library begins receiving two copies of all works deposited for copyright.

1871　Librarian Spofford suggests to Congress that the Library be separated physically from the Capitol and moved into its own building.

1886　Congress authorizes the construction of a separate Library of Congress building.

1895　Librarian Spofford presents a reorganization plan.

1896　Congress holds hearings on the organization and future role of the Library.

1897　Congress approves a reorganization and expansion of the Library that gives the Librarian of Congress sole responsibility for establishing rules and making appointments.

　　　John Russell Young becomes Librarian of Congress.

　　　The monumental new Library building, located across the east plaza from the Capitol, is opened.

1899　Herbert Putnam becomes Librarian of Congress.

1901　Congress extends the use of the Library to "duly qualified individuals" outside the District of Columbia.